SHI'ISM AND THE DEMOCRATISATION PROCESS
IN IRAN

Ibrahim Moussawi

Shi'ism and the Democratisation Process in Iran

With a focus on *Wilayat al-Faqih*

SAQI

ISBN 978-0-86356-470-3

First published 2011 by Saqi Books

A full CIP record for this book is available from the British Library.
A full CIP record for this book is available from the Library of Congress.

Manufactured in Lebanon

SAQI
26 Westbourne Grove, London W2 5RH
www.saqibooks.com

Contents

Introduction

With the emergence of the Islamic Republic of Iran in 1979, and the introduction of what was perceived as a new political ideology, observers, particularly in the West, were faced with several questions, the most basic of which were: What does this concept of *wilayat al-faqih* mean, where did it come from and what are the implications of its implementation in Iran?

Events surrounding the disputed elections of 2009, moreover, threw into sharp relief the debate over whether Islam and democracy could cohere. To some observers, it even called into question the philosophy of *wilayat al-faqih* itself. Coming as it did just after Iran had celebrated the thirtieth anniversary of the 1979 revolution, the contested re-election of Ahmadinejad as president prompted unprecedented levels of protests. Some were directed at political shortcomings in the running of the election, some at the sense of officially sanctioned dishonesty, some at the personalities of the politicians involved. Other protestors even seemed to question the system adopted in 1979, and advanced since the death in 1989 of Imam Ruhollah Khomeini. There was also talk that the crushing of the revolt and the arrest and occasional execution of dissidents signalled a curbing of democracy. Likewise some analysts described the return to power of Ahmadinejad as a coup by younger military and radical factions over previous power-holders, including large sections of the *ulama* (Islamic clergy). Conversely, the survival of both the supreme guide and the president – and the assent of other parliamentarians and official councils – appeared to signal that the system was stronger than foes had expected. Arguably, ran this view, *wilayat al-faqih* still enjoyed the support of a 'silent majority' of ordinary Iranians.

Literally translated *wilayat al-faqih* means 'mandate of the (Islamic) jurist' or 'guardianship of the jurist', '*wilaya*' meaning government or legal authority, combined with '*faqih*' which is the standard Islamic term for someone who interprets the law. The concept as elaborated by Imam Syed Ruhollah Khomeini (1900–89) is a forthright attempt to legitimise governance by Shi'i clergy in the temporal as well as the spiritual realm. Concretely speaking, it implied that the highest authority of the Islamic Revolution, namely the Guide or Leader (*rahbar*), should be one of the highest religious authorities (*marja' al-taqlid* or 'authority of emulation') and the political leader, who 'understands his time' and therefore could lead a mass movement.

Some observers have described the concept of *wilayat al-faqih*, or guardianship of the jurist, as a rigidly tyrannical system of governance, an authoritarian and highly centralised leadership structure that gives precedence to the whims of the *rahbar*. From this perspective, it is impossible to imagine a genuine process of democratisation taking root and flourishing inside the Islamic Republic of Iran. However, a careful examination of the principles of *wilayat al-faqih* allows for a more nuanced understanding of both the concept itself and its fluidity and ability to evolve and adapt to changing socio-political circumstances. To begin such an analysis, we must first define democratisation, which is itself a contested term, particularly in the post-11 September world.

ONE VIEW OF DEMOCRATISATION

Mahmud Haydar,[1] a Lebanese journalist and intellectual, contends that democratisation, as a concept, entered the political and philosophical sphere in the framework of the late development of modernity. That is to say, capitalist societies in the West deemed democratisation as a necessary road that developing countries have to travel in order to reach the level of modernisation and prosperity that the First World countries enjoy. By this method, Western nations attempted to generalise their experience and impose their political, social, economic and cultural models on third world countries.

Haydar stresses that democratisation linguistically means 'making what is not democratic, democratic', or 'activating (*taf'il*) a community that is lacking in political, economic, and social democratic practices to become on par with Western democratic practices'. However, he clarifies that it is not necessary for the would-be democratic society to either follow the same path toward democracy or become a spitting image of democracy as practised in capitalist developed countries, such as the G7, for instance.

According to Haydar, the trend of promoting democratisation emerged after the end of the Cold War, which resulted in the ascendance of American liberalism as a hegemonic model over the 'global village'. Haydar purports that the real objective of promoting democratisation is to prepare the ground for the targeted communities and countries to become amenable to fast and huge flows of capital.

---

1   Mahmud Haydar, Lebanese intellectual, journalist and editor-in-chief of *Madarat*. Interviewed by the author, Beirut, 5 May 2007.

From this perspective, Western nations employed the terminology of democratisation as a tool to expand their hegemony over Third World countries. If this is the objective of democratisation, then the ensuing relationship would be one between an oppressor (developed countries) and oppressed (developing countries), resulting in hegemony of the strong over the weak, which runs counter to the aims of democracy.

Thus, Haydar contends, democratisation became a global phenomenon serving the interests of the Western hegemonic powers, who opted to promote 'radical reform' in the targeted countries in order to make them able to properly function in the global capitalist system. Through this networking, democratisation not only targets political reform and periodic elections, but also extends its domains to dealing with lifestyles, proper behaviour, even religious practices. Islamic movements term this as 'cultural invasion', which should be stopped at all costs.

Haydar adds that after 11 September, the discourse on democratisation reached an unprecedented peak. This was concomitant with the hegemony of the neoconservatives over US foreign policy, investing in the so-called 'democratisation' of the Middle East as a means of achieving political and security objectives. Michael Ledeen, a scholar at the American Enterprise Institute, contended[1] that the US should employ its political, ethical and military capabilities in order to sustain a global democratisation revolution, which would emancipate the Middle East from tyranny, as he put it. Two leading neoconservative thinkers, William Kristol, editor of *The Weekly Standard*, and Robert Kagan, had argued earlier that 'today's international system is built not around a balance of power but around American hegemony' and that 'in the post-Cold War era, the maintenance of a decent and hospitable international order requires continued American leadership in resisting, and where possible undermining, rising dictators and hostile ideologies; in supporting American interests and liberal democratic principles; and in providing assistance to those struggling against the more extreme manifestations of human evil.'[2] Thus the neoconservative thinkers began conflating the idea of democratisation with the notion of external force.

Haydar concludes that because of the wars in Iraq and Afghanistan, the terminology of 'democratisation' became conflated with the terminology of military force in the political discourse after 11 September, and thus the very idea of democratisation became based on mutual suspicion and mistrust, especially when it comes to the overall objectives of America's promotion of democratisation.

---

1 See his article in the *Wall Street Journal*, 4 September 2002.
2 William Kristol and Robert Kagan, 'Toward a Neo-Reaganite Foreign Policy' in *Foreign Affairs* 75, 4, 1996: pp. 18–32. Also see Kristol and Kagan, *Present Dangers: Crisis and Opportunity in American and Defense Policy*, San Francisco, 2000.

From this perspective, 'democratisation' implies an act that is carried out by an external agent for the purpose of specific gains that can run contrary to those of local societies, and therefore ought to be resisted.

ANOTHER PERSPECTIVE ON DEMOCRATISATION

An alternative view sees democratisation as an organic process that emerges naturally in a society as a result of the collective will of the people and smoothly guides a system of governance toward greater degrees of democracy. Richard Haass,[1] in his speech entitled, 'Towards a Better Democracy in the Arab World', delivered to the Council on Foreign Relations in the United States, emphasised that democratisation is a process directed by citizens and members of society. If the US or any other country attempted to impose democratic principles on a certain country, then the end product would be an unviable democracy. Haass stressed that for democracy to take root in any society it should be a local, domestic production.

Building on Haass's argument, the question then becomes whether a citizen-directed or society-driven democratisation process can occur within the context of *wilayat al-faqih*. Furthermore, does *wilayat al-faqih* provide democratic principles – such as freedom, consensus, accountability, pluralism, checks and balances, etc. – of its own? And indeed, can these principles be applied in such a way that *wilayat al-faqih* eventually results in a viable, indigenous and authentic manifestation of democracy?

METHODOLOGICAL APPROACH

It is misleading to assume that the process of democratisation in developing countries such as Iran would necessarily mirror that of Western societies; rather, we could expect that an organic democratisation process would build upon and evolve from existing societal structures. Revolutionary Iran developed its own political system and conception of Islamic democracy. While this system may have drawn from certain ideas from the West such as the social contract, as well as what could be called either democratic participation or public participation, it also built upon ideas that originated in Iran itself or in the Islamic world. Nevertheless, the Iranian version of democracy is not completely dissimilar to Western democracy; though it has its own specificities, it draws a great deal from Western systems of governance, most notably the constitution of the French Fifth Republic.

---

1   He has been the president of the Council on Foreign Relations since July 2003.

Any evaluation of Iran's system of governance requires an understanding of this system in terms of Islamic parameters, not as ethnocentrism dictates; in other words, understanding the ideas or practices of another culture in terms of those of one's own culture. If we were to limit our study of democratisation in Iran to Western concepts of democracy and democratisation, the end result would be an ethocentric analysis. Ethnocentrism refers 'to the tendency to assume that one's culture and way of life are superior to all others. The ethnocentric person sees his or her own group as the centre or defining point of culture and views all other cultures as deviations from what is 'normal'.'[1] The assumption that the Western model of secular democracy is the best and most advanced and that it ought to be universally applied everywhere, even in Third World or Muslim countries, will inevitably result in an ethnocentric analysis and lead to premature judgements based on stereotyping and prejduce. As such, it is necessary to acknowledge that Iran has its own specificity that precludes a blind application of the so-called Western model of democrcay without examining the specific context of the Islamic Republic's notion of theocratic democracy (see Surush, Kadivar in later references). With this approach, it is possible to identify how democracy can develop endogenously (from the inside), rather than being imposed exogenously (from the outside).

From this perspective, we can evaluate whether the political system in Iran contains structures and mechanisms that are inherently democratic and would lend themselves to an organic process of democratisation. In Khomeini's contemporary thought, Islam is not an end in itself but a means to an end, which is social justice. In this conception, man does not serve Islam but Islam serves man; it is in the service of humanity. Indeed, there are problems with *wilayat al-faqih*, but it is not a question of whether the concept itself is in diametric opposition to that of democracy. The ongoing debates about *wilayat al-faqih*, including whether it is absolute or relative, reveal its fluidity and adaptability to various models of governance and imply that its inclusion in the Iranian political system does not necessarily make that system averse to democratisation.

In order to avoid an ethnocentric analysis of the Iranian experience, this book does not rely exclusively on Western theories of democracy and democratisation. Rather, it attempts to synthesise two models or different sets of critera: one being the basic human rights enshrined in the United Nations Declaration of Rights, which includes civil and political rights[2] and serves as a benchmark for measuring democratic freedom in Iran; and the other is the Khomeiniest school of thought,

---

1   Richard T. Schafer and Robert P. Lamm, *Sociology*, sixth edn, US 1998, p. 84.

2   Civil and political rights would include the freedom of religious expression, freedom of assembly, etc., with the qualifications being any threat to national security or grave offence to public morals.

which is used by all Iranian political groups in the path of the Imam (*khat al-imam*) to debate policies. This synthesis forms the basis of a new paradigm for studying democratisation in Iran, one that includes Islam on the one hand, and democracy on the other. To begin, there is an exploration of the commonalities between Western concepts of democracy and the concept of *wilayat al-faqih*.

WESTERN THINKERS ON DEMOCRACY

The British philosopher John Stuart Mill (1806–73), in his *Essay on Liberty*, described the nature and limits of the separation between the private and public spheres or domains. He included in the private sphere those actions that do not have harmful consequences and he argued that the public sphere should be responsible for these consequences. Mill tried to describe the appropriate form of government that would realise the advantages of each sphere.[1] Likewise Imam Khomeini argued that the Islamic government that he envisaged and that was given legitimacy by way of public referendum had earned public consent and aimed at achieving the public good (*al-salih al'amm*). In Khomeini's view, political goals are determined by their effect on public affairs and the efficiency and abilities of the citizen. For Mill the goals of the rulers and the ruled are the same since what connects the public and the private spheres is representative government. Those who exercise authority should have the consent of the people. This concept resonates to a certain extent when compared with the workings of the system in the Islamic Republic. In addition to the *Majlis al-Shura*, which roughly corresponds to a parliament, there are other bodies that act as checks and balances on the whole system and serve to safeguard it as an embodiment of the public will. For instance, the Council of Experts, all of whose members are elected by the people, maintains the authority of choosing and ousting the *rahbar*.

According to Mill, the job of the parliament is to review and control the executive but the balance between executive and legislative authority depends on the will of the people. This implies democratic or popular sovereignty exercised through universal suffrage, a concept embodied in Imam Khomeini's conduct of a referendum to ratify the Iranian Constitution. In order to avoid the tyranny of the majority, Mill was the first to argue for pluralism based on institutionalism. He argued that democracy should be based on popular opinion (referendum). He advocated freedom of press and speech, and governmental intervention in the economy only to regulate social exchanges, selling and commercial activities that necessarily affect the interest of others.

---

1   John Stuart Mill, *Essay on Politics and Society*. Ed. J.M. Robson. Toronto, University of Toronto Press, 1977, p. 64.

By insisting on the regulatory role of government, he was to some extent advocating government paternalism.

The French Enlightenment political writer Charles-Louis Montesquieu (1689–1755) confines the concept of natural law to the state of nature before the establishment of civil society. His near contemporary, the English thinker John Locke (1632–1704) broadly concurs. However, liberty was the most important of all the inalienable rights of nature, considered Montesquieu, because he was haunted by the fear of tyranny that had undermined constitutional principles. Contrary to Hobbes,[1] Montesquieu argued that nature provides a standard of absolute justice prior to positive law. This means that the law in general is the human reason which governs the earth. Accordingly, the political and civil law of each nation ought to be the only particular case in which human reason is applied. Montesquieu favored the separation of powers among the executive, legislative and judiciary bodies, as well as limited government through his concept of negative state. Its function is to maintain law and order to protect liberty and property: 'the good government is the government that governs least.'

Positive law is sometimes viewed as contradictory to divine law. But if positive law is intended to ward off tyranny and concentration of authority, giving primacy to liberty, then it is a welcome occurrence. In Islam in general, and subsequently in the Islamic Republic, there is a distinction between positive man-made law (*al-qwanin al-wad'iyya*) on the one hand, and the divine law (Shari'a) on the other. Positive law is enacted by men to suit their purposes for a particular time frame, and as such these laws are transient and need constant revision and updating; while divine law is immutable, permanent across time and space. In the Islamic Republic of Iran, there exists the common separation of powers as indicated by Montesquieu; however this is also networked through a host of interrelated councils in order to insure thorough checks and balance, division of labour and specialisation of tasks.

Montesquieu's approach in this regard overlaps with the Islamic notion of *fitra* (fine instinct). According to Islam the human *fitra* is so pure and almost impeccable, that even without the presence of a Prophet or religion to lead, the love of good and the hate of injustice is innate. This *fitra* provides the supreme and most primal and pivotal compass on an individual level from within, that is to be consolidated later by the religion from without. From here springs human absolute commitment to liberty and his vehement attack against tyranny.

Like Locke and Hobbes, the Franco-Swiss philosopher and writer Jean-Jacques Rousseau (1712–1778) subjects political authority to a social contract. Unlike them, his concept of contract is not based on reason, rather on instinct. Rousseau's contract requires that civil society must be organised like the state of

---

1   Thomas Hobbes, author of *Leviathan* (1588–1679).

nature: simplicity, equality and freedom must be brought into society because on them depends man's moral development and happiness. The individual surrenders his rights completely to the community. Freedom is secured if the individual is made dependent on the collectivity: 'He who gives himself to all, gives himself to none.' Society as a moral entity makes choices as does the individual; it has a will. Through shared interest and shared moral values the individual is identical with society; this is his concept of general will.

The theory of power according to the concept of *wilayat al-faqih* is based upon conceptual principles, which could be constructed and applied in different ways. Furthermore, we can build a democratic *wilayat al-faqih* or a theocratic democracy based upon the historical-realistic approach because it serves as a bridge-builder to the other approaches as it is capable of assimilating and reconciling all the due results brought by the other approaches.

A very important process is to break down the elements that build up *wilayat al-faqih* into individual elements, such as: ideological roots, value system, set of duties and rights, and the mechanisms of the power and the question of its limitations and legitimacy. After that, we can clearly see that there is ample room for reconciliation or adaptation between Islam and democracy, and indeed between democracy and *wilayat al-faqih*, and further, that an organic process of democratisation can take place in the Islamic Republic.

The aim of this book is to dispel the commonly held view which suggests that *wilayat al-faqih* is predisposed to tyranny, and thus cannot allow for a natural democratisation process, because its religio-political nature and heritage do not allow for that possibility. Taking Iran as a case study, this book will study the vivid tendencies and the dynamics of Shi'i jurisprudence, its flexibility and adaptability in accommodating different situations, and the way that it has evolved and remained opened to new interpretations, which allow the Iranian system of governance to respond and adapt to different challenges of various natures.

The major questions are the following: Is *wilayat al-faqih* a despotic form of governance, one that precludes openness, tolerance, pluralism, freedom, equality, accountability and the rule of law? Or does it have room for democratisation, and can it be flexible and open to interpretations? Put another way, can viable, indigenous and authentic democratic practices and democratisation thrive in Iran, or does *wilayat al-faqih* inevitably contradict democratic principles such as freedom, consensus, accountability, pluralism, or checks and balances? Can citizens really have their voices heard in a state founded on religious principles, and can republicanism and Islamism coexist in a modern state?

This book will analyse the theoretical and conceptual framework which forms the backbone of the system of governance in Iran, *wilayat al-faqih*. It will also examine the different religious (*shar'i*) doctrinal foundations, as well as religious edicts (fatwas) that relate to this system of governance to see how these unfold in practice and how they are manifested in the various legislative, executive and judicial institutions in Iran.

One major line of argument is that first, Shi'i Islam and its jurisprudence are progressive in nature, and allow for independent reasoning (*ijtihad*), thus entailing a continuous evolution in religious thinking. Thus, Shi'i Islam, by virtue of its dynamism and adaptability, does not automatically preclude democracy or democratisation. Secondly, *wilayat al-faqih* is not a fixed, closed system, but rather is a fluid concept that is open to a wide range of interpretations by a variety of Islamic clerics and scholars and draws from republican concepts such as constitutionalism, separation of powers, etc. Thirdly, consultation (*shura*) is a key concept and practice in Islamic governance that reflects the central role of the populace. Fourthly, the Islamic Republic ensures the central role of the populace and the individual through the application of Islamic concepts of *shura* and *umma*, while simultaneously preserving the rights of the community, by also applying the concept of *maslaha* in the system of governance and guaranteeing pluralism (*ikhtilaf*). Fifthly, Iran's system of governance is not based on a dichotomy between divine and mundane values; rather, it stresses the concordance between the two, and the Islamic Republic is founded upon the fusion of Islamic and republican concepts. Sixthly, the jurisprudent (*wali al-faqih*) is not a dictator, and *wilayat al-faqih* includes many mechanisms and safety valves that aim to guarantee that the *wilayat* does not lead to tyranny. Finally, Iran is witnessing a society-driven process of democratisation within the context of *wilayat al-faqih*, and although that process has been fraught with slowdowns and setbacks, it nonetheless remains a force that is shaping the ever-evolving system of governance in the Islamic Republic of Iran.

Bearing in mind the aforementioned line of argument, chapter one discusses the main principles of Shi'i Islam. Chapter two explores Shi'i jurisprudence in relation to *wilayat al-faqih*. Chapter three discusses the concept of *shura*, or 'consultation', which is praised twice in the Qur'an, and its relationship to the concept of democracy, as well as its centrality in Islamic systems of governance. Chapter four explains how the Islamic concepts of *shura*, *umma*, *maslaha* and pluralism (*ikhtilaf*) are applied in the Islamic Republic of Iran. Chapter five investigates the possibility of *wilayat al-faqih* of degenerating into despotism, and surveys the safety valves that act against this possibility. Chapter six sheds light on Islamism and republicanism as two concepts of different natures, and analyses how in the final analysis they converge and overlap in contemporary Iran. Chapter seven discusses the process of democratisation in the Islamic Republic, as a case study with likely applications elsewhere. This chapter also considers the emergence of an Iranian 'reform movement'; and, by way of a postscript, the final chapter considers the events of the disputed election of 2009, their repercussions and their possible implications for the future.

An important conclusion is that democracy is neither handed down nor imported wholesale from outside. Rather, democracy as a concept is always negotiated, in any context, including the Western one. In essence democracy is the concern of people who come from all walks of life ranging from clerics to civil servants; students to workers; women and others. Thus, the leadership and people, hand in hand, developed a democratic system that is specific to the Iranian case without encroaching on its political and cultural importance. It is never an elite decision but always a popular demand (bottom up not top down). As such, it cannot be imposed from the outside. A popular and dynamic movement, democratisation is necessarily a culturally relative process. Democracy is best reached when it is nurtured steadily and applied endogenously and not imposed as a ready recipe exogenously.

There is no universal model that fits all cultures, and the Iranian example has its own peculiarities. Nonetheless Iranians seem to have steered an organic, society-driven process of democratisation within the context of *wilayat al-faqih*. As a religious-based system of governance, *wilayat al-faqih* remains open to criticism and new interpretations, while preserving the Islamic character of Iranian society. This is not to deny the recent crackdown on public liberties in the early 2000s and especially surrounding the contested elections of 2009, which coincided with the thirtieth anniversary of the Iranian Revolution of 1979.

Yet in comparison with many countries in the Middle East, Iran still enjoys a considerable degree of freedom, and remains one of the few states in the Gulf region where democratic elections regularly take place. While this book focuses on the internal mechanisms of the Islamic Republic, future researchers might wish to study the relationship between democratisation and external factors, such as sanctions and military threats. Such a study might help inform policymakers in the West that Iranians would be best left to steadily nurture their own nascent democratic practices.

The debate over democracy will not cease, and the Iranian case illustrates how progressive interpretations of Shi'i Islam render it not merely reconcilable with democratic processes, but open to the very concept of democracy.

CHAPTER ONE

Principles in Shi'i Islam

INTRODUCTION

An analysis of the doctrinal foundations of Shi'ism reveals several important shifts in theological interpretation that resulted in changes in Shi'i political culture. This dynamism in the conceptualisation of the faith suggests that there is ample space for democratisation to take place within the context of Shi'i Islam, and indeed *wilayat al-faqih*. This chapter will examine the basic principles of Shi'i Islam, the evolving interpretation of these principles in various eras and the coinciding evolution of political culture. A discussion of the periods of Lesser Occultation and Greater Occultation will show that while the prior was characterised by political quietism, the latter has seen the emergence of political activism. Finally, this chapter will explore the making and choosing of the Marja', a process which is not based on privilege, inheritance, nepotism or cronyism, but rather is firmly rooted in meritocracy, demonstrated ability, intelligence and competence.

FOUR SOURCES OF ISLAMIC LAW

Shi'i Islam, like Sunni Islam, acknowledges four sources of Islamic Law, or Shari'a. In Sunni Islam, Shari'a is based upon the Qur'an, the Sunna of the Prophet (Traditions), the consensus (*ijma*) of the *umma*, and analogical reasoning (*qiyas*). However, Twelver or Imami Shi'ism is based upon the following four sacred sources of Islamic legislation: the Qur'an, the Sunna of the Prophet and the Hadiths of the Twelve Imams, the consensus (*ijma*) of the jurists (*fuqaha*), and reason (*al-'aql*).

1. The Qur'an

Like the Sunnis, Shi'is consider the Qur'an the primary source of legislation, the infallible and impeccable revelation from Allah to his Prophet Muhammad. Both sects view the Qur'an as *hujja* (an apodictic proof), since it is the revealed word of God to the Prophet. Most of the fatwas or religious edicts that are based on the Qur'an are binding on the whole Muslim population, unless there is a difference in interpretation over the Qur'anic verse in question.

There are two types of verses in the Qur'an: *ayat muhkamat* or 'verses that are unequivocal in meaning', and *ayat mutashabihat*, 'verses that require allegorical interpretation'. Only God and erudite Muslim scholars are capable of rendering a hermeneutic interpretation of Qur'anic verses. In both Shi'i and Sunni jurisprudence, there is a consensus that the *ayat muhkamat* are those that state the clear Islamic injunctions (*ayat al-ahkam*) in subjects such as prayer, fasting, pilgrimage, alms giving, and personal status, etc.[1] These verses do not exceed 500.[2]

Both Shi'is and Sunnis view the Qur'an as the foundational and uncontested text in Islam, which abrogates any other text in cases of conflict. The Sixth Imam, Ja'afar al-Sadiq, advised that 'If the community of believers are faced with two different Hadiths, then they should juxtapose these to the Qur'an. Those that are in conformity with the Qur'an should be accepted and those which are in contradiction to it should be rejected or abrogated.'[3] In another account, al-Sadiq affirms that the final recourse is always God's book and his Traditions, and every Hadith that is not in conformity with the Qur'an should be abrogated.[4]

2. The Sunna

Unlike the Qur'an, the Sunna, which literally translates as the 'trodden path', has been a domain of contestation among Muslims. Though Shi'is and Sunnis agree on the saliency of the Hadith as an irrefutable source of legislation, they differ over which Hadith ought to be included within the abode of Sunna. While Sunnis only acknowledge the Hadiths of the Prophet and his four rightly guided Caliphs, the Shi'is include the Hadith of the Twelve Imams, starting from the Fourth Caliph Imam 'Ali, and his eleven descendants, beginning with Imam Hassan and ending with Imam al-Mahdi. This is the case because Shi'is consider the Twelve Imams infallible and impeccable. The only difference, in their

---

1 Al-Sheikh Murtada Al-Ansari, *Fara'id Al-Usul*, (FAU) volume two, Qom, 1405 AH (1984) pp. 108–111.
2 According to Fu'ad Ibrahim, most Islamic schools of law have limited their research to these verses; it seems that no serious study has been reported in relation to the other *ayat*. Fu'ad Ibrahim, *Al-Faqih wa Al-Dawla: Al-Fikar Al-Siyasi Al-Shi'i* (The Jurisprudent and the State Shi'i Political Thought), Beirut 1998.
3 Fu'ad Ibrahim, pp. 26–32.
4 Ibid.

view, between the Imams and the Prophet is that the latter received the revelation from Archangel Gabriel and the miracle of the Qur'an. According to Etan Kohlberg, 'the belief that Muhammad was the seal (that is the last) of the prophets is common to Imamis and Sunnis; but in contrast to the Sunnis, the Imamis in their law give the Imam a status identical to that of the Prophet. In other words, while both Sunnis and Imamis regard the Prophet's utterances and actions as the second source of Islamic law (after the Qur'an which is the word of God), the Imamis add to this source the utterances and actions of the Imams.'[1]

This difference in interpretation stems from the fact that Shi'is and Sunnis disagree on the centrality in Islam of *ahl al-bayt*, or literally 'the people of the house' or household of the Prophet Muhammad. The focal point of the disagreement emanates from a certain Hadith, *hadith al-thaqalayyn*, attributed to the Prophet Muhammad about the issue. Shi'is narrate the Hadith as saying: 'I order you after my death to adhere to two principles: The book of God (Qur'an) and my successors (*itra*), *ahl al-bayt*.' Sunnis narrate the Hadith the same way save one vital difference: the Sunnis replace *ahl al-bayt* with 'Sunna', or tradition.

In Twelver Shi'ism, the traditions of the Prophet and the Twelve Imams are considered as *hujja* or evidence. Traditions entail both the sayings and the deeds of the Prophet and the Imams. Shi'i jurists rely on these to derive *maqasid al-shari'a* (purposes of the Shari'a) and to come out with their injunctions. The Shi'i Hadith are compiled in four authoritative books, which contain the jurisprudential stipulations in different eras. These are: *Al-Kafi, Man La Yahdurhu Al-Faqih, Al-Tahdhib,* and *Al-Istibsar*. The Sixth Imam, Ja'afar al-Sadiq, enjoined the believers not to accept a Hadith unless it conforms to the book and traditions and falls in concordance with an earlier Hadith uttered by him or the previous five Imams.[2] Thus, he urged that it should be in conformity with the Qur'an and the Hadith.

3. Ijma'

Both Sunnis and Shi'is view *ijma'* as a source of Islamic legislation. In Sunni Islam, *ijma'* refers to the consensus of the *ulama*, or Islamic scholars. This argument is based on the Hadith of Muhammad that says: 'It is second to impossible that my *umma* agrees on aberration,' although traditionally, '*umma*' has been narrowly interpreted to include only the *ulama*. In Shi'i Islam, *ijma'* is confined to the jurisprudents (*fuqaha*) and not the lay people who are not well versed in interpreting the Divine truth. This view is based on the centrality of the doctrine of *ahl al-bayt* in Shi'i Islam.

In Twelver Shi'ism the Imam, who is a direct descendant of the Prophet Muhammad and 'Ali, the first Imam, is considered 'both sinless and absolutely

---

1   Etan Kohlberg, *Belief and Law in Imami Shi'ism,* Great Britain 1991, p. 5.
2   Al-Ansari, pp. 108-111.

infallible in his pronouncements on dogma and, indeed, in all matters.'[1] According to the late Ayatollah Murtaza Mutahhari, the *wilayat* or leadership of the Imam has four dimensions, stemming from the Qu'ranic verse 42:23[2] which states: 'Loving the *ahl al-bayt* is one of the *daruriyyat ad-din* (the essential parts of the Islamic faith)':

— *wilayat al-mahabba*, the right of love and devotion, which places Muslims under the obligation of loving the *ahl al-bayt*;

— *wilayat al-imama*, authority in spiritual guidance, which reflects the power and authority of the *ahl al-bayt* in guiding their followers in spiritual matters;

— *wilayat al-za'ama*, the authority in socio-political guidance, which reflects the right of *ahl al-bayt* to lead Muslims in all social and political aspects of life;

— *wilayat at-tasarruf*, the authority of the universal nature, which reflects the power over the entire universe that the Prophet and the *ahl al-bayt* have been vested with, by the grace of Almighty Allah.

According to the contemporary Usuli[3] Shi'i interpretation, *ijma'* signifies the agreement of a great number of *mujtahidin* (jurists who practice *ijtihad* or independent reasoning) or a substantial number of *fuqaha* in a certain era to adjudicate in such a way as to achieve the religious decree or fatwa.

The Shi'i scholars stood their ground against consensus from a Sunni perspective, as they deemed it incapable of conveying the true meaning of Tradition. According to al-Sharif al-Mutrada (966–1044 CE), a renowned Shi'i jurisprudent, consensus branches into three categories: the consensus of the *umma* that believes in Prophet Muhammad, the consensus of the community of devout believers, and the consensus of the *fuqaha*.[4] According to Sheikh Murtada al-Ansari (1799–1864) known as the father of all the *fuqaha*, these types of consensus in the doctrine of the Imamate do not constitute *hujja* unless they include the opinion of the Infallible Imam: 'the consensus of the Imamate is *hujja*, hence it includes the judgement of the Infallible Imam, as it has been established throughout the ages that there will never be a time without the presence of the Infallible Imam.' Contrary to the Sunnis, who sanctioned the abrogation of one *ijma'* by another, the Shi'is prohibited the abrogation of the *ijma'* because it entails the judgement of the Infallible Imam.[5] Thus, a close reading of Shi'i jurisprudence from the start of the Greater Occultation till our current time has

---

1   Fazlur Rahman, *Islam*, London: Weidenfeld and Nicholson, 1966, p. 173.
2   http://www.al-islam.org/wilayat/5.htm, Dr. Abdulaziz Sachedina, 'Appointment of 'Ali: Explicit or Implicit?' p. 1.
3   The majority denomination within Twelver Shi'ism.
4   Al-Sharif Al-Murtada, *Al-Shari'a fi Usul Al-Shi'i*, vol 1, Tehran, pp. 604–631.
5   Al-Sayyid Muhammad Taqi Al-Hakim, *Al-Usul al-'Amah lil-l-Fiqh al-Muqaran*, Beirut: Mu'assasat al-Bayt li-l-Tiba'ah wa al-Nashr, second edition, 1979, pp. 253 ff.

revealed that the debates over the issue of *ijma'* led to doubting and weakening its normative status.[1]

4. Al-'Aql

Devout Shi'is believe that God in His superabundantly omnibenevolent nature has endowed human beings with *al-'aql*, an independent capacity to differentiate between right and wrong, good and bad. There are many verses in the Qur'an that convey the prominence of *al-'aql*, or reasoning in Islam. One of the most salient is the following (39:9): 'It is those who are endued with understanding that receive admonition.'

There are also many Hadiths that convey a similar meaning, such as the Qudsi Hadith, when Allah said: 'When God created the human mind and endowed it with reasoning, he ordered it to come, and then to go. Then, God swore: "by my majesty and grace I never created a more beloved creation to me. With you [reasoning] I punish, with you I reward."' The Prophetic Hadith also highlights the importance of reasoning as follows: 'Goodness is entirely perceived by reasoning; he who has no reasoning has no religion.' Another Prophetic Hadith says: 'An hour of reasoning is better than sixty years of worship.' These three Hadiths demonstrate the saliency of reasoning in Islam because reasoning is considered the fulcrum of Islam.

Islamic Shari'a does not sanction its followers to believe what reason rejects or finds appalling. Moreover, Imam 'Ali said: 'Reasoning is to say what you know and to do what you utter.' In addition, the Iranian cleric Muhammad Reyshahri argues: 'Reasoning is the life of the soul.' He considers that reasoning has life and death and that man's moral and material dimensions are complementary to each other. Furthermore, reasoning is interpreted by light, and light is considered as a principle for the existence of reasoning. As such reasoning is looked at as 'a divine gift from which mankind originates'.[2]

Scholastic theology, or *'ilm al-kalam*, intervenes in weighing the evidential role of reason by transforming it from a dialectical concept to a jurisprudential concept in order to lend weight to reasoning in the jurisprudential (*fiqhi*) dimension. This is achieved by employing the discourses that centre on *al-tahsin wa al-taqbih al-'aqliyyayn wa al-shar'iyyayn*, which basically means that either reason or Shari'a is by itself is capable of determining independently whether something is good or bad. Reaching the dialectical connection between reason (*al-'aql*) and religion (*al-shar'*) boils down to the following reconciliation: 'what reason has sanctioned, religion has sanctioned.'[3]

1 Fu'ad Ibrahim, pp. 26–32.
2 Muhammad Rishahri, *Al-'Aql wa al-Jahil fi al-Kitab wa al-Sunna* (Reasoning and Ignorance in the Qur'an and the Sunna), Beirut 2000, pp. 17–19.
3 Fu'ad Ibrahim, ibid, pp. 26–32.

However, during the period of the Greater Occultation, a strong consensus has emerged among the Shiʻi *fuqaha* stressing that reason is not a form of independent evidence in its own right; rather it performs the function of uncovering or illuminating evidence.[1] Basing their argument on the understanding that reason is capable of recognizing the advantages and disadvantages of many things, Shiʻi jurists conceded that reason remains ignorant of numerous issues and therefore it cannot construe a lot of injunctions, in a positive or negative sense, unless aided by the Shariʻa .

Nevertheless, reason, although restricted within the confines of religious text, has ushered in a distinguished role by the creative usage of its capacities to analyse and research, leading to tangible results vis-à-vis Shariʻa injunctions and evidence. Employing reason to highlight the text has led to expanding the horizon of interpretation. Based upon the classical denotative meaning of *al-ʻaql* as light, reason has been recently regarded as functioning in its full capacity in order to find a compromise to emerging problems that do not have a clear injunction from the Qurʾan or the Hadith.[2]

To summarise, Shiʻi jurisprudence relies on the Qurʾan, especially the injunction verses (*ayat al-ahkam*), which throughout the history of Shiʻi jurisprudence have hardly undergone any change pertaining to interpretation. Traditions and reason as well were to take the primacy within the function and research of the Shiʻi *fuqaha*, thus widely opening the doors of *ijtihad* (independent reasoning) and its diverse perspectives and conclusions.[3]

THE PROBLEM OF SUCCESSION

Beyond theological schisms, a historical division also emerged between Sunnis and Shiʻis; the usurpation of Imam ʻAliʼs Caliphate and the subsequent martyrdom of the Third Imam Husayn, is vital in understanding the Shiʻis downtrodden status in history and pervasive sense of indignation, to the extent that the martyrdom of Imam Husayn succeeded in moulding a Shiʻi political culture and institutionalising the doctrine of Imamology.

According to Sunni tradition, Prophet Muhammad died without naming a

1   Fuʾad Ibrahim, ibid.
2   Muhammad Jawad Mughniyeh, *ʻilm Usul Al-fiqh fi Thawbihi Al-Jadid* (The Science of the Principles of Jurisprudence in its New Garment),   second edn, Beirut 1980, pp. 225–263; Muhammad Baqir Assadr, *Durus fi ʻIlm Al-Usul*, (Studies in the Principles of Jurisprudence), vol. 1, pp. 243 ff.
3   Al-Sheikh Murtada Al-Ansari, Faraid alUsul, *Muassasat Al-nashr Al-Islami Altabiʻa LiJamaʻat Almudarressin* (Principles of Jurisprudence), vol. 2, Qom, Iran 1405 AH,Volume 2, 275ff, section on ijmaʻ.

successor, and thus the leaders of the Muslim community, known as the people who bind and loose (*ahl al-hal wa al-'aqd*), met and reached a consensus (*ijma'*) that Abu Bakr, the father of the Prophet's wife 'Aisha and the eldest among the Prophet's companions, should become Caliph. He ruled from 632 to 634 CE. When Abu Bakr was on his death bed, he named 'Umar as his successor; thus he became the second of the four 'rightly guided caliphs', ruling from 634 to 644 CE. After the assassination of 'Umar, the people who bind and loose met and named 'Uthman as the third rightly guided caliph; his reign lasted from 644 till 656 CE. After 'Uthman was murdered, the nascent Islamic community plunged into civil war. 'Aisha, along with her brothers-in-law Talha and Zubayr (two of the Prophet's close companions), fought Imam 'Ali in the Battle of the Camel in the year 656 CE. Imam 'Ali won and he consolidated his leadership of the community of the faithful.

However, the Islamic community plunged again into civil war after Mu'awiyya challenged Imam 'Ali's leadership. They met in the Battle of Siffin in the year 657 CE, which witnessed an ebb and flow until the tide started to turn in the direction of 'Ali's forces. The shrewd Mu'awiyya ordered his army to raise the Qur'an on the top of their swords, asking for a truce in order to find a just arbitration between them. Imam 'Ali conceded to arbitration after his army was split between his faithful followers, the Shi'is, and the secessionists (the Khawarij). The Khawarij fought him and lost. As retribution, a Kharajite killed Imam 'Ali in the year 661, and as such Mu'awiyya became the uncontested leader of the community, especially after Imam Hassan, 'Ali's son, abdicated to him.[1]

The Sunnis, unlike the Shi'is, believe that after the death of the Prophet, his successors wielded only political and not religious authority. According to the Sunni tradition, during the period that has been termed by some scholars as the Golden Age of Islam, that is the ten-year rule of the Prophet in Madina from 622 till 632 CE, the year of his death, religious and political authority were both consummated in the Prophet himself.

According to the Shi'i tradition, the problem of succession of the Prophet has been neatly solved since the Prophet during his lifetime had appointed Imam 'Ali and his two sons Hassan and Husayn as his successors[2] and named all the twelve Imams till Imam al-Mahdi. As such the Shi'is believe that their leadership had been duped from their divine and inalienable right of succession after the death of the Prophet. They exercised patience and *taqiyya* (expedient dissimulation)

---

1   Bertold Spuler, *The Age of The Caliphs: A History of the Muslim World,* Princeton 1999, pp. 1–34. See also Ira M. Lapidus, *A History of Islamic Societies,* Cambridge University Press, 2005, pp. 1–30; pp. 45–47.

2   Devout Shi'is believe in the precedent of the people of the cloak (*ahl al-kisa'*), whereby the Prophet after covering Imams Ali, Hasan and Husayn with his cloak has specifically designated them as his successors and favourites.

and conceded to the Caliphate of Abu Bakr, 'Umar and 'Uthman in order to preclude the community of the faithful from plunging into civil war and schisms. They patiently waited for Imam 'Ali to become the leader of the faithful, but he was cheated and killed out of his rightful rule. As such, the Shi'is' only chance to lead the *umma* ceased to be and the Sunnis monopolised political power, maintaining it throughout the Umayyad and 'Abbasid dynasties.[1]

1. The Martyrdom of Imam Husayn

Briefly, as the only Shi'i Imam who actively pursued his claim to the Caliphate, Husayn's martyrdom acquired additional political purport.[2] Husayn's brother Hassan, the Second Imam, had been compelled to relinquish his claim to power to Mu'awiyya, the Umayyad governor of Syria, after a very brief period of rule.[3] Husayn initially shunned political activity, in deference to the treaty Hassan had made with Mu'awiyya. However, upon Mu'awiyya's death, and the accession to power by his son Yazid, Husayn was no longer bound to the pact. While the pious among the Sunnis had reconciled themselves to tyrannical Umayyad rule for the sake of Islamic unity,[4] Husayn could not accept Yazid's flagrant impiety and despotism, even on a de facto basis.

Against this background, Husayn readily heeded the people of Kufa's request to assume leadership there despite their notoriously fickle character.[5] Accompanied by just over seventy companions, Husayn embarked on his ill-fated mission to Kufa, along the route to which his party was intercepted by 4,000 of Yazid's troops at Karbala on the tenth day of the month of Muharram (in Arabic, *'ashura muharram*) in 680 CE. According to Shi'i belief, Husayn's baby was first killed, after which Husayn fought a heroic battle that culminated in his decapitation. In addition, the men who fought alongside him were also beheaded, and their heads were raised on stakes along with Husayn's, at Yazid's request.[6]

For Shi'is, the leitmotiv of injustice and suffering inherent in the tale of Husayn's martyrdom provides them with a cultural lexicon that was applicable to all times and places: 'Every day is 'Ashura and every place is Karbala', was

1   Moojan Momen, *An Introduction to Shi'i Islam: The History and Doctrines of Twelver Shi'ism* (AISI), Yale USA 1985, pp. 11–60.
2   Hamid Enayat, 'Martyrdom' in Nasr, Seyyed Hossein, Hamid Dabashi and Seyyed Vali Reza Nasr, eds. (1989) *Expectation of the Millennium: Shi'ism in History*, New York: State University of New York Press, p. 52.
3   Abdulaziz Sachedina, 'Activist Shi'ism in Iran, Iraq and Lebanon', in Martin E. Marty and R. Scott Appleby, eds., *Fundamentalisms Observed*, The Fundamentalist Project, vol. 1, Chicago and London 1991, p. 409.
4   Enayat, 'Martyrdom', p. 50.
5   Momen, AISI, p. 29.
6   Fouad Ajami, *The Vanished Imam: Musa al-Sadr and the Shi'i of Lebanon*, London 1986, p. 141.

the resonant theme.[1] This event would have varying manifestations in different periods of Shi'i history. For example, in the early 1970s, it served as a revolutionary exemplar and an indispensable mechanism for communal political mobilisation.

2. The pre-Occultation (Ghayba) Period

The interim phase between the martyrdom of Husayn and the Occultation of the Twelfth Imam who is believed to have gone into *ghayba*, or hiding, in the ninth century, is one which best epitomises the accommodationist strand of Shi'i political culture. On the doctrinal level, the Karbala drama was conceived as a soteriology by the pre-Ghayba Shi'is; Husayn had intentionally died in order to redeem the Muslim community, just as Christ had done for humanity.[2] On the political level, the blame for Husayn's death, as well as the deaths of all successive Imams,[3] fell squarely on the Sunni Caliphate and all subsequent rulers were perceived as illegitimate.

The perception of the Sunni Caliphs as morally bankrupt was pitted against the conceptualisation of the Shi'i Imams as eminently virtuous. In part, this view was facilitated by the Imams' exclusion from political power, which enabled them to preserve their moral integrity. More significantly, the doctrine of Imamology contributed to this moral dualism, as it embraces the principle of *'isma,* or infallibility of the Twelve Imams.[4] The apotheosis of the Imams underlies the staunch allegiance paid to them by their believers and by the same token, the sanctity of their teachings and injunctions.

Against this backdrop, the Imams – the Fifth,Sixth and Eighth in particular – were empowered with the ability to depoliticise their Shi'i adherents in the face of Umayyad and Abbasid repression.[5] Beginning with Zaynul 'Abidin, the Fourth Imam, a policy of political quietism was instituted. That Muhammad al-Baqir, the Fifth Imam, cautioned one of his followers against participating in 'Ali ibn Zayd's resistance to the Ummayads, was taken as an indication of endorsement of his father's policy.[6] By the mid-eighth century, Shi'i depoliticisation became firmly established by the Sixth Imam, Ja'far al-Sadiq. By declaring *taqiyya*

---

1   Nazih Ayubi, 'State Islam and Communal Plurality', *Annals of the American Academy of Political and Social Science* 524, November 1992, p. 86.

2   Enayat, ibid, p. 53.

3   Shahrough Akhavi, 'The Ideology and Praxis of Shi'ism in the Iranian Revolution', in *Comparative Studies in Society and History* 25, April 1983, p. 203.

4   Khalid Khishtainy, 'Shi'ism and the Islamic Revolution', *Contemporary Review* 247, 1985, p. 64.

5   Ervand Abrahamian, *Khomeinism: Essays on the Islamic Republic,* 1993, London: I.B. Taurus & Co. Ltd. p. 113.

6   Jassim Hussein, 'Messianism and the Mahdi', in Nasr, Seyyed Hossein, Hamid Dabashi & Seyyed Vali Reza Nasr, eds. *Expectation of the Millenium: Shi'ism in History,* 1989, New York: State University of New York Press. p. 17.

(precautionary dissimulation) is my religion and the religion of my forefathers,' al-Sadiq laid the doctrinal basis of political quietism.[1] Combined with the relinquishment of political rule and the indeterminate suspension of the Imam's political functions,[2] Shi'i depoliticisation was institutionalised on both a de jure and a de facto basis.

The renunciation of political power coupled with the preservation of the Imamate's moral authority was translated practically as submission to Abbasid rule without according it any legitimacy.[3] The moral logic behind this political realism was that Shi'i militancy against the Abbasids would be futile and self-destructive. According to one historian, the Imams did not feel that their adherents had the necessary degree of political awareness or loyalty for political activism.[4] As such, al-Sadiq and his successors devolved the revolutionary task onto an unspecified member of their own al-Qa'im[5] or al-Mahdi (the rightly guided one)[6] – whose *qiyam*, or rise, was foretold by the Prophet Muhammad.[7]

Ever since Imam al-Mahdi (also known as the Hidden Imam) was identified with the Twelfth Imamate during the Tenth Imam's lifetime,[8] every generation of Shi'is has awaited his *zuhur*, or appearance.[9] Born in 868 CE in Samarra, Muhammad Abul-Qasim (the Twelfth Imam) succeeded his father as Imam in 874 CE but went into hiding that same year after making only one appearance as a young boy.[10] For the next sixty-seven years, known as the 'Lesser Occultation', the Twelfth Imam communicated with the Shi'i community through four different agents, or, as they were called by the Shi'is, *sufara,* or deputies. A few days before the death of the fourth deputy, Muhammad as-Samarra in 941 CE, the Imam is believed to have declared the end of the Lesser Occultation, and hence all communication with the community, and the commencement of the Greater Occultation.[11] This second Occultation (Al-Ghayba) would persist for an indefinite period of time until God so willed his *raj'a*, or return.

As an article of the Shi'i faith, the doctrine of *raj'a* is based on the messianic belief that upon his *qiyam*, or rise, the Mahdi will Islamicise the whole world and

1   Mangol Bayat, 'Khomeinism', in *Expectation of the Millenium: Shi'ism in History*, p. 354.
2   Ibid., p. 348.
3   Sami Zubaida, *Islam: The People and the State,* London and New York 1993, p. 27.
4   Hussein, 'Messianism and the Mahdi', p. 20.
5   Ibid., 21.
6   David Rapoport, 'Messianic Sanctions for Terror', in *Comparative Politics,* vol. 20, New York: January 1988, p. 202.
7   Hussein, 'Messianism and the Mahdi', p. 14.
8   Ibid., p. 20.
9   Abdulaziz Sachedina, 'Messianism and the Mahdi' in Nasr, Seyyed Hossein, Hamid Dabashi & Seyyed Vali Reza Nasr, eds. *Expectation of the Millenium: Shi'ism in History,* 1989, New York: State University of New York Press. p. 30.
10   Momen, ibid., p. 161.
11   Ibid., p. 164.

institute a rule of justice on earth[1] that will represent the Shi'is' golden age. This Islamicisation process necessarily entails the use of force as signified by one of the Mahdi's aliases: Sayyid al-Sayf, or master of the sword.[2] Like Imam Husayn, he will use the sword to fight oppression but unlike him, the Mahdi will be driven by a vendetta, especially against Husayn's slayers.[3] The direct corollary of this theme is the concept of *faraj*, or freedom from grief; after centuries of unbearable suffering and persecution, the Mahdi will come to redeem the Shi'is[4] when the world is consumed by tyranny and injustice.[5]

3. The Post-Ghayba Period

Although the Ghayba doctrine could, in theory, justify both politically activist and politically quietist courses of action,[6] the Occultation of the Twelfth Imam had the practical effect of shifting what little emphasis there was on politics – in the pre-Ghayba period – to theology.[7] Based on a 'suffering and passion' ethos, the post-Ghayba Shi'is resigned themselves to political fatalism; their emancipation would only come about at the end of time when the Mahdi would root out all evil and tyranny.[8]

In a similar vein, the politically passive interpretation of the Karbala drama obscured the revolutionary symbolism implicit in the narrative. As in the pre-Ghayba period, Husayn's martyrdom was construed as an act of redemption. The suffering and affliction he consequently endured, supposedly passively, rendered him highly noble and virtuous. Such was the teaching of the *ta'ziyya*, or 'Ashura ceremony promoted by the Safavid and Qajar ruling elites, who hoped to instil their subjects with a sense of political apathy.[9]

What further reinforced the Shi'i community's sense of political resignation was its staunch allegiance to a conservative religious leadership – dominated by the Akhbaris until the late eighteenth century, a group which had divested itself of political and religious authority. According to this school of jurisprudence, the *akhbar*, or reports of the Shi'i Imams, constituted the fundamentals of the Shi'i faith and as such, were to be observed dogmatically.[10] Having ruled out legal ration-

---

1 Sachedina, 'Messianism and the Mahdi', etc. p. 39.
2 Ibid., p. 40.
3 Ibid., p. 30.
4 Sachedina, 'Messianism and the Mahdi', p. 38.
5 Momen, ibid., p. 166.
6 Sachedina, 'Activist Shi'ism in Iran, Iraq and Lebanon', p. 423.
7 Esposito, John, L., ed., *The Iranian Revolution: Its Global Impact*, Miami: Florida International University Press, 1990.
8 Sachedina, 'Activist Shi'ism in Iran, Iraq and Lebanon', p. 403.
9 Enayat, pp. 53–54.
10 Juan R.I. Cole and Nikki R. Keddie, 'Introduction', eds., *Shi'ism and Social Protest*, New Haven and London 1986, p. 6.

alism as a jurisprudential procedure, there was no attempt to systematise government. In fact, the only juristic deliberation they permitted themselves was in the realm of political accommodation.[1] Thus, while all governments were perceived as illegitimate, on account of the fact that the Twelfth Imam did not head them,[2] they were granted a de facto recognition that sanctioned a variety of options.[3]

Under tenth-century Buyyid rule,[4] the argument was put forward that since only the Twelfth Imam could implement the Shari'a, it could not be fully executed in his absence. Correspondingly, the politically relevant functions of the Imam had 'lapsed'. Such a line of reasoning meant that while the government was illegitimately perceived, active opposition to it was barred.[5] Rather than preach the absolute eschewal of political power, the Shi'i jurists rationalised that participation in an illegitimate government could be deemed justifiable if it 'benefited the brethren in faith'.[6]

By the early sixteenth century when Twelver Shi'ism[7] became established as state religion by the Safavids, accommodation had become the norm. Some *ulama*, or religious scholars, even upheld the view the Safavid Sheikhs[8] were owed obedience on account of their status as the 'shadows of God on earth'.[9] While this perception of the Sheikhs was not generalised, the religious institution as a whole did not view the Safavid monarchy as illegitimate[10] and accordingly proscribed political opposition.[11] However, this political deference was countered by religious independence as evidenced by the *na'ib al-'amm*, or general delegate concept advanced by the prominent Shi'i scholar, Sheikh Zaynud-Din ibn 'Ali al-Juba'i, known as *Shahid ath-Thani*, or the Second Martyr (d.1558).[12] By transferring the religious prerogatives of the Hidden Imam – such as the collection

---

1   Norman Calder, 'Accommodation and Revolution in Imami Shi'i Jurisprudence: Khomeini and the Classical Tradition', *Middle East Studies*, vol. 18, 1982, p. 1 and p. 5.

2   Gregory Rose, 'Velayet-e-Faqih and the Recovery of Islamic Identity in the Thought of Ayatollah Khomeini', in Nikki Keddie, ed., *Religion and Politics in Iran*, New Haven and London 1983, p. 171.

3   Calder, 'Accommodation and Revolution', p. 6.

4   The Buyyid Dynasty was a Shi'i Persian dynasty that lasted from 934 to 1055 and encompassed territory extending across most of modern-day Iran and Iraq.

5   Calder, 'Accommodation and Revolution', p. 4.

6   Sachedina, 'Activist Shi'ism', etc., p. 409.

7   So named because adherents believe that the Twelfth Imam is the promised Mahdi. By contrast, one faction of Ismaili Shi'is are deemed Seveners, because they see the Seventh Imam as the Mahdi. Twelvers are also variously known as *Ithna-'Ashari* in Arabic, or Imami Shi'is, or Ja'afari Shi'is, after the name of their legal school. They make up some 85 percent of the global Shi'i community. Thus when a person uses the term 'Shi'i' he or she invariably means a Twelver Shi'i, unless qualified by another term, such as Ismaili or Zaidi.

8   Religious figures or political rulers.

9   Abrahamian, p. 19.

10 Zubaida, p. 31.

11 Bayat, 'The Iranian Revolution', p. 35.

12 See Calder, 'Accommodation and Revolution', p. 4 and Momen, p. 190.

and distribution of religious taxes and the call for a defensive jihad – to the Shi'i *ulama*, the religious leadership's authority was greatly enhanced. However, such authority remained a doctrinal abstraction until the Qajar period.[1] The elevated religious standing of the *ulama* under Qajar rule was further bolstered by the victory of the Usulis over the Akhbaris in the late eighteenth century, as will be elaborated in the next section.

By institutionalising *ijtihad*, the Hidden Imam's general deputies now had a much-enlarged scope of authority.[2] Moreover, the principle of *ijtihad* bought with it a religious hierarchy that further inflated the authority of some *ulama* who became *mujtahidin* (those who practised *ijtihad*) or more prominent still, *marji' at-taqlid*, or models of emulation.[3] But most significant was the creation of the centralised role of the *marja' al-akbar* which was to be filled by a pre-eminent *Marja' at-taqlid*.[4] The upshot of these developments was the cultivation of a unique relationship between believers and religious leaders[5] whose charismatic authority was inextricably bound to the Hidden Imam.[6]

Parallel to this consolidation of religious authority, was the palpably opposi-tional position of the *ulama* vis-à-vis the Qajar rulers.[7] However, this political stand did not stem from the conviction that the political authority and temporal rule inherent in their deputyship were theirs to seize.[8] Rather, their opposition assumed the form of protests against specific issues related to justice and Islamic morality. One such instance was the fatwa issued by one of the first universally recognised *marji' at-taqlid*, Ayatollah Muhammad Hasan Shirazi, banning the consumption of tobacco, in protest against the British Tobacco Concession of 1892.[9]

While such protests served to assert the *ulama*'s independence from Qajar rule, the same purpose was also served by the *ulama*'s bestowal of a much-cov-eted legitimacy upon the Qajar rulers. Thus, although Fath 'Ali Shah, the second Qajar ruler, was accorded with a 'derived de jure legitimacy' in light of Sheikh Ja'far Kashiful-Ghita's declaration of jihad against the Russians,[10] the 'retractable' nature of this legitimacy underlined the growing influence enjoyed by the *ulama*.

---

1 Momen, p. 190.
2 Cole and Keddie, p. 7.
3 Sivan, Emmanuel. *Radical Islam, Medieval Theology, and Modern Politics*. New Haven and London: Yale University Press, 1985.
4 'Abbas Kelidar, 'The Shi'i Imami Community and Politics in the Arab East', in *Middle East Studies* vol. 19, 1983, p. 1 and p.7.
5 Sachedina, "Activist Shi'ism", etc., p. 424.
6 Sivan, ibid., p 10.
7 Zubaida, p. 28.
8 Momen, p. 195.
9 Rose, 'Velayet-e-Faqih', p. 175.
10 Momen, p. 194.

The newfound ability to withhold and offer support at whim rendered the *ulama* a 'potential resistance' as opposed to an active one.[1]

While the Lesser Occultation lasted for under seventy years, the Greater Occultation is indefinite. Unlike the period of the Lesser Occultation, upon the declaration of the Greater Occultation there were no *sufara* to disseminate the directives and teachings of Imam Mahdi. The *sufara* here have come to be represented by the Grand Marja's, the *wali al-faqihs*, or leader jurisprudents who have shouldered responsibility for guiding people. The Greater and the Lesser Occultation periods have in turn been characterised by debate within Imami Shi'ism. This debate has in turn led to the emergence of two basic sects in Shi'i Islam: pacifists who advocate waiting peacefully for the Mahdi; and activists who believe there is a primordial role to be played by Shi'is to help pave the way for the Mahdi to return.

The pacifists comprise religious scholars, intellectuals and lay people who base their belief on the idea that, since the Mahdi will not appear until oppression and tyranny prevail in the world, the ideal approach is to wait patiently. They believe this attitude will hasten the reappearance of the Hidden Imam, who will eventually come to eradicate oppression and lay the foundation for a heavenly state of justice and equality.

Activists on the other hand are convinced that they should do everything possible to help pave the way for the Imam. They have been active in fighting oppression and bear responsibility of Shi'i mobilisation and activism. They have come to be known as *al-mumahidun*, or those who pave the way for the advent of the Mahdi.

Ayatollah al-Khu'i (1899–1992), a *Marja' at-taqlid* who 'is reported to have opposed Imam Khomeini's political activity',[2] exemplifies the former, while Ayatollah al-'Uzma, Imam Khomeini (1902–1989), *Marja' al-tajdid* or authority of innovation, represent the latter. Imam Khomeini's contribution in this field consists in his blatant rejection of *taqiyya*, or expedient dissimulation, which he considers to be one of the major sources of passivity of the Shi'is. His alternative was opting for mobilisation and political activism; thus, he rejected the *taqiyya* of some *ulama* who argued that sins should proliferate for the Mahdi to appear in order to redress injustice. By contending that if sins did not proliferate then the Twelveth Imam would not appear, they retreated from their role as guides. And so Khomeini considered the practice of *taqiyya* legitimate only if it is intended to safeguard the self and others from dangers resulting from the application of religious rules, rites and practices. However, if Islam is in danger, then there is no room for passivity; he also enjoined the *ulama* not to practise *taqiyya* and not to work for an unrighteous government.

---

1   Calder, 'Accommodation and Revolution', p. 7.
2   Moojan Momen, *An Introduction to Shi'i Islam: The History and Doctrines of Twelver Shi'ism* (AISI), Yale USA 1985, p. 262.

Moreover, according to Imam Khomeini another factor that contributed to the passivity of the Shi'is was their belief that government in the absence of the Imam is perverted and unjust even if headed by a Shi'i.[1] As a result, the Shi'i *ulama* used to recommend to their followers not to get involved in government and to refuse governmental positions as these governments were deemed unjust or *kuffar*, or apostate governments anathema to the political order.[2] This somewhat explains why the Shi'is until recent decades were not fairly represented in governmental positions; their negative attitude towards established government made them passive and hampered their active participation in public and political life.[3]

However, with the introduction of the doctrine of *wilayat al-faqih*, the leadership of the divine jurisprudent, this practice was radically changed if not completely uprooted: this doctrine made possible the establishment of a just government in the absence of the Hidden Imam. This turned out to be a springboard of political activism as it conferred upon the Shi'is the duty to establish such a government. As such, the *ulama* were not passive any more; on the contrary, they resorted to political activism, being regarded as successors of the Hidden Imam, thus engendering complete allegiance from the masses.

USULI AND AKHBARI SCHOOLS OF SHI'I ISLAM

The Usuli school has stressed the necessity of the presence of a Marja' for the believers to emulate. By emulating the Marja's, the believers are guided in their religious affairs as well as their daily dealings, even those matters pertaining to marriage, inheritance, prayer, fasting, pilgrimage, alms giving and the like. These authoritative views have been elaborated into something like a comprehensive theory in the wake of the Qajari era and the advent of the constitutional revolution, of which a leading jurist was Sayyid Muhammad Husayn al-Na'ini. Since then, the central issue does not only centre upon the following of the fatwas of the Marja's, but rather emphasises the importance of the participation of the *ulama* and *marja' al-taqlid* in the authority itself as al-Na'ini has stipulated.

In contrast, the Akhbaris stressed the holiness of the Hadith of the Imams as an obligatory grace that believers should abide by without any distortion or hermeneutic interpretation or the use of rational sciences. Al-Akhbaris stressed the importance of being aloof from politics during the Occultation period of the Infallible Imam.

The controversy between the Usuli and Akhbari schools became prominent during the seventeenth and eighteenth centuries when the Usuli school prevailed

---

1   The Shah's government fell into this category.
2   Imam Khomeini, *Al-Hukuma Al-Islamiyya*, Beirut 1991, p. 66 ff.
3   This was the case of the majority of the Shi'is in Lebanon till the advent of Imam Musa al-Sadr.

over the Akhbari school that went into demise. The Akhabris were against *ijtihad* and rendering a salient stance to the *mujtahidin*; they based Shi'i jurisprudence on *akhbar* or traditions and not on rational principles or the *usul* of *fiqh* that are used in *ijtihad*, thus rejecting rational principles upon which *ijtihad* and *fiqh* were based. By this, the Akhbaris moved towards Sunni principles of jurisprudence. In essence the difference between the Usuli and Akhbari schools can be summarised as such:

— The Usuli school acknowledges four sources of the Shari'a: the Qur'an, the traditions of the Prophet and the Twelve Imams, *ijm'a* and *'aql*. On the other hand, the Akhbaris only accept the first two stressing that the Qur'an can only be construed by way of traditions of the Prophet and the Imams.

— The Usuli school holds that by employing *'aql* one can construe the meaning of Qur'an and traditions, while the Akhbari school stresses that the Qur'an and traditions can only be construed by the exegeses and hermeneutic interpretation of the imams.

— The Usuli school claims that the four referential books of jurisprudence (*Al-Kafi, Man La Yahdurhu Al-Faqih, Al-Tahdhib,* and *Al-Istibsar*) are filled with many controversial traditions and unfounded Hadith, while the Akhbaris consider these four books as canonical.

— The Usulis believe that the Qur'an and the Traditions are in harmony with what can be derived from rational principles. On the contrary, the Akhbaris give precedence to the former over the latter.[1]

After the victory of the Usuli School, which came to be known as the Ja'afari School, religious seminaries across the Shi'i world adopted universal guidelines that were set in order to choose the leading *mujtahid*, who after passing stringent theological requirements becomes a Marja' (authority of emulation).

THE MAKING AND CHOOSING OF A MARJA'

Although much has been written and said about the Marja's in Shi'i literature, scant academic attention has been accorded to the role of the Marja's in the Shi'i community. While some researchers have touched upon some relevant intellectual themes, hardly any have conducted a comprehensive study that encompasses all of them into a single framework of analysis. Moreover, although 'Marja' observers' have explored some aspects of this role, only a few have examined it with the aim of discerning the degree to which it is compatible with the secular world. The lack of literature on the matter should invite no astonishment, as the Marja' itself, as a concept and as an institution, has been a topic of mounting debate, especially

---

1   Ali Khalifa Al-Kawtharani, et. al., *Al-Istibdad fi Nuzum Al-Hukm Al-Arabiyya Al-Muasira* (Tyranny in Contemporary Arab Political Systems), Beirut 2005, pp. 67–72.

since the establishment of the Islamic Republic of Iran which the Shi'is regard as the first Islamic Republic since the death of Prophet Muhammad. The debate has been heated ever since the death of Imam Khomeini who was the grand Marja', the leader and the governor of Iran, and who has a substantial following across the Shi'i Islamic world.

Shi'is have always taken pride in the Najaf religious school. This college considers itself as the forerunner in teaching religious aspects, partly due to the longevity of the city as a centre of Shi'i learning. Najaf is the Shi'i equivalent of Cairo's Al-Azhar for Sunnis. Unlike Najaf, Azhar was a recognised centre of Islamic learning celebrated worldwide. Arab Shi'is believe that their city deserves equal status, having been founded as a place for learning in the year 1056, when Cairo was barely fifty years old as a city, and Al-Azhar was still in its infancy. To become a Marja', one has to complete three levels of studies to become a *mujtahid*, and after that a programme of study and research to manifest excellence and eligibility, which will be detailed in the coming pages.

1. Qualities of the Marja'

The Encyclopedia of Islam states that the essential function of the Marja', also called *muqallad*, is to guide the community of those who 'imitate' his teachings, in particular concerning the application of the rules of the Shari'a, *furu'idin* and *ahkam*, judicial solutions or legal qualifications in regard to the problems of contemporary life. Imitation of the Marja' has no connection in principle with *usul al-din* or the principles of faith and from *yaqin* (deep inner conviction). The *mujtahid* established as Marja' must pronounce fatwas, or judicial decisions and write one or more books to guide his *muqallidin*, or followers, in the form of a *risala amaliyya*, a kind of a practical treatise.[1]

One of the best illustrations of the qualities of a Marja' is what Sheikh Tubrusi states in his book *Al-Ihtijaj*, quoting an anonymous Imam, 'He of the *fuqaha*, or legal experts, who is self-preserving (*sa'nann linafsihi*), religion preserving, against his desires, conforming to God's will, then the lay people should emulate him.'[2] There is a consensus among the *fuqaha* that anyone who wants to become a Marja' should acquire the following three principal qualifications: *al-'adala* (justice), *al-a'lamiyya* (the highest knowledge), and *al-hayat* (life) which will be discussed in order.

Al-'adala refers in one sense to *istiqama* or straightforwardness, as employed by the *fuqaha*. According to Muhammad Baqir al-Sadr, justice boils down to

---

1   *The Encyclopedia of Islam*, New edition edited by C.E. Bosworth, E.Van Donzel, B. Lewis and Ch. Pellat. Volume 6 Leiden E.J. Brill 1991.
2   Ali Ahmad Al-Bahadli, *Al-Hawza Al-'Ilmiyya fi Al-Najaf: Ma'alimaha wa Harakataha Al-Islahiyya (1920–1980)* (The Religious Seminary in Najaf: Features and Reformist Trends), Beirut 1993, p. 201.

'straightforwardness according to God's Shari'a and way.'[1] There are at least two Qur'anic verses that substantiate the aforementioned: 'Stand firm (in the straight path)' (11:112) and 'If they had only remained on the right way' (72:16). Sheikh Muhammad Husayn Kashif al-Ghita' defines justice as a '*malaka*,' or instinct 'with which the individual abstains from sins and performs one's duty. Its ultimate manifestation is reverence of God.'[2] For his part, Imam Khomeini defined justice as: 'an imprinted instinct leading to adherence to piety, refraining from vice and enjoining [religious] duties.'[3] Ayatollah al-Khu'i deals with the problem of proving how a Marja' becomes just by stating that in order to prove the justice of a certain Marja' the following stipulations must be taken into account: experiential knowledge; the testimonies of two just individuals, one just individual, or a well-entrusted individual and reputation. However, according to Imam Khomeini: 'the attribute of justice is eliminated by having a big vice (*kabira*), insistence on small vices, or even by committing small ones.'[4]

According to the late Sheikh Muhammad Mahdi Shamseddine, the *fuqaha* gave two *'adilla 'aqliyya*, or rational substantiations for the indispensability of *'adalat* or justice, *Marja' al-taqlid*. The first *dalil*, or sign, *al-awlawiyya al-'aqliyya*, or the primacy of reason, is the sense that if justice is a basic requirement for the Imam al-Jama'a, the Sheikh leading the prayers, and in the divorce-witness, then it is more needed in *marja' at-taqlid*. The second *dalil* is *al-istib' ad al-'aqli wa al-dhawqi*, or conceptual distancing from predilection [i.e. so as to be objective] for fear that the absence of *al-'adala* in *Marja' at-taqlid* would lead to grave consequences in legislating the religious law.[5] For his part Imam Ghazali commented on conditioning *al-'adala* in the *mujtahid*, saying, 'It is a condition to accept his [*mujtahid*] fatwa, but not his *ijtihad* ... so if he breached his *'adala* by committing a vice, then he reappropriated the characteristic of *al-'adal*, he would be eligible to embrace Marja's and issue fatwas.'[6]

According to a consensus among the *fuqaha*, the practitioner of *al-a'lamiyya* is well versed in *istinbat*, or logical reasoning. In distinguishing between the most knowledgeable and others, Imam Ghazali states: 'I would rather follow the most knowledgeable. He who believes that the Shafi'i is the most knowledgeable, and that his *madhhab* [school] is the right one, is not entitled to embrace any other *madhhab*, out of favoritism.'[7] Al-Muhaqiq al-Karaki contends that there

---

1   Ibid., p. 214.
2   Ibid., p. 215.
3   Ibid.
4   Ibid., p. 216.
5   Sheikh Muhammad Mahdi Shamseddine, *Al-Ijtihad wa Al-Taqlid: Bahith Fuqhi Istidlali Muqaran* (Ijtihad and Emulation: A Comparative Fuqhi Istidlali Research), Beirut 1998, p. 290.
6   Ibid., p. 287.
7   Al-Bahadli, *Al-Hawza*, etc. p. 221.

is consensus among the Shi'i *fuqaha* concerning the primacy and necessity of *al-a'lamiyya*. The stipulation of *al-a'lamiyya* in the Marja' serves as an incentive for more research and religious learning, in conformity with God's saying: 'of knowledge it is only a little that is communicated to you, (O men)' (17: 85). The fatwas of the Najafi *ulama* serve the same purpose: if there has been a conflict in the fatwas among the *mujtahidin*, then the *muqallidin* should refer to the most knowledgeable. Another fatwa states that if the most knowledgeable was refuted by another, then the *muqallidin* refer back to the *A'lam* (most knowledgeable).[1]

It is worth noting that the renowned Lebanese Shi'i Marja' Sayyid Muhammad Husayn Fadlallah stressed that being most knowledgeable in fiqh, or the practice of Islamic law, does not necessarily mean that the Marja' is most knowledgeable in the socio-political spheres, which he deems as an essential criterion for Marja's. Other jurists say that emulating the most knowledgeable does not necessarily mean 'the most knowledgeable in the entire world,' rather the most feasibly reached.[2]

Al-hayat, or life, is the third primary condition that should be present in the Marja's. The Shi'i *fuqaha* stipulated this condition to ensure renovation in intellectual legislative life. Unlike the Sunnis who confine *taqlid*, or acceptance of a religious ruling to four schools of law, the Shi'is purport that all the intellectual production of the Sunnis lacks authenticity and creativity, while the Shi'i *ulama* have achieved remarkable progress in conforming with the eras in which they live.[3] A substantial disagreement between Shi'i and Sunni *fuqaha* arose in connection with stipulating life as a primary condition in the Marja'. The Shi'i *fuqaha* have, in their majority, agreed that once embarking upon emulation, the emulated Marja' should be alive. Emulating a dead Marja' is prohibited in principle. Contrary to this, the Sunni *fuqaha* have not stipulated life as a condition to start emulating a Marja' and approve of the emulation a dead Marja'. Imam ash-Shafi'i said, '*al-madhahib la tamut bi mawti arbabiha*,' or 'schools do not die with the death of their founders.' This is what led later on to the confining of their schools of law to the four traditional ones, namely Hanafi, Shafi'i, Hanbali and Maliki. (Thus, the Sunnis had closed the doors of *ijtihad*, while the Shi'is never closed the doors of *ijtihad*; on the contrary, for them *ijtihad* is an ever-continuing process.) It is worth mentioning that Sheikh Shamseddine sanctioned the emulation of a dead Marja', in the sense that emulating a dead Marja' is not an emulation of the person, rather the fatwas that he issued during his lifetime, which do not become obsolete upon his death. The other Shi'i *fuqaha* allowed the *muqallidin* to emulate a dead Marja' if he had started emulating him during his life in issues that he remembers.[4]

---

1   Ibid., p. 222.
2   Shamseddine, *Al-Ijtihad wa Al-Taqlid* ..., p. 367.
3   Al-Bahadli, *Al-Hawza*, etc., p. 220.
4   Shamseddine, *Al-Ijtiihad*, pp. 336–7.

Although the aforementioned constitute the primary criteria for the Marja', the *fuqaha* have mentioned other conditions albeit with less assertion. These are: memorisation of the Qur'an; memorisation of the Sunna, *al-dabit*, or strong retentive memory; *bulugh*, or reaching puberty; *'aql*, or intellect; *hurriya*, or freedom; *taharit al-mawlid*, or clear birth; and *dhukoura*, or male gender.

Some *fuqaha* contended that if the Marja' is a *hafiz*, someone who memorises the entire Qur'an, then he would be more capable of *istinbat*, or soliciting the religious law. Others confined the issue to memorising only *ayat al-ahkam*, or verses of order. The same applies to the memorisation of the Sunna or Hadith, where they agreed on the necessity of memorising *ahadith al-akham*. Nevertheless a thorny issue arose here in relation to the number of Hadith to be memorised. Some *fuqaha* say that they amount to 300,000, while others contend that they are only 500.[1] Concerning *al-dabit*, or strong retentive memory, the Marja' should be distinguished in memorisation, especially if he works in adjudication or *qada*. Ayatollah al-Khu'i states: 'The Marja' should have an average standard in *al-dabit*,' in the sense that he is not known for his forgetfulness.[2]

According to the *fuqaha*, *bulugh* implies *bulugh al-shar'i*, in which one of two distinguished features is recognised: reaching puberty, or completing fifteen lunar years.[3] There is an overwhelming consensus among the *fuqaha* on the saliency of *'aql*. Sayyid Muhammad Baqir al-Sadr defines *'aql* as 'a sense of reason and maturity to feel responsible and committed'.[4]

Regarding *huriyaa*, some define freedom in relationship to slavery. They contend that a slave can't completely detach himself from being affected by his prevailing circumstances, which influence his judgement. Other leading Marja's, like Khomeini, Khu'i and Muhammad Baqir al-Sadr, did not approve it as a condition.[5]

Regarding *taharit al-mawlid*, or clear birth, Muslim scholars have long defined the status of the offspring born of illicit intercourse (also called *ibn zina*) as impure and possessing 'despicable qualities'. The Twelver or Imami Shi'ism in particular poses a more serious issue in this regard. The Fifth Imam Muhammad al-Baqir is quoted as saying that the *ibn zina*, or son of an adulteress, is a product of *zani*, an adulterer and the devil, both of whom participate in the sexual act. Other Imami Hadiths convey a basic message that the hallmark of the *ibn zina* is hatred of the *ahl al-bayt*. As such, they will not enter paradise, and thus cannot be Marja's.[6]

---

1   Ibid., p. 352.
2   Ibid., p. 352.
3   Al-Bahadli, *Al-Hawza* p. 312.
4   Sadr, *Al-Fatawa Al-Wadiha* (Clear Decrees) Najaf, 1976. p. 127.
5   Ibid., pp. 216–217.
6   Kohlberg, *Belief and Law in Imami Shi'ism*, pp. 237–239.

Regarding *dhukoura,* or male gender, many *fuqaha* have long agreed that the Marja' should be male, thus marginalising the role of women in this regard. They base their argument on the Hadith that says: 'Those who give their command to a woman are truly the losers.' Ayatollah al-Khu'i contended that women are not allowed to be Marja's since they are prohibited from mixing with men, or assuming public office. Recently, things have started to change with certain scholarly voices debating the issue. Shamseddine quotes both al-Muhaqiq al-Asfahani, who says, 'there is no evidence that women are prohibited to be Marja's,' and al-Sayyid al-Hakim who argues, 'many *muhaqiqeen* (jurisprudents who are authorities in a certain branch of *fiqh*) have issued fatwas allowing women to be emulated.' Shamseddine further supports his argument with a quotation from Ibn Jurayr: 'Since women are allowed to be muftis, so she is allowed to be a judge.'[1]

2. Choosing the Marja'

Here lies one of the most hotly debated issues, yet to be resolved. Currently, there is no clear-cut method for choosing the Marja'. Instead the process is influenced by factors ranging from political, social and even geographical considerations. Another point of contention has to do with ethnicity, for instance being an Arab or a Farsi. Being a graduate of the Najaf or seminary or the Qom seminary is also a factor, considering the two have been in fierce competition over leadership. Usually the would-be Marja', who is a *mujtahid*, is 'marketed' by a narrow clique which constitutes his entourage, who are usually his disciples or relatives. He is often promoted to attract more *muqaliddin*, or followers who emulate his religious authority, and thus pay the *khums*. Although the *hawza*, or seminary, has not standardised a method in choosing a Marja', two very important elements are accounted for; firstly, the number of *muqaliddin* and their proximity; secondly, the number of would-be *mujtahidin* attending his lectures. A third less salient factor to be regarded is his publications. Upon the aforementioned premises, the Marja' establishes *shaya'*, or a wide reputation, enabling him to join the club of grand Marja's, who could also have a say in establishing him as such.

3. Stages of Ijtihad as a Precursor to Becoming a Marja'

A would-be Marja' should fulfil certain scholarly requirements to attain the degree of Marja's. Basically, he has to cover the following three levels: *al-muqaddimat*, or the prolegomena, *sutuh* or surfaces, and *bahth al-kharij*, or outside research. In *al-muqaddimat* the student learns grammar, rhetoric and logic. 'According to Bahr al-'ulum, a student spends an average of three to five years in the prolegomena stage.'[2]

---

1   Shamseddine, *Al-Ijtiihad,* pp. 282–85.
2   Chibli Mallat, *The Renewal of Islamic Law: Muhammad Baqer as-Sadr, Najaf and the Shi'i International,* Cambridge University Press, 1993, pp. 39–40.

In the *sutuh* the student is not required to grasps the inner core of the books, rather only the superficial meaning.[1] *Sutuh* introduces the study of the substance of *al-fiqh al-istidlali*, or deductive jurisprudence. Generally courses are arranged in a series and conducted on a tutorial basis, in groups of seven to ten students, rarely more than twenty. The student spends three to six years in this stage, where he could freely choose the books he wants to study preparing him for *ijtihad*.

Bahth al-kharij is the third and final stage of religious study in which the graduate student heavily participates in a seminar setting in the ongoing debates taking place in the *hawza*. The system at this stage is completely different; instead of tutorials the student attends important public lectures of the most prominent *mujtahidin* of Najaf who conduct their discussions as seminars organised in a series over a period of months or years. Discussion is free in the class, but the lectures are generally intricate, and sometimes result in books being compiled by the students and eventually published.

Muhammad Bahr al-'Ulum mentions three levels in *bahth al-kharij*. At the first level, formed by the students who have just completed the study of *sutuh*, it is common to address the chapters of a legal treatise in a general manner, without insisting on the sequential logic of the text, and to add in some commentaries by other *ulama*. The teacher will thus train his students with the logic of a given work and introduce them to his own method.

At the second stage of *bahth-al kharij*, exposition is more elaborate. For instance, the second part of Khurasani's *Kifaya* can give way to lengthy analyses. Texts are thus presented, discussed and choices are made by the teacher as to the most cogent interpretations.

The third stage, which is the most advanced in the curriculum, is what has made the teaching at Najaf famous and has allowed for great renovation and progress in Shi'i *ijtihad*. The teacher at this third stage is free to arrange his own course; adopt the arguments that he prefers; and devise an opinion different from his predecessors.

It is worth mentioning that this stage is referred to as *bahth al-kharij* because it is extracurricular in nature.[2] After fulfilling these criteria, the student acquires the title of *mujtahid*. It is only after the *mujtahid* publishes his fatwas that he becomes a Marja'.

---

1   Al-Bahadli, *Al-Hawza*, p. 274.
2   Al-Bahadli, *Al-Hawza*, p. 275.

CHAPTER TWO

Basic Principles:
Wilayat al-Faqih and Shiʻi Jurisprudence

FOUR STAGES OF SHIʻI JURISPRUDENCE AND WILAYAT AL-FAQIH

When *wilayat al-faqih* was first announced as a system of governance in the Islamic Republic of Iran in 1979, many in the Islamic world, Shiʻis and Sunnis alike, were taken by the new terminology that has become a catch phrase, but was an innovative concept at the time. Some who were not well versed in Shiʻi jurisprudence regarded *wilayat al-faqih* as a pillar and a fundamental asset of Shiʻism. Some Sunni scholars, especially those who were seeking a route to political Islam, were fascinated by this innovation, which was considered the foundation of the Islamic government.

However, basing his argument on primary sources, the renowned Iranian intellectual, cleric, philosopher and university lecturer Muhsin Kadivar, in his book entitled *The Progress of Shiʻi Political Thought,* points out that Shiʻi jurisprudence did not independently touch upon concepts such as *wilayat,* emirate, and political governance in general before the thirteenth century AH (nineteenth century CE). Prior to this date, political issues were included under the doctrine of 'enjoining the good and prohibiting the evil', which extended to ritual practices (*ʻibadat*) and daily dealings (*muʻamalat*). Kadivar attributes the lack of Shiʻi engagement in politics and issues pertaining to governance to the absence of the sense of urgency to tackle these matters in the Great Occultation period. He further concludes that the then-prevailing belief and attitude towards the waywardness of any system of governance or political order during the Great Occultation had eventually led to the stagnancy in Shi'i political thought.[1]

Based upon the aforementioned, Kadivar classifies the development of Shi'i political thought across the following four stages:

— He labels the first one as 'the age of the flourishing of individual jurisprudence' during which due attention was not given by the general jurisprudence to political issues and basic individual rights. This stage is the longest since it has lasted from the beginning of the fourth century to the end of the tenth century AH.

— He dubs the second stage as 'the age of sultanate and *wilayat*', which lasted for around four centuries. On the whole, it was an Iranian stage, which was inaugurated by the ascension to power of Shah Isma'il, the head of the Safavid dynasty, and ended with the advent of the constitutional revolution in 1905 CE. The Safavid period established Twelver Shi'ism as state religion. The book demonstrates that *wilayat al-faqih* at that time did not constitute a theory of governance in its own right. Rather, it was confined to the issues of religiously sanctioned and religiously prohibited. Also, the Shi'i jurisprudents rarely touched upon the political *wilayat* or the government of *fuqaha* when they came across the concept of *wilayat al-faqih*.

— The third stage labelled by Kadivar as 'the age of constitutionalism and supervision' (*mashruta* and *nazara*), originated at the beginning of the fourteenth century AH. During this period, the constitutional movement came to light and succeeded in establishing the constitution and its amendments and altering the authority of the kings and their absolute power. During this era, Shi'i jurisprudents or *fuqaha* split into two main camps: the first rejected the democratic practice and favoured traditionalism which upholds a dichotomy between religion and politics. The second camp, however, went as far as calling for progress in order to reconcile between constitutionalism (*mashruta*) and legitimacy (*mashtu'a*),[2] while at the same time safeguarding that the established state requires the general legitimisation from the *fuqaha*.

— The fourth stage corresponds to the era of the Islamic Republic which started in the beginning of the fourteenth century AH, where Imam Khomeini is considered the first Shi'i Faqih who succeeded in establishing an Islamic order. As such, *wilayat al-faqih* as a theory of governance is a modern theory which Imam Khomeini envisaged four decades ago and which materialised with the

---

1   Khaykh Muhsin Kadivar, *Nazariyyat Al-Dawla fi Al-Fiqh Al-Shi'i: Buhuth fi Wilawat Al-Faqih* (The Theory of the State in the Shi'i Jurisprudence: Research in the Rule of the Religious Jurist), Beirut 2000, pp. 19–41.

2   According to the political jargon that the book employs, the *mashruta* refers to the temporal authority, and the *mashru'a* refers to the religious authority.

victory of the Islamic Revolution and the establishing of the Islamic Republic in Iran.[1]

In an interview conducted with Kadivar in 2002, he contended that dictatorship could not originate from a good ruler. He argued that during Khomeini's lifetime, due to his charismatic authority, there was no crisis in the constitutional functioning of the Islamic Republic since the initiator of the Islamic Revolution was himself the ruler. His charisma coupled with his piety guaranteed that his outlook and vision were in concordance with that of the populace. Khomeini not only did not abuse the power delegated to him by *wilayat al-faqih*, he did not need to do that because of his stance as the *rahbar*, or leader. However, in Kadivar's view, after the death of Imam Khomeini, things changed dramatically, and it was very difficult to find a successor of his erudition.

Ayatollah Husayn Ali Montazari, who was once the heir apparent of the Islamic Revolution before falling foul of Imam Khomeini, initially stressed the institutionalisation of *wilayat al-faqih* by way of incorporating its major doctrines in the Constitution, as such making it the fulcrum of the Constitution and a precursor for the political life in Iran. Later on, however, he revised his position in such a way as to delineate *wilayat al-faqih* within the narrow confines of the law, thus attempting to abolish Khomeini's theory of absolute *wilayat* that grants the *wali al-faqih* absolute powers. Montazari considered the law as a covenant between the Faqih and the Muslims. This is one of the reasons why he fell out of favour with Khomeini, was stripped of his succession title, and, in later years, was confined to house arrest.

NINE THEORIES OF WILAYAT AL-FAQIH AND THE ATTEMPT TO RECONCILE IT WITH DEMOCRACY[2]

Kadivar, in his book entitled *Governance Theories in the Shi'i Jurisprudence: Studies in Wilayat al-Faqih*, presents several theories about *wilayat al-faqih*, which have the following common principles: the concept of *hakimiyya* (God's governance) over people as well as the universe is first and foremost, for any government that does not acquire God's authorisation is illegitimate; the Infallible Imams who are endowed with foreknowledge and forecast future events are the most capable to lead the nation religiously, politically, and administratively; the necessity of establishing a just governmental order is indispensable; the government must be in accordance with and abide by Islamic laws and injunctions and it is incumbent

---

1   Kadivar, pp. 19–21.
2   Ibid., pp. 67–191.

upon it to provide the suitable milieu for the progress of the Muslims towards the sublime religious goals; and the fundamental criteria for the Islamic ruler are the following: faith, credibility, justice, management, merit and function.[1]

Kadivar classifies the theories in two main categories: theories of state that are based upon God's divine governance and the theory of authorisation for the private owners of the common property (*masha'*). In turn, the former branches into four subdivisions, the most salient of which is the theory of absolute authority of the *fuqaha*, which is considered the brainchild of Imam Khomeini's innovative theory of Shi'i jurisprudence or *wilayat al-faqih* which constitutes the backbone of the Islamic Republic's Constitution.[2] The latter is in turn divided into three theories.

First: The theory of Imam Khomeini: according to Kadivar, this theory is based on four basic principles:

— The necessity of Islam of founding a state in order to execute its divine injunctions.

— It is incumbent as a religious duty upon the just *fuqaha* to establish an Islamic government where public opposition to the oppressors is a precursor to its founding. It is incumbent upon people to abide by the injunctions of the *fuqaha* from the stance of a religious legal obligation.

— The Islamic government connotes that the just *fuqaha* have every right to exercise their *wilayat* and governmental authority in line with the Prophetic tradition and the Infallible Imams.

— The Islamic government and the laws that emanate from it are considered as primary ordinances, which have precedence over secondary ordinances (cf. Imam Khomeini's 1988 fatwa), and maintaining order is regarded as a legal religious duty (*wajib shar'i*).[3]

It goes without saying that if Khomeini's theory served as jurisprudential base for the mobilisation towards the success of the Islamic Revolution, then the second theory, as articulated by Mahdi al-Ha'iri, might lead to a constitutional deadlock, rendering the absolute *wilayat* as tyrannical.[4]

The second theory of authorisation (*wikala*) developed by Mahdi al-Ha'iri is based upon three basic principles:

— The citizens' personal ownership of the common property (*mash'a*) constitutes the foundation of legitimacy.

— People are the source of legitimacy and by this virtue they authorise the government to rule them.

---

1   Ibid., pp. 62–5.
2   Ibid., pp. 62 ff.
3   Ibid., pp. 29–30.
4   Ibid., pp. 119–23.

— The Islamic doctrine of the unity of religion (*din*) and state (*dawla*): or from a jurisprudential perspective the two are one in Islam.[1]

From the perspective of legitimacy, the theory of *wikala* conceives of government in the sense of the art of administering the country and managing the internal and external affairs of the state, and it should not be construed as leadership, authority or governance of the subjects which are considered as subcategories of wisdom and practical reason. The government is an experimental result of the progress of life. Every individual has an inalienable right to private ownership. Out of this, through a social contract the citizens delegate their rights to a government which will protect their private property by means of justly managing their everyday affairs. Thus, the concept of fiduciary trust emerged whereby the people have rights and they are the truster and the beneficiary, and the government as trustee has only duties to instate the authority of the state based on Islamic injunctions, whereby it prevents the tyranny of the majority and upholds the rights of the minority from the perspective of its trusteeship function.[2]

The third principle of the theory of *wikala* highlights the distinction between the religious sphere and the mundane one in the sense that the government and all its institutions constitute a trenchant, positive and mutable entity as opposed to the immutable, permanent divine injunctions. In other words, statesmanship falls outside the framework of the general divine injunctions.[3]

KADIVAR AND SOROUSH ON 'THEOCRATIC DEMOCRACY'

According to Muhsin Kadivar,[4] the concept of democratic theocracy or 'Islamic democracy' is one of the main foundational trends in contemporary Islamic political thought, especially in Iran. This is a relatively modern concept that also ties with the concept of modernity as such.

Islamic democracy is a system for political life of the Muslims in the modern world. The use of the word Islam does not necessarily mean that everything is derived from the Qur'an and Sunna (Traditions); rather that it is an intellectual trend that does not contradict the basic norms of Islam. It is a means used by the Muslims to order their lives; Islamic thought is capable of supplying the philosophical edifice for theocratic democracy. From another perspective, theocratic

---

1   Ibid., pp. 192 ff.
2   Ibid., pp. 195–196.
3   Ibid., pp. 198–199.
4   Tawfiq al-Sayf, ed., *Addimyqratiyya fi Balad Muslim* (Democracy in a Muslim Country), Al-Qatif, Saudi Arabia 2007, pp. 41–68.

democracy is one of the forms of 'religious government' since Islamic government is based upon democracy derived from the sovereignty of the people as is the case in the Islamic Republic of Iran.

The concept of legitimacy is the ethical foundation that conveys the authority of the government in any Islamic system and gives it the right to enact laws and policies, and to impose duties and obligations upon the citizens. Based on this the government obtains the obedience and the loyalty of the populace, which considers the work of the policy makers moral and acceptable. Kadivar distinguishes between two versions of religious legitimacy. The first states that God Almighty has delegated to the jurisprudents the right to govern directly, without any intercession or intervention from the people. In effect, that means that people have no role in generating political legitimacy. Based on this perspective, the right to govern is in the hands of the just jurisprudent whom God Himself has installed as a governor over the people. The second version is that of the religious-popular legitimacy or 'popular legitimacy based upon religious norms'. According to this theory, God has delegated *tadbir* (ordering) of the political system in terms of public and administrative affairs based upon public interest vis-à-vis religious standards. According to this view, the human being has an absolute right in self-determination and to choose his way of life, as God has given this right to the individual as well as the community. No one has the right to forfeit this religious right. The populace exercises this right by defining the major policies of the government and electing its ministers as well as the deputies in parliament.

Democratic theocracy has nine major characteristics:

(1) Islamic democracy could be applied in Muslim societies where the majority of the population approves it and it is not to be imposed by any other way.

(2) Irrespective of their colour, race, religion, political doctrine, ethnicity, etc., all members of the community are equal in front of the law and have the same rights and duties, according to the equal opportunity dictum.

(3) Based upon Godly sanctioning, the will of the people (as described by Rousseau) is the only legitimate source of political practice.

(4) Every decision that the populace does not participate in is considered null and void. On the contrary, democratic practice stipulates the largest possible participation in decision making, especially those that pertain to public life according to promulgated standing laws.

(5) One of the basic differences between theocratic democracy and other forms of democracy is that in the former, the community is committed to religious ethics and its stipulations, accepting these as the bases of public law.

(6) The state manages the natural resources of the country and its capacity as representative of the people and public interest.

(7) Upholding meritocracy based on the principle of free and just elections.

(8) The Muslim religious scholars who are elected by the people or their

representatives give due course to the religious dimensions of the system in the sense of making sure that it does not diverge from the basic principle of Islamic Shari'a or law.

(9) Theocratic democracy is a system bound by law and both the rulers and the ruled are under the law.

According to Abdolkarim Soroush,[1] the problem with democratic theocracy is finding a viable balance in political work that is capable of satisfying both the creator and the created. Also, there should be equilibrium between the religious dimension and the mundane dimension, while organising its policies and works in such a way to aspire for the human and religion perfection. Soroush acknowledges that the tasks incumbent upon theocratic democracy are difficult to accomplish in comparison to other forms of government. For smooth functioning of theocratic democracy there should be a reconciliation between reason (*'aql*) and Islamic Shari'a or law.

According to Soroush, the fusion between democracy and religion as a historical model for reconciliation between *'aql* (reason) and *shar'* (religion) contends that every success that is achieved on a theoretical basis could be implemented on a practical basis.

Soroush adds that understanding religion requires more than religious knowledge, which is a fact that cannot be ignored by Muslim religious scholars. They also cannot ignore the necessity of finding a balance between the religious ingredient of the world on the one hand, and the *rifi* (traditional) and *'aqli* (reasoned) dimension on the other. Certain preconceived ideas and characteristics attributed to religion, such as being just humanistic, are being explored and diagnosed outside the bounds of religion. From another perspective, the evidence that is presented to prove the righteousness of religion and its justice are all rational human evidences; they are not textual or revealed, and if it were so then it would have fallen under the previous controversy. He concludes that rational human evidences are central to understanding religion.

Based on the aforementioned, Soroush argues that the development of a religious government into a theocratic democracy hinges upon a primary condition which is the transformation of religious understanding by way of fostering and increasing the role of reason in it. By 'reason', what is meant is the public participation of all the citizens through a general will (a concept paralleling that of Rousseau).

---

1 Dr Soroush (b. 1945) is a contemporary religious academic and currently a visiting scholar at George Washington University, Washington DC. See for example, Soroush, *Reason, Freedom, and Democracy in Islam*, Mahmoud Sadri and Ahmad Sadri (Translators), New York: Oxford University Press, 2002.

Democratic governments are governments that give primacy to the general will or public reason as the sole arbitrator in conflict resolution. However, religious governments, while they are based upon religion or the revealed text, do not afford these the rule of the judge (umpire); instead such systems also draw from rational effort.

In conclusion, religious certainty should not by any means be used as a pretext to hinder or sideline the need to rethink the interpretation of religion and the use of independent reason which according to Soroush is based upon knowledge outside the framework of religion. Thus religiosity and reason (*'aql*) are the two main pillars on which democratic theocracy is based upon.

AL-FAQIH AND SHURA DURING THE GREATER OCCULTATION PERIOD

Shura in *jahiliyya*[1] had a completely different connotation after Islam was revealed and later through the association between *shura* and *wilaya*. However, one has to include *shura* under the concept of *hakimiyya*, since God is the one who appoints the governor through *nass*, or sacred text. In this section we will review and comment on these ideas and highlight the domains of *shura* in the Occultation period, questioning whether the governor is the result of *shura*, or if *shura* during the time of the Infallible Imam is the same as in the period of the Greater Occultation. 'And consult with them upon the conduct of affairs. And when thou art resolved, then put thy trust in Allah. Lo! Allah loveth those who put their trust (in Him).' (3:159) In the light of this verse, it is necessary to ask, who is the genuine *wali* who is addressed in this verse? According to Kadivar, this is the Prophet, and the Infallible Imams. Thus, there is a necessary continuation from the era of Prophethood to the era of Imamhood which requires that the governor should not be a consequence of *shura* in the Occultation period; from this perspective, it does not make much sense to discuss the role of the *umma* and *shura* without touching upon *wilaya* in the Occultation period because based upon the rational evidences that support the necessity of *wilaya* in every era, in addition to the Hadith of the Imams, it is self-evident that humanity cannot give away religious injunctions that require the necessity of a concordance between the ruler and the people where he promulgates and executes the laws and administers the people through them. This is done because of the impossibility of the king to promulgate these laws to the people since there is no direct connection between the two: 'And had We made him an angel, We would have certainly made him look like a man', (6:9) because not every individual has the capacity to

---

1   Pre-Islamic period of ignorance from 500 to 610 CE.

become conversant of these laws. This is substantiated by the reasoning that God has safeguarded this knowledge through a canopy of doors, where it is impossible for common people to construe and have knowledge of it except if they enter all of these doors: 'So go to the houses by the gates thereof, and observe your duty to Allah, that ye may be successful.' (2:89)

Twelver Shi'is have a consensus that it is incumbent upon the Imam to take the leadership of the *umma* after the Prophet, as revealed by God Almighty through *nass* (sacred text). However, the nuances and differences came to the fore during the Greater Occultation period, when some scholars interpreted the leadership as equivalent to the *wilaya* of the *umma* on itself, whereas others interpreted it as delegating all the prerogatives of the Infallible Imam to the *faqih* in the latter's capacity as his deputy. The history of *marj'iyya* passed through two main interpretations, the Usuli and Akhbari schools of jurisprudence, where the Akhabri school contended that the *faqih* has the primary function of transmitting the Hadith and has no jurisdiction to perform independent reasoning or *ijtihad*. According to them, the relationship between the *faqih* and common people is on an equal par (*'am illa'am*). The justification of this reasoning by the Akhbaris is what they attribute to one of their prominent scholars, Al-Muhaqiq Al-Khuasani, who argued: 'If we uphold their Hadith we will remain infallible; however, if we do not then we will go astray.'[1]

Even in the Usuli school, there are those who held a similar view of the role of the *faqih* save one distinction which is his jurisdiction to practise *ijtihad* within the domain and rules of the jurisprudential injunctions.

The *wilaya* of the *umma* on itself does not necessarily imply that the *umma* produces its governor or *hakim* through the principle of *shura* since any action performed by the *umma* should be agreed upon by the *wali al-faqih*, which implies that no legitimacy can be accorded to the work of the *umma* without being legitimised by the *faqih*. The aforementioned has been elaborated upon by Muhammad Baqir Al-Sadr, who held the view that it is feasible from the aforementioned to deduce that Islam is always inclined to uphold the sphere of *'isma* (infallibility) as much as possible. But since there is no infallible individual present to take the lead and as the *umma* has not been able to achieve an infallible vision then it is an absolute necessity for the *umma* and the Marja' to exercise a common role in exercising God's providence.[2]

The contention that *shura* is binding to the *faqih* is not by a causal nexus between *shura* and its results as might be construed from the divine delegation

---

1   See *Dairat Almarif Al-Shi'iyyah Al-Islamiyyah* (The Encyclopedia of Shi'i Islam), vol. 1, Third Hadith, p. 27.
2   Sayyed Muhammad Baqir al-Sadr, *Al-Islam Yaqoud Al-Hayat* (Islam Guides Life), Beirut, 1979. pp. 51–5.

to the Imam or his deputy that they are bound to consult; however, they are not bound to abide by the results of this consultation. The *faqih* has the prerogative to accept the opinion of the majority after consultation or he can do what he deems right to do. According to Sheikh Hashemi Rafsanjani,[1] the *wilaya* entails that the final say in all the societal and leadership exercises lies in the hands of the *wali al-faqih* whose authority is absolute and irrevocable, thus it should be completely abided by.[2]

One of the salient verses on *wilaya* is the following: 'But no, by your Lord, they will not believe until they call you to arbitrate in their dispute; then they will not be embarrassed regarding your verdict and will submit fully'. (4:65)

AL-NA'INI AND CONSTITUTIONALISM[3]

Sayyid Muhammad Husayn al-Na'ini[4] based his thesis on adopting the parliamentary constitutional system based on many considerations; the most salient is the one that regards authority as a divine right. Thus, the person who practises this authority violates this right from God, from the people, and from the Infallible Imam who has the right in this *wilaya* according to the Shi'i doctrine. Based on the aforementioned, every authority aside from that of the Infallible Imam is considered tyrannical.

Al-Na'ini based his second major concept on the principle of confining the tyranny and usurpation of the power system in the most restricted area possible. As such, absolute *wilaya* is limited by constitutionalism; as a result, the governor concedes many of his prerogatives in such a way to make his authority within the narrow confines of safeguarding the state, its constitution and its institutions.

Based on the aforementioned, the governor's authority is limited by the following mechanisms: constitution, various monitoring bodies, and the separation of powers.

In al-Na'ini's view, the most important monitoring body is the legislative authority that is elected by the people, that is, the parliament or the Shura Council which forms the backbone of a representative democracy, in which all the people take part in electing the body, thus ensuring its legitimacy.

---

1   Ayatollah Akbar Hashemi Rafsanjani (b. 1934) is an influential cleric, writer and politician, and was Iran's fourth president under the Islamic Republic.
2   Mahmoud Alhashemmi, *Masdr Al-Tashree Wanizam Al-Hokm* (The Source of Legislation and Governance System), p. 83.
3   Husayn Rahhal, *Ishkaliyyat al-Tajdid: Dirasah fi Daw 'ilm ijtima'a alma'rifah* (The Dialectic of Modernity: A Study in the Domain of the Sociology of Knowledge), Beirut 2004, pp. 225–228.
4   Rashid Al-Khayun, *Al-Mashruta wa Al-Mustabidda* (The Constitution and Dicatorship). Beirut: Iraqi Institute for Strategic Studies, 1007.

1. Separation of Powers

In any governing system, the separation of powers between the executive, legislative and judicial branches helps to ensure freedom and equality, the two most important pillars of just governance. Al-Na'ini argued further that placing the Shura Council or the parliament under the supervision of the people or the *umma* at large enhances accountability and improves the system of checks and balances.[1] Based upon freedom and equality, al-Nai'ini argued that justice or tyranny is not confined to the person of the governor, but rather to the seeds of despotism that are present in tyrannical states. That is why he argued for the necessity of the constitution as the law of the land and the *shura* warranty through a permanent legislative institution – in other words, a parliament where representatives are elected on the concept of merit through a rotation policy, in order to ensure that everybody is represented.

Al-Na'ini's most striking innovation in thinking was represented in his concept of the preponderant majority (*akthariyya murajjiha*), as seen in his unwavering support for the legitimacy of considering the opinion of the majority.[2]

According to al-Na'ini, *shura* is a comprehensive 'democratic' system where all the populace, irrespective of their ethnic and religious belonging, are real partners in the state. This implies that the parliament is not composed only of Muslims but also non-Muslim minorities who take part in elections since they are partners in the state with all its affairs and institutions.[3]

In spite of the fact that al-Na'ini did not mention democracy as such but labelled it '*shura*' or 'constitutional system' (*al-mashruta*), he was fully aware that the democratic system is not a political recipe that can be disseminated from one country into another, but rather depends greatly on the special circumstances of every society, its social network, and the patterns of interaction among its components. It seems that as early as 1906, Al-Na'ini was fully aware of the discrepancy between theory and practice concerning the application of the concepts of *shura* and democracy.

2. Al-Na'ini

Concerning the stance of the majority from an Islamic perspective, al-Na'ini was able to come up with rationalistic, jurisprudential legitimisation for majority decision by making it binding. Further, he was able to construe the mechanisms of the functions of the institutions in the modern state. Also al-Na'ini was unequivocal in his recognition of the salient role of the modern state and the dialectical relationship between Western colonialist democracies and their foreign

---

1   Tawfik al-Sayf, *Did al-Istibdad* (Against Tyranny), Beirut, pp. 285–298.
2   Ibid., p. 322.
3   Ibid., p. 329.

policy towards the Third World countries. This led him to acknowledge the Western democratic constituents, while at the same time rejecting their foreign policy and mobilising people to confront their colonialism but to disseminate their democratic values in Muslim countries.

Al-Na'ini was revolutionary in highlighting the danger of despotism, especially that emanating from the clergy. He characterised religious tyranny as the most dangerous form of despotism that should be warded off at all costs. Al-Na'ini emphasised the need for establishing justice through abiding by the constitution, a well-functioning elected institutional apparatus that confines the prerogatives of the governor and limits his authority. By this, al-Na'ini comes up with institutional safeguards to limit the authority of those in power by acknowledging that they will abuse people's trust and blindly pursue wealth, power and material well-being at the expense of the state interest and the populace interest; that is why he tied the ruler to an elaborate system of constitutional checks and balances. In this sense, his *wilayat al-faqih* is democratic, although his overall thesis is based upon Shi'i jurisprudence and rationalistic and jurisprudential Shari'a evidences rendering his thesis as not only Islamic but also humanitarian since he fuses democracy with the *wilayat al-faqih* doctrine from the perspective of cultural and jurisprudential Shi'i concept incumbent upon the deputy of the hidden Imam, as personified in the figure of Imam Khomeini.

Based on the religious framework of the imamate, al-Na'ini produces a non-religious conception of authority. Al-Na'ini assumes that infallibility and wisdom are important personal traits of the imami ruler, and it is the guarantee for righteous rule to reach its end: equality and freedom, even in the absence of the Infallible Imam. And thus in the absence of the aforementioned traits, the alternative is to find other external means that do not depend on the personal traits of the ruler. Among these is to institute a written constitution, a *shura* council and the separation of powers, making it possible for the *umma* to practise various kinds of checks and balances that render despotic rule difficult, if not impossible. By this, al-Na'ini endeavours to transfer the infallibility of the imam to the authority as a whole whose fulcrum is the populace. When the ruler delegates his authority to others as a trusteeship, he has transferred the authority from the person of the infallible ruler to the institutions of society, basing its functioning on clear mechanisms that limit the 'waywardness' of the ruler.[1]

Al-Na'ini builds upon a development in Shi'i jurisprudence which took place in the beginning of the nineteenth century which was built upon old Shi'i jurisprudents such as al-Mufid, al-Tusi, al-Murtada and Ibn Idris, who considered that the ruler usurped two rights: the right of the Imam, and the right of the people.

---

1   Al-Sayf, pp. 256 ff.

Al-Na'ini relies upon such distinction in order to come up with a jurisprudential solution that settles the ambiguity between the holy and divine authority on the one hand, and the human one on the other. In adumbrating the latter, that is, the right of the people, al-Na'ini resorts to *shura*, which allows the person who took the reins of government not to usurp the right of the people and the *umma* by exploiting the concept of trusteeship (*al-wikala* or *al-'inaba*) that they bestowed him with. Concerning the former aspect, the right of the Infallible Imam, the issue of usurpation could be surmounted by obtaining the legitimacy from the deputy of the Imam, or the *wali al-faqih*, by taking his permission and consent on the principle and form of government. This is based upon the jurisprudential rule of rationalistic expediency and abomination (*qa'idat al-husn wa alqubh al-'aqliyyayn*).

This is a well-known Usuli concept among the *fuqaha*, where there are two schools of thought: one embraced by the Shi'is and the Mu'tazilites, on the one hand, and the other is followed by the Ash'arites. The first school believes that aside from the religious injunctions and whether religion existed or not, human reasoning is capable of clear differentiation between right and wrong, or good and bad. The *fuqaha* give an example that human reasoning is capable of recognising that cheating and lying are bad as much as it is capable of recognising that truthfulness is good. As such, they elaborate to say that if some people, due to any reason, did not hear about messengers of God or Prophets, then this does not absolve them from being responsible for their acts before God. This is precisely so because God has privileged and endowed them with reasoning which is capable of recognising the difference between right and wrong, thus abiding by what sound, rational thinking, and reasoning dictate upon them. In short, the Shi'is and the Mu'tazilites consider that most of the moral values and norms are embedded in the nature of man. On the contrary, the Ash'arites believe that religion (*shar'*) is the source of legislation and that good is what the *shar'* deems as good, and bad what it considers as bad.

Al-Na'ini elaborates upon this distinction in order to remove the sacredness of the authority without trespassing on the concept of the Imamate and its diverse prerogatives; rather he presents a theory that is in conformity with it even if it tilts towards consolidating 'humanism' in the formation of authority. This ultimately leads to increasing the margin between the sanctioned (*al-muhallal*), which is based upon the principles of jurisprudence (*'ilm usul al-fiqh*), and scholastic theology (*'ilm al-kalam*).

Al-Na'ini begins his argument by stressing the self-evident fact that governance is a necessity for the community in order to uphold its general order (*nizam 'am*) and the people's salient interests. He stresses that this has nothing to do with ritual worship (*'ibadat*), which people refer to the jurisprudents in order to construe the humanistic and the civil dimension of the authority (*bashariyyat wa madaniyyat al-sulta*).

Al-Na'ini emphasises people's ownership of the state because he considers that the rulers govern on the concept of trusteeship and deputyship (*wikalah*) which is susceptible to change. This theoretical conception for a humanistic authority allows an important induction, namely the consideration that the ownership of the state by the people, since they are financially contributing and becoming partners to the governor, irrespective of the religious belonging of the populace. This ultimately leads to the inculcation and application of the concept of citizenship (*al-muwatana*) and the conception of the state for all its citizens irrespective of their religious denomination. This implies that the non-Muslims are equal partners to the Muslims in the Islamic state as envisaged by Al-Na'ini.

Al-Na'ini legislated the concept of majority in an unprecedented manner that has not been done before by any *faqih*. He based this innovative thinking on the *fiqhi* concept of the 'mark of fame' (*imarat al-shuhra*) and its likelihood to validate the legitimacy of majority decision.[1] *Imarat al-shuhra* is another *usuli* and *fiqhi* research field where certain fatwas are being issued or accepted, even though they lack the genuine *shar'i* evidence in the Hadith about them. As such, and because a certain fatwa is circulated among the *fuqaha* without any rejection or objection, this credit given by the *fuqaha* is considered enough to validate the fatwa and supply it with enough legitimacy to be adopted. Contrary to the majority of the Shi'i *fuqaha*, Sayyid al-Khu'i rejected this, arguing that the *fuqaha* are not legislators, and thus they should only depend on the Hadith to validate their fatwas.

Al-Na'ini was able to transfer the legitimacy of the authority from the Hidden Imam to the *umma*, the community, and the populace by stipulating humanistic mechanisms and institutions (as opposed to the transcendental or idealistic morality) that limit the tendency of the ruler towards coercion and tyranny. Thus, al-Na'ini has presented a religious vision for a democratic state based on *shura*, linked to the society and a product of it while at the same time allowing the Shi'i to take part in the contemporary political system, and thus not keeping their political-societal effectiveness paralysed awaiting the return of the Hidden Imam who is the real wielder of power.

RELIGIOUS AND POLITICAL LEGITIMACY

Since the early days of the Islamic Republic, the infrastructure of the political system and a pattern of an elected government as envisaged by Islam were the

---

1   Al-Na'ini also builds upon the Prophetic tradition resorting to Qur'anic texts which attest to the aforementioned legitimacy.

main concern of the intellectuals and the political community.[1] Historical studies have indicated that the concept of republicanism as an imagined and cultural community had penetrated the Iranian political culture for more than 150 years, as early as the Qajari period.[2] The Islamic Republic represents a new theory in the sphere of existing political systems which were labelled as theocratic democracy. Establishing an Islamic Republic has to meticulously delineate the role of *wilayat al-faqih* as a bridge of communication and coordination between republicanism and Islamism, and as an instrument of fusion between the two.[3]

Mixing elements linked to the tyrannical model and the exoteric democratic model and the democratic model in the edifice of the authority or power in the Islamic Republic has become the primary source of contradictions, changes and different interpretations to the nature of this regime. The edifice of the Constitution of the Islamic Republic, like some old mixed constitutions, is an amalgamation of different theocratic elements of representative democracy, aristocracy or the rule of the elite, in this case the *ulama*, and direct democracy, that is, the direct election of the president and the parliament. In addition, the regime of the Islamic Republic has special ideological and structural traits of the state, such as the comprehensibility of the authority on the one hand, and some democratic touches on the other.[4]

According to the French scholar Olivier Roy, the Islamic Revolution in Iran has since its inception built upon an organic linkage between two kinds of legitimacy: religious and political, as conveyed through the conception of *wilayat al-faqih*. This implied that the higher authority of the Islamic Republic, the *rahbar*, has to be chosen from the highest religious authorities so that he can also be the political leader. Roy contends the amalgamation of *wilaya* and Islamism has led to serious complications in the political system.[5]

WILAYAT AL-FAQIH AND WILAYAT AL-UMMA

The fusion between the *faqih* and the *shura* is vague in its own right because it entails a discussion of two *wilayat* – *wilayat al-faqih* and *wilayat al-umma*

---

1 Mohammad Soroush, 'Republicanism? Islamism?', in *Iranian Echo Monthly* 3.9, April\May 2002, pp. 4 ff.
2 Saeed Hajarian, 'Republicanism as a Framework for Freedom', in *Sunlight Monthly*, vol. 13, March 2002, pp. 4 ff.
3 Habib Sa'i, 'Islamic Republic?' in *Iranian Echo Monthly*, vol. 3, 10 July/August 2002, pp. 10–11.
4 Husayn Bashiriyyeh, *A Contribution in Iranian Political Sociology: The Stage of The Islamic Republic*, Tehran 2002, pp. 50–51.
5 Olivier Roy, 'The Crisis of Religious Legitimacy in Iran', in *Middle East Journal*, vol. 53, 2 (Spring 1999), p. 201.

– without any prescription for how the legitimacy of *wilaya* is inculcated. If it is a dual *wilaya* then is it the *faqih* who renders legitimacy to it? Or does the *umma* give legitimacy to the *faqih* in exercising his role. If he doesn't abide by the consequences of the *shura* does his legitimacy collapse? Those who argue for a fusion between the *faqih* and the *shura* cannot produce a convincing answer on how to fuse the two concepts as long as the *umma* has the right to choose and does choose, yet the *wali al-faqih* has the right to abrogate and annul. If the *faqih* refuses to ratify something then he does not reject the choice of the *umma* if it is righteous and serving the public good, but he will argue that righteousness according to his vision and that of the *umma*.[1]

The aforementioned constitutes a real concession from almost all the *fuqaha* that the vision of the *faqih* is the basis of what the *umma* accepts or rejects. This implies that the *faqih* is rejecting the *wilaya* of the *umma* on itself or that the legitimacy of the *faqih* is tied to the *shura* of the *umma* that is abiding to him; this means that if the *shura* of the *umma* led to something that the *faqih* deemed unrighteous then it is his right to decline it, and by this, the *faqih* is the one who gives legitimacy to the *umma* in exercising its role. However, some *fuqaha* are adamant in the *hakimiyya* of the *shura* for the *wali*, because it leads to 'assurance' (*itminan*).[2]

Muhammad Baqir al-Sadr did not clearly delineate how the *faqih* can render legitimacy to the *umma* in exercising its role. On the other hand, he discusses *hakimiyyat al-shura* for the *faqih*, in the sense that his judgement is the basis of what the *umma* accepts or rejects. The exoteric interpretation of the aforementioned, according to Muhammad Baqir al-Sadr, is: 'in this way we know that the role of the Marja' witnessing on the *umma* is a lordship delegated role that can not be given away. His role in the framework of the general succession of man on earth is a socio-humanistic role inculcating its value and depth from the influence of the *faqih* in the *umma* and its trust in his wise social and political leadership.'[3]

Some researchers' conflation in construing *wilaya* and *shura* in the period of Occultation emanates from not limiting *shura* to *wilaya*. Previously we argued that the separation between the two concepts will gradually lead the *umma* to independence in its decisions without the *faqih* witnessing on them. And since God Almighty did not will the temporal *shura* to be the sole governor, in the same token, He did not will the *faqih* to be far away from the *umma* or not in interaction with it; rather, he has to be a witness on it since the *faqih* is the bearer of succession. The shar'i evidence has proven that the *faqih* has a *wilaya* that entails him to execute this role and shoulder this responsibility. Any consultation

---

1   Al Muntalaq, Op. cit., vol. 110, 1995.
2   Ibid.
3   Sayyed Muhammad Baqir al-Sadr, *Khilafat Al-Insan Wa Shahadat Al-Anbiyya*, (Men's Caliphate and the Witnessing of the Prophets). Al-Islam Yaqwod al-Hayat, Iran: Islamic Ministry of Guidance, n.d.

that is done without recourse to him or intends to constrain him in things that are not dictated by the *shura* amounts to severing the line of *wilaya* and exercising the influence of *shura* as has been the case throughout Islamic history when *wilaya* was isolated from *shura*; this led to the alienation of people from Islam and the production of rulers who downgraded *wilaya* under the heading of *shura*, as Imam 'Ali was murdered under the banner of 'There is no governance except for God'.

According to Sheikh Muhammad Mahdi Shamseddine, *bay'a* or homage, is not a precondition for being a Muslim, but a materialistic expression of the political commitment.¹ Those who say that the way to Imama goes through *bay'a* are on the same par with those who say it goes through *shura*; they both need guidance and saviours to lead them along the true path. Imam 'Ali's involvement in the *shura* was a way to reinstitute the sacred text. According to Muhammad Baqir al-Sadar, the *bay'a* to the Infallible Imam is a *wajib shar'i* (religious duty) that cannot be neglected; he argues that Islam has stipulated this and insisted on it as a contract between the leader and the *umma* to further theoretically and psychologically the concept of general *wilaya* of the *umma*.²

1. Legitimisation of Wilayat al-Faqih

'It is incumbent upon the just jurisprudents to conduct the affairs of the community that were in the hands of the prophets ... since Islamic government is the government of law, then law scholars and religious scholars or jurisprudents are the ones who should institute it.'

IMAM KHOMEINI

2. Dialectics on Imama in Wilayat al-Faqih

The Sunni and Shi'i jurisprudents hold a consensus on the concept of the imamate and its importance in organising an Islamic political community; however, this consensus ceases to be when they interpret it. For the Sunnis, the caliph or the Imam is completely different from the Infallible Imam of the Shi'is. For the Sunnis, the caliph is chosen by the consensus of *ahl al-hal wa al-'aqd* (the people who bind and loose); that is why the caliph could be isolated if he does not abide by the content of *bay'a* (homage). The Shi'is, however, believe in divine appointment, so that the stance of the imam is the same as that of the Prophet; that is why

---

1   Farah Musa, *Shamseddine Bein Wahj Al-Islam Wajaleed Al-madheb* (Shamseddine between the Glare of Islam and the Freeze of the (Islamic) Schools of Law), Beirut 1993, p. 106.
2   Sayyed Muhammad Baqir al-Sadr, *Al-Islam Yaqoud Al-Hayat* (Islam Guides Life), Beirut, 1979, pp. 146 ff.

he cannot be isolated. From the aforementioned, it could be fairly stated that the imamate of the Shi'is[1] is one of the main principles of faith (*usul al-din*), while for the Sunnis it is a subsidiary principle.

Wilayat al-faqih founded a jurisprudential solution to the issue of *wilaya* for the Shi'is, whose religious consciousness has dictated to them the stance that there is no *wilaya* but for Imam Mahdi, to the possibility of dealing with the tyrannical governors without recognising their legitimacy, to the stance of the necessity of establishing the *wilaya* of the deputies of the infallible imam, that is, the jurisprudents who hold specific credentials. Upon this point, the Shi'i stance split into two opinions. One view held the illegitimacy of establishing Islamic governance in the period of the Greater Occultation, as this would entail exercising the general *wilaya*, which they only delegated to the Prophet or Infallible Imam. According to them, the jurisprudent, or Marja', has a minimal mandate which does not render him eligible to exercise the general *wilaya*. However, the opposing view holds that the general *wilaya* is one of the prerogatives of the jurisprudent, and it is feasible to establish an Islamic government on the basis of religious injunctions. *Wilayat al-faqih* falls under the second view as elaborated by Imam Khomeini in the late sixties. After the Islamic Revolution it became the basic foundation for the theory of governance in Iran. Nevertheless, Khomeini's contribution is not totally revolutionary because it had been anticipated by many religious scholars before him. Imam Khomeini merely reformulated it in a new revolutionary light with Montazari and others.[2]

3. Three Pillars of Wilayat al-Faqih

Wilayat al-faqih has three basic pillars: the need of Muslims for government; the meaning of the *wilayat al-faqih* and the limitations of this *wilaya*; and the meaning of Islamic government.

The Need of Muslims for a Government

The Shi'i jurisprudents who are for *wilayat al-faqih* stress the necessity of *wilaya* as a basis of their *madhab*, or school of thought: 'The belief in the necessity of establishing Islamic government and the founding of executive and administrative authority as part of this *wilaya*, as well as the strife and struggle to establish it are also among the beliefs in the *wilaya*.'[3]

---

1   Muhammad Hussein Al-Ansari, *Al-imama Wal-Hokomua fi Al-Islam* (Imamate and Governance in Islam), Tehran 1998, p. 25.
2   Husayn Montazari, *Dirasat fi Wilayat al-Faqih wafikh Addawlah Al-Islamiyyah* (Studies in Wilayat al-Faqih and The Jurisprudence of The Islamic State), vol. 4, second edn, Beirut 1998.
3   Imam Khomeini, *Al-Hokouma Al-Islamiyyah* (Islamic Government), second edn, Beirut 1999, p. 56.

According to Sheikh Ahmad Naraqi[1], *wilaya* has to do with God's providence to his subjects: 'It is an immutable doctrine passed through His Prophet and His Infallible Imamas ... and they are the true governors of people since in their hands lies the leadership of the people through God's grace. *Wilayat al-faqih* cannot be practised save by the Prophet, the Infallible Imams, and their guided successors. Only in this case the ruler is considered a *wali* over what God himself has asked him to govern.'[2]

However, the Prophet and his rightful descendants do not have the right to general *wilaya* which means political *wilaya*. This implies that all those who governed after the Prophet and the Infallible Imams do not have the legitimacy to do so since they are not divinely appointed for this post. According to Shi'i jurisprudence they are labelled as tyrannical governors. And since the immutable *wilaya* was for the Prophet and for the Infallible Imams, then it is incumbent upon him and them to establish such a government. This is precisely what he has done when he established a government and named the successor after him by divine providence. By this act, the message of Islam is kept on the right path since it is not only legislating and preaching of the injunctions, rather their execution too.[3]

This foundation was Khomeini's starting point to the necessity and duty of establishing an Islamic government: 'It is self-evident that the necessity of executing God's governance has led the Prophet to establish his government, which is not confined to his time, but rather is an everlasting necessity after his passing away', because of its absolute importance to prevent chaos and corruption. 'Then establishing an Islamic government is inevitable, not only at the time of the prophet and Imam 'Ali but also from the stance of reason and Shari'a, which exhort the establishment of a government and an executive and administrative authority in our time also.[4]

The question that comes to mind has to do with the legitimacy of establishing an Islamic government by those who are not entitled to *wilaya*, meaning those who are not included among the Prophet and Infallible Imams. This was the stance of the old Shi'i jurisprudence which stressed that during the Greater Occultation *wilaya* cannot be incumbent upon any individual except the Infallible Imams. However, contemporary Shi'i political jurisprudence includes

---

1   An Iranian Shi'i *muhaqiq* (religious investigator), who lived in the eighteenth century CE (1185–1245 AH). He founded a large religious seminary at his hometown of Naraq, where leading Shi'i jurisprudents graduated, among them Shaykkh Murtada Al-Ansari. Al-Naraqi is considered the first *mujtahid* who founded the doctrine of *wilayat al-faqih*, and Khomeini later developed it from him.

2   Ahmad Al-Naraqi, *Wilayat Al-Faqih*, Introduction and commentary by Yassine Musawi, Beirut 1990, pp. 29 ff.

3   Ibid., p. 62.

4   Ibid., pp. 62–3.

the *marja' al-tadlid* among those who can establish Islamic government since it is delegated to them and incumbent upon them to establish such a government.[1]

Imam Khomeini discussed the legitimacy of establishing an Islamic government during the occultation period. He argued: 'Should the Islamic injunctions stay without implementation in the post-Lesser Occultation period which is a thousand years till now, and it could be another hundred thousand years before it is due for Imam Mahdi to appear again? So should the injunctions stay without implementation, where chaos spreads and everyone does as he likes? So, were all the laws and regulations that the Prophet struggled hard to educate and preach during twenty-three years limited to a certain period of time only? And has Islam abandoned all its preaching and injunctions in the post-Lesser Occultation period? Such a belief is far worse than the belief that Islam was abrogated.'[2]

According to Khomeini, this is unacceptable, because the Islamic injunctions are immutable, and they are incumbent upon Muslims in every time and place, and they cannot be implemented or put into effect save by political governance. As such, the same divine assignment during the presence of the Prophet and the Infallible Imams continues during the Occultation period.

The Meaning of the Wilayat al-Faqih and the Limitations of this Wilaya

Wilayat al-faqih prescribes the delegation of the authorities and jurisdictions of the Infallible Imams to the jurisprudents who are assigned as their deputies to execute their authority. It is an absolute necessity during the Greater Occultation for Muslims to conduct their affairs based upon religion, as Shi'i Islam does through the leadership of a Marja'. Imam Khomeini goes as far as stating that there is no practical difference in the performance of the *wilaya* and executing governance between the Prophet, the Infallible Imams and the jurisprudent: 'It is incumbent upon the Marja'iyya to execute all the issues that were in the custody of prophets.'[3]

According to Imam Khomeini as ascribed to Sheikh Ahmad Naraqi, the jurist-consult's mandate is not only confined to the *hisbi wilaya* (or the *wilayat* of the wali on the property of the mentally disabled or orphans) but extends to general *wilaya*, because as such the sum total of functions ascribed to the imam become included under the jurisdiction of the Marja'iyya as stipulated by *wilayat al-faqih*.

The Meaning of Islamic Government

According to Imam Khomeini, the Islamic government is the government that the populace longs for, but this does not amount to a civil government, rather a

---

1   Ibid., p. 121.
2   Ibid., pp. 63–4.
3   Ibid., p. 115.

religious government that is chosen by the Muslim populace among other forms of governments. Khomeini clarified this by characterising the government as a 'religious government' that is 'in accordance with God's governance', and the government that he longs for is 'governed by the righteous and the pious'.[1]

When Imam Khomeini called for establishment of an Islamic Republic, he clarified that the concept of republicanism is a clear concept to the populace and it entails the necessity of taking the public opinion into consideration; Islamism means commitment to Islamic principles. Khomeini posed the rhetorical question, 'Do you accept that the government be republican, and reject it being Islamic?' He concluded that as long as public opinion is Islamic then the republican nature of the government does not contradict its Islamism.[2]

The Islamic government is different in its content from other governments: it is not despotic, rather confined to the injunctions of Islam and its laws. From this perspective it is 'the government of implementing the divine law on people'.[3]

4. Evaluation of Wilayat al-Faqih

Sayyid Muhammad Husayn al-Na'ini is considered the first modern Shi'i thinker who produced a dialectical treatise on the traditional Shi'i view of the imamate on the outskirts of the twentieth century. In his article, he went all the way to bestow legitimacy to establish a modern constitutional state because of the difficulty, even the impossibility, of leaving the reign of governance of the imam vacant in the period of Occultation. Al-Na'ini was well conversant in *wilayat al-faqih*; he partially acknowledged it in its *hisbi* and ritual practices domain (*'ibadat*), but he did not extend it to the political domain in the sense of absolute *wilaya* as Imam Khomeini has done. Rather the crux of his argument was the *wilayat* of the *umma* on itself. From this perspective it is a fallacy to assume that there is continuity between Al-Na'ini's discourse and that of Imam Khomeini in relation to *wilayat al-faqih*.[4]

Al-Naini has placed this theory of *wilayat al-umma* on its own outside the political sphere, in order to establish a modern theory of government which stresses that the *umma* can take care of itself, and it is the source of authority, and the framework of reference of this authority is the constitution and that *shura* is the basis of this political system.

It is alleged that Ayatollah Montazari has built upon al-Na'ini's theory in order to criticise *wilayat al-faqih*. Although *wilayat al-faqih* became the ideology of the

---

1 Imam Khomeini, *Al-Kawther: A Collection Of Imam Khomeini's Speeches*, vol. 3, Tehran 1996, pp. 12–13 and p. 339.
2 Ibid., p. 431.
3 Khomeini, *Al-Hokouma Al-Islamiyyah*, p. 82.
4 Muhammad Al-Husseini, 'The Different Lutherism and the Alleged Secularism Project', in *Alhadaf,* 22 November 1992, p. 41.

Iranian state, many Shi'i Marja'iyya have criticised it in recent years, mostly from jurisprudential perspective, which also questioned its alleged political infrastructure. Among these are Ayatollah Muhammad Mahdi Shamseddine and Marja' Sayyid Muhammad Husayn Fadlallah.[1]

Fadlallah acknowledges the doctrine of *wilayat al-faqih*, but like Al-Na'ini, confines it to the *ibadi* and *hisbi* domains.[2]

Even though Fadlallah does not specify the linkage between *wilayat al-faqih*, on the one hand, and *shura* and democracy and the right of the *umma* to administer its affairs on the other, he stresses that the *umma* cannot be without a leadership that governs it and this leadership is not subjugated to the whims of the people and their choice.[3] Fadlallah talked about the 'coercive implementation' in the Ghayba period, by which he means that the governor has the right to employ the state's apparatus from the stance of *wilayat al-umma* by itself. Thus the *umma* bears its responsibility through the divine *taklif* (assigning) to the Prophet and the Infallible Imams. Beyond this domain, the issue of governance becomes the prerogative of the *umma* in such a way that any person is barred from subjugating it and tyrannically ruling it, even if he is the just *faqih*. This opens the floor for *shura*.[4]

In turn, Sheikh Shamseddine has openly criticised *wilayat al-faqih* in reference to an imamate basic origin (*asl-awwali*) which is: 'The illegitimacy of a person to coerce others'. Like Fadlallah, Shamseddine finds evidence for the necessity to establish an authority to uphold law and order but within the domain of the *asl-awwali*.[5]

Those who argued against the legitimacy of *wilayat al-faqih* have indirectly proven that the Shi'i political mind is not enslaved to this theory, even though it has become a considerate state's ideology; as such the political choices of the state in the Shi'i political thought are much greater than *wilayat al-faqih* on its own right.

---

1   Ayatollah Shamseddine (1936–2001) was a famous Twelver Shi'i scholar. Born in Najaf, Iraq, he returned to Lebanon in 1969, and that year co-founded the Supreme Islamic Shi'i Council with Musa Sadr. He was the president of the council from 1994 until his death. Marja' Fadlallah (1934–2010) was also born in Najaf and from a Lebanese family. A founder of numerous institutions and highly influential in religious and political circles, he was regarded as the leading Shi'i scholar in Lebanon at the time of his death. Media reports that he was the 'spiritual mentor' of Hizballah have been disputed.

2   Fadlullah, 'Islamic Leadership inside the State', in *Al-Thaqafa Al-Islamiyyah*, vol. 37, May/June 1991, p. 41.

3   Ibid., p. 53.

4   Ibid., pp. 40–44.

5   Shaykh Muhammad Mahdi Shamseddine, *Nizam Al-Hukum wa Al-Idara fi Al-Islam* (The Order of Governance and Administration in Islam). Seventh edition, Beirut: Al-Mu'assasa Al-Dawliyya lil Dirasat wa Al-Nashr, 2000, p. 448.

5. Wilayat al-Faqih in the Islamic Republic

Wilayat al-faqih constitutes the ideology of the Islamic Republic of Iran, and this ideology has played a primary and continuous role since the victory of the Islamic Revolution in 1979 till now. *Wilayat al-faqih* has stipulated the constitutional foundations for erecting a progressive Islamic Republic and the nature of the political system (Islamic Republic) based upon the constituents of absolute *wilaya*. The Islamic state had to conduct two complementary alterations in order to consolidate *wilayat al-faqih*. The first alteration was to supersede the national kingship or heritage that is based upon racial belonging and which had for a long time defined the Iranian national identity. The Islamic state replaced that identity with an Islamic one, based upon *wilayat al-faqih*, which does not stipulate race as a basis of a religious state. It was very important to surpass national oppression that was practised by the kingship against other Arab, Turkish and Kurdish minorities. This translated itself positively on the Shi'i population especially in areas where religious sentiment is high, such as Iraq and Turkey.

The second alteration had to do with the Shi'is who lived beyond the geographical boundaries of the Islamic state in order to found the greatest rallying behind the Islamic Republic and *wilayat al-faqih*. This in turn branched into two domains:

— Building a central Marja'iyya, or structured hierarchy of clerical authority, for the Shi'is in order to cut down on polarisation and competing Marja'iyyas outside the borders of the Islamic state as was the case during the Safavid and Qajari eras.

— A political dimension aimed at putting the Shi'is in the forefront of the operations of *wilayat al-faqih* and this is by far the most important objective of exporting the revolution.

A deep understanding of these two alterations is defined under the light of examining the formation of the new Iranian identity, which is not a mono-dimensional identity, in the sense that Shi'ism is not the sole ingredient of the Iranian identity as was the case to a great extent in the Safavid dynasty. On the domestic scene Iran is witnessing an ebb and flow of intellectual, social, political, religious and economic ideas which seem to be in line with Western modernisation in the Pahlavi era[1] in spite of the Islamic state's endeavours to diminish the influence of the old heritage in the current Iranian society.

The historical development of Shi'i political jurisprudence has been ripe with different interpretations of Islamic governance, passing through al-Na'ini, al-Khu'i,

---

1   The name adopted by the father-and-son dynasty that ruled Persia/Iran from 1925 until it was toppled by the Islamic Revolution of 1979.

Muhammad al-Shirazi, Muhammad Baqir al-Sadr,[1] Husayn Ali Montazari and others. All of these distinguished between two types of jurisprudence:
— The aim of the earlier Shi'i jurisprudents such as Sheikh Al-Mufid, Al-Sayyid Al- Murtada, Sheikh Al-Tusi, etc. was the interpretation of the legitimate authority (*al-imama alilahiyya al-nassiyya*) or Al-Mahdi's Islamic order.
— However, the objective of the recent Shi'i jurisprudents is the realisation of altering the current authority and establishing an alternative one based on the application of Shari'a.

This distinction makes the former the bearer of the epistemic ways of knowledge. However, the latter becomes a positive partner and a competitor in establishing an Islamic order. Since the latter jurisprudents call first and foremost for change by endeavouring to adapt their thesis to reality, they are thus being pragmatic and flexible.

Upon reading al-Sadr's categorisations in political thought it could be inferred that there is a combination of three elements: (1) the culture of political Shi'i jurisprudence (*fiqh sultani Shi'i*); (2) special awareness for the religious text, and the Qur'an par excellence; (3) the assimilation of modern political thought.

In the first stage al-Sadr started the visualisation of the Islamic state, parting with the historical context of the Shi'i political jurisprudence that denies the existence of the Islamic state in the era of the Greater Occultation, arguing that it is totally illegitimate. However, al-Sadr strongly argues that it is a legitimate duty to establish an Islamic state in the period of the Greater Occultation: 'The Islamic state is not only a religious necessity (*darura shar'iyya*) rather it is also a cililisational necessity.'[2]

He added, 'The establishment of Islamic governance is the fulcrum of Islam.'[3]

In another book he argues that 'the primary objective of Islamic political work is to found an Islamic community and an Islamic state ... i.e. an Islamic state that is based on the foundations of Islam taking all its legislation from it.'[4]

On the level of the private awareness of the Qur'anic religious text, al-Sadr's vision could be patched together from his different books which centre upon the concept of succession (*istikhlaf*) as the basic essential concept of the Islamic state. This concept leads first and foremost to authenticating the right of the *umma* in espousing its own authority and sovereignty on itself. It could be inferred that

---

1   Muhammad Baqir al-Sadr (1935–80), Iraqi Grand Ayatollah and founder of the Islamic Dawa Party.
2   Muhammad Baqir al-Sadr, *Manabi Al-kodra fi Aldawla Al Islamiyyah (The Sources of Power in the Islamic State),* Beirut 1979, p. 13.
3   Mohammad Baqir al-Sadr, *Thaqafat Al-Dawaa Al-Islamiyya, Hizb Al-Dawaa Al-Islamiyyah, Al-Qism Al-Siayasi* (The culture of the Islamic call, Al Dawaa Islamic Party, the political wing), vol. 2, Iran, 1984, p. 375.
4   Ibid., vol. 1, p. 90.

succession as a Qur'anic concept, as elaborated and developed by al-Sadr, is equivalent to the Rousseauean social contract. This interpretation is clearly visible in
al-Sadr's outlining of the concept of succession. Thus, al-Sadr, who undermines
the classical Shi'i political jurisprudence, conveys a progressive understanding of
the religious text which acts as the foundation of the theocratic state.

Al-Sadr bases his political vision on the Qur'anic verse (2:30) 'When your
Lord said to the angels: "I am placing a deputy on earth", they said: "Will you
place one who will make mischief in it and shed blood, while we sing Your praise
and glorify your sanctity?" He said: "I know what you do not know." Inspired by
this verse al-Sadr interprets it as, 'God's successor on earth has providence over
all these things, the earth, the human beings, the animals, and all four-hoofed
animals that are spread on the four corners of the globe. From this perspective
succession in the Qur'an is regarded as a basis for governance and governing
people is a subsidiary to succession.' Based on that, he argues, 'When human
beings represented by Adam were accorded this succession, then it is assigned to
shepherd the globe and to manage people's affairs and leading humanity towards
the designed road of religious succession'. Al-Sadr concludes, 'God Almighty has
delegated to human beings the governance and the leadership of the globe and
to develop it in the social and natural realms. Building on that, he establishes the
theory of people governing themselves and the legitimacy of the human race to
govern itself in its capacity as being created by God.'[1]

Al-Sadr's interpretation is not only at variance with the Shi'i political jurisprudence, classical or modern, but also with Islamic political thought in general. The
reason is that it is a progressive vision that is almost equivalent to the Western
concept of social contract, save al-Sadr's conclusion on succession in which he
stipulated that the community in this context does not govern independently.
Rather, it exercises the responsible succession, so it bears the religious responsibility (*amana*), which is in opposition to the concept of community that governs
itself based upon an agreement or social contract, as is the case in the Western
democratic political systems.

In spite of that, there is a clear indication in the aforementioned text, which
stresses that the *umma* has the right in exercising the legislative and executive
authority, and this right is the right of succession and care derived from the real
source of authority, that is, God Almighty.[2] Moreover, the state in Islam in its
capacity as a prophetic phenomenon, as al-Sadr put it, was designed to put the
reins of governance in the hands of the *umma*, which is capable of directing and

---

1   Al-Sadr, *Khilafat Al-Insan*..., p. 14.
2   Al-Sadr, *Lamha Tamhidiyyah an Mashrou Dostour Ajjamhouriyyah Al-Islamiyyah: Al-Islam
    Yakud Al-Hayat*. (A Preliminary Insight on the Project of Islamic Republic Constitution; Islam
    Guides Life), second edn, Beirut 1979, p. 19.

executing its affairs through its own devices. This progressive interpretation is the sole characteristic of al-Sadr which completely distinguished him from the traditional *fiqhi* circle and placed him in the philosophical sphere along the lines of philosophers such as Ibn Rushd, Ibn Sina and al-Farabi in realising the communal nature of the political community, which is not based upon religious text from the Qur'an and traditions; rather he conceived it as a human phenomenon that could be realised by human intellect since it is an implied social revelation. That is why al-Sadr delved into the meaning of Prophethood and interpreted its socio-political implications.

Istikhlaf as constructed by al-Sadr is implicated with a series of theological and historical speculations, thus casting a religious label on the issue of political will (*nisab*). This construction issue becomes clearer when al-Sadr discusses the *istikhlaf* issue, starting by God's ownership and delegating man to run this ownership of God through two things which ultimately fall under the contract concept. The first is the *istikhlaf* of the good mankind as a whole. The second is the *istikhlaf* of the individual by the majority, which is based upon the jurisprudential and legal dimension in terms of private property. Al-Sadr affirms in this respect: 'private property cannot be legitimised if it is not in accordance with the general will and its right to appropriate wealth'.[1]

Al-Sadr conveys the essence of the social contract in which he bases his doctrine of *istikhlaf* in such a way that the state that he strives to establish is characterised by a dualism between the human and divine. The state is not an independent social phenomenon in human history because it is based upon a rich heritage of the community.

6. Tabataba'i and Maghniyye's Views

Sayyed Muhammad Husayn Tabataba'i[2] in his theory on politics and governance in Islam stated that the issue of government and governance is not confined to a particular era or to certain specificity; rather it covers the whole Occultation era. Tabataba'i stressed explaining who is incumbent upon ruling the Muslim society. He explained that the issue of Islamic government after the death of the Prophet and the Occultation of the Imam till our modern time is an absolute necessity. It is incumbent upon people to find a just ruler along the lines of the prophetic tradition, the imams and the rightly guided ones. These are the only people capable of upholding the injunctions and establishing social justice.[3]

---

1   Mohammad Baqir al-Sadr, *Sura 'an Iqtisad Al-mojtamaa Al-Islami, sulsulat Al-Islam Yaqud Al-Hayat* (An Image about the Economy of the Islamic Society: Series of Islam Guiding Life), Beirut 979, pp. 15–16.

2   Sayyed Muhammad Husayn Tabataba'i (1892-1981) is considered among the most prominent thinkers of philosophy and contemporary Shi'i Islam.

3   Sayyed Mohammad Hussein Tabataba'i, *Nazariyyat Assiyasah Wal Hokm fi Islam* (The Theory of

Sheikh Mohammad Jawad Maghniyye, in his book *The Shi'i and Governance*, argues that the Shi'is vehemently support from a religious perspective the establishment of a temporal state in this era or in previous historical epochs if it governs by the consent of the people and according to their general will and performs its duty as a good state that preserves law and order and gives each one his rights and protects the borders from enemies.[1]

7. Debates on Wilayat al-Faqih

It has become clear that *wilayat al-faqih* represents the ideology of the Iranian Islamic Republic. This ideology has played a continuous pivotal and central role since the advent of the Islamic Revolution in Iran in 1979 till today. It is the same *wilayat al-faqih* that defined the constitutional formulations of the construction of the Islamic Republic in Iran and the nature of the political system (the Islamic Republic), stemming from the content and essence of the absolute *Wilayat al-Faqih*.

It is worth mentioning that the *wilayat al-faqih* is not a Khomeini-made theory; rather its roots dig deep into history for a period of time which extends at least two centuries before Khomeini. What Khomeini did was simply reproduce the writings of the fore-founders of the absolute *wilayat al-faqih* theory.

But, despite all that has been said about *wilayat al-faqih* as a Shi'i translation of the Islamic state, and despite the intensive media coverage of the theory, there is a wide spectrum of opponent jurisprudents (*fuqaha*) concerning the entirety of this theory. A delicate scrutiny of this theory starting by the fourth century AH (tenth century CE) till now reveals that only scarce attention if any has been paid to this theory, and if we were to look into the categories of Marja'iyya in the last two centuries we will discover that it was completely unknown among their ranks. The *fuqaha* of the constitutional movement in Iran such as al-Na'ini, Akhund, Mazenderani, Sayyid Abdullah Bahbahani, Sayyed Muhammad Tabatabi and Sheikh Isma'il Mahallati have not paid much attention or agreed to the absolute *wilayat al-faqih*; rather, they vehemently advocated a parliamentary government.

Even the *fuqaha* of this century did not agree on this wide mandate of the *wilayat*. Among the names that could be mentioned in this regard are the following: Sayyid Abu al-Hasan Al Asfahani, Sayyid Kadhim Yazdi, Agha Dia' Iraqi,

---

Politics and Power in Islam), Beirut 1982, p. 67.

1   Sheikh Muhammad Jawad Mughniyeh, *Asshia Walhakimoun* (The Shi'is and the Rulers), Beirut 1992, p. 9. This characterisation sounds like the nineteenth-century liberal night watchman state where civil freedom of the citizens consisted of the freedom to pursue what the law allows such as the liberty to buy, sell, contract with one another, choose their own abode, diet, trade, and raise their children according to the private judgement of individuals. In turn, the state defines and enforces property rights, maintains social peace, system of courts, and defends society against foreign powers. This theorisation started with the social contract tradition, namely, by theoreticians such as Hobbes, Locke, Rousseau, Montsequieu and Robert Nozick (1938–2002).

Sayyid Mahmud Shahrurdi, Sheikh Murtada Al Yasin, Sheikh Muhammad Kashif Al-Ghita', Sayyid Hadi Al-Milani, Sayyid Ahmad Al Khunsari, Sayyid Muhsin Al Hakim, Sayyid Khadim Shari'at Madari, Sayyid Kulbaykani, Sayyid Shihabeddine Marashi Najafi, Sayyid Husayn Tabatabi Qommi, Sayyid Mohammad Al-Ruhani, Sayyid Abdulaala Al-Sebzawari and Sayyid Ali Sistani; none of the aforementioned advocates the absolute or comprehensive *wilayat al-faqih*. In this context it is worth mentioning that Imam Khomeini did not base his argument to validate the full and comprehensive *wilayat al-faqih* on clear and strong Hadith, but rather resorted to reason and rational evidence to support his argument.

At any rate, the triumph of the comprehensive *wilayat al-faqih*, as theorised by Imam Khomeini in the Shi'i arena, and its stipulation in the Constitution of the Islamic Republic, that *wilayat al-faqih* is the highest constitutional authority in the country, do not conceal the fact that the nature of the authority which emerges from this theory and its mechanics continue to be ambiguous. In his speeches during the ascending eruption of the Islamic Revolution in 1977–9, extending to the victory of the revolution and establishment of the Islamic Republic in 1979, Imam Khomeini provided only faint and feeble glimpses about the *wilaya*. These glimpses indicated the legal right of the *wilayat al-faqih* to appoint the officials in the government. What added more ambiguity and obscurity to the issue is that Imam Khomeini did not introduce the *wilaya* position in the state bureaucracy; rather, he placed it outside the activity of the state and its bureaucracy. The *faqih*'s role, as the files and the literature of the Imam suggest, is limited to supervising and guiding the power system and checking its legal procedures under the religious light, without any direct involvement in its affairs.

On the practical level as well, what has not become clear – even so many years after the victory of the Islamic Revolution – are the limitations and boundaries between the state and the *faqih*, particularly given that the overwhelming majority of the Shi'i population inside and outside Iran have not received enough education about the *wilayat al-faqih* theory. One of the prominent events in this regard happened after the formation of the Council of Experts, as it was the first time that the theory of the *wilayat al-faqih* was presented to the Iranian public as one of the basic principles of the Islamic system, a concept which generated wide and dynamic debate within the Iranian Parliament. Some parties went as far to say that *wilayat al-faqih* is the confiscation of power by the clergy. At that time, Imam Khomeini limited his activity to defending *wilayat al-faqih* without preaching it or presenting it to the public. Khomeini's basic aim was limited to refuting the accusations that regarded the theory as a new form of dictatorship. The following section will provide an idea about the kind of defensive efforts made towards this end.

8. Imam Khomeini's Theory and Implications

Political Freedom

Unlike Machiavelli, Imam Khomeini emphasised that politics is not tantamount to deception, rather to reality and truth. According to him, politics is real in the sense of administering the affairs of the state; Islam is political Islam and political realism is not deception. Khomeini argued against the Western secular tradition that separates religion from politics, contending in argument that this is against the logic of Islam, since political engagement is one of the religious duties incumbent upon Muslims.[1]

He added that every member of the populace has the absolute right to question and criticise the Muslim governor. In turn, it is incumbent upon the Muslim governor to produce satisfactory and convincing answers. In the event that the governor did not act in conformity with his Islamic duties, he will be immediately discharged of his office. He added that there are constitutional safeguards and mechanisms to deal with this problem.[2] According to Khomeini, freedom can never be given; freedom is for the people; the law bestows freedom; God is the one who has given freedom to the people; Islam rendered freedom to every individual, and no one has the right to deny this inalienable right to anybody.[3] He added that since sovereignty is vested in the hands of the people, then the people are the real governors: the people are the ones who give legitimacy to the state's institutions and apparatus. (After the constitution was ratified, Imam Khomeini ordered a public referendum in order to confirm its legitimacy in the view of the people.[4])

Islamic Shura Council and the Council of Experts

Khomeini clarified that the consensus of the people in opposition to God's governance is waywardness.[5] The formation of Islamic Shura Council aims at finding harmony and consensus between state interests and holistic divine law, on the one hand, and supervision (*raqaba*) on the other: 'The Islamic Shura Council considers that God is the only legislator, and the council's duty is not to legislate, rather to plan.' As for the Council of Experts, Imam Khomeini stressed that if the populace elected the Council in order to elect a just *mujtahid* to lead their government, then the experts nominate a person in order to assume the leadership. In this case, authority is accepted by the

---

1 Imam Khomeini, *Al Hukuma al Islamiyyah wa Wilayat al-Faqih*. Mu'assast Tanzim wa Nashr Athar al-Imam al Khomeini. Tehran 2006, pp. 19–22.
2 Ibid., p. 681.
3 Ibid., p. 406.
4 Ibid., p. 702.
5 Ibid., p. 365.

people and the *wali* becomes elected by the people and his rule has legal force.[1]

Taklif

Khomeini emphasised that every work without *taklif* (legal-religious obligation) is illegitimate and groundless: the president of the Islamic Republic should always be appointed by the *faqih* according to God's stipulations or else the appointment is illegitimate. In case the appointment becomes illegitimate, then this is tantamount to tyranny, and obeying the president is the same as obeying a despot.[2] Imam Khomeini questions how some people could say that Islam did not highlight the religious duty (*taklif*) of forming a government. If this is the case, then how did Prophet Muhammad form a government?[3] Was this contradictory to the religious teachings? And if so, how can the Prophet and the Imam engage in a practice which is contradictory to the religion and the Shari'a?[4]

'Islam Is More Sublime Than All Democracies'[5]

When naming the Islamic Republic, Khomeini vehemently rejected the addition of the word democracy to the word Islamic, considering it an insult to Islam which implies that Islam is an undemocratic religion. According to Imam Khomeini, labelling Iran an Islamic democratic republic is rejected by the populace. 'They say Democratic Islamic Republic, but what do we mean by republic? Democracy has changed its attire through different historical epochs. Democracy in the West has a different meaning from that of the East; the same applies to the conception of democracy as laid down by Greek philosophers such as Plato and Aristotle.'

According to Imam Khomeini Islam is the religion of justice, the justice that had prevailed among the rulers of early Islam like the justice of the leader of the faithful Imam 'Ali bin Abi Talib. Khomeini adds, 'The meaning of the Republic is that people have the right to express their opinion and elect their representatives.' He rejected the juxtaposition of democracy and Islam arguing, that this is an insult to Islam. Imam Khomeini asserted also that when someone places the word Islamic next to democracy, then it is as if he is saying Islam is not democratic, while Islam, to him, is far more sublime and graceful than all democracies. From this perspective he refused to say Islamic Democracy; he further stressed that when someone places the word Islamic next to the word democracy, it is as if he

---

1   Ibid., p. 536.
2   Ibid., p. 127.
3   This refers to the ten-year rule of Prophet Muhammad in Madina from 622 to 632, where both the political and religious authority were consummated in him.
4   Khomeini, *Al Hukuma*, etc., p. 88.
5   Ibid., pp. 64 ff.

has placed the word justice next to the word Islamic Republic, so this tantamount to saying a just Islamic Republic; this is again an insult of Islam because justice is the essence of Islam. Likewise, he concluded that it is an insult to Islam to add the word democracy to the word Islamic, because this would be equivalent to saying that Islam is undemocratic.

According to Khomeini, the Islamic government is a government which relies on justice and democracy and is based upon the regulations and laws of Islam. Khomeini stressed the need for an Islamic Republic, where the populace would determine the form of the government, and Islam would determine its content based on the Divine Laws. In such a government, it is absolutely the duty of the governor to take recourse in the legislators because they represent the populace; in case the parliamentarians differed with him, he cannot take the decisions on his own. He added that the Islamic government is the government of law, and if the leader of the Islamic government has committed any infringement then he would be discharged of his position; 'if he committed injustices and violations then the Islamic system has the mechanisms to discharge him, and he will not have the credibility to be a ruler.'[1]

'There is no legitimacy without Islam'

Imam Khomeini stressed that if the affairs of the state are conducted without divine legitimacy, then the state in all its institutions is tyrannical, illegitimate and dealing with it is prohibited.[2] He added that *wilayat al-faqih* is not an issue created by the Council of Experts; rather it is decreed from God. The difficulty in forming a government does not affect the mandate of the jurisprudents because they are appointed by God, thus *wilayat* does not cease to be.[3]

The Salient Characteristics of Wilayat al-Faqih

The competent incumbent to govern should have the basic traits of knowledge (*'ilm*) and justice (*'adala*). If this person forms the government, then this is tantamount to the *wilayat* that was present during the life of the Prophet and his way in administering society, etc. Based on this, the populace has the duty to obey him.

It is a mistake and nugatory (*batil*) to assume that the prerogatives of the government of the Prophet are more than those of the leader of the faithful (Imam 'Ali), or that the prerogatives of Imam 'Ali were greater than those of the *faqih*. Khomeini concedes that the virtues of the Prophet are more than anyone that came after him; the same applies to Imam 'Ali. Thus, Imam Khomeini stresses the

---

1   Ibid., pp. 54–62.
2   Ibid., pp. 127–8.
3   Ibid., p. 230.

virtues rather than the prerogatives. *Wilayat al-faqih* pertaining to rational considerations (*al-umur al-'itibariyya al-'aqliyya*) amounts to sacred text and divine
appointment (*al-nass wa al-t'ayyin*).[1]

Imam Khomeini stressed that if the *wali al-faqih* imposed his will by sheer
force, then his *wilaya* becomes illegitimate According to him, Islam entails democratic aspects and people have the total freedom in practising their religious and
social rights.[2]

---

1   Ibid., p. 231.
2   Imam Khomeini's message in *Sahifat al-Nur*, vol. 4, p. 234.

CHAPTER THREE

Democratisation Processes in the Islamic Republic of Iran: The Role of *shura* in the Democratisation Process

'Democracy presents the best mechanism of governance that the citizens could have recourse to, especially in practising basic rights as well as political rights'.

RASHID AL-GHANUSHI, a Tunisian Islamist

'Many social scientists have distorted the conception of *shura*, especially some modernists who have equated *shura* with democracy, which is considered a degradation of Islamic thought and a deflection from the authentic meaning of *shura*'.

FATHI YAKAN, a Lebanese Sunni Islamist

BACKGROUND ON SHURA

Most contemporary Islamists seem to have reached a consensus on the centrality of *shura* in Islam, especially in organising the political system. However, they interpret *shura* differently, in both theory and application, but they seem all to agree on the importance of Islamic awareness as inculcated in the concept of *shura* as a foundation for the Islamic outlook for politics. According to Hasan al-Turabi, a Sudanese Islamist, contemporary Islamic literature is what has spread the concept of *shura* and has bestowed upon it value and content, after old jurisprudential books did not give it due regard because the exercise of political *shura* was neither prevalent nor hazardous to Islamic history.[1]

Although the idea of *shura* is as old as political directives in Islam, the concept of *shura* is a contemporary ideology. According to Radwan al-Sayyid, a Lebanese intellectual, *shura* is a genuine Islamic specificity, and also a Qur'anic text. However, its political dimension in the first two centuries of Hijra dwindled in the third century and was replaced by its ethical and social dimensions until the late Egyptian scholar Rifa'at Tahtawi and the founding father of Islamic modernism Jamal ad-Din al-Afghani discovered it, or discovered its political dimension under the influence of getting acquainted with Western constitutions, especially the French Constitution in the nineteenth century. From this perspective, Tahtawi, as well as Muslim reformists, regarded *shura* as synonymous with constitutional governance.[2]

According to Muhammad al-Ghazali and Abd al-Salam Yassin, *shura* is not a ready-made recipe in Islamic texts, but rather a concept relegated to *ijtihad*.[3]

In turn, the influential contemporary Sunni Egyptian scholar Sheikh Yusuf al-Qaradawi builds upon the aforementioned to deduce that the Islamic state is a constitutional state, the state of rights and freedoms. Thus, according to him, it is a grave mistake to assume that *shura* amounts to civil governance where people exercise their consensus over the principles, laws and treaties at their own accord, without any recourse to their religious authority. The aforementioned does not go in accordance with the logic of the Islamic state which is based on the authority of the Shari'a in its sociopolitical order. Right in the Islamic state, the state of Shari'a and *shura* is not a civil right, rather a divine right. It is the inalienable right of every Muslim not to abide by what contradicts the Shari'a even if the ruler orders him to do so, since this amounts to an opposition between the right of the governor, on the one hand, and God's right, on the other. It goes without saying that God's right always has precedence over the governor's right.[4]

In turn, Sayyid Qutb stressed that it is, 'Either *hakimiyyat* Allah or *jahiliyya*: Either governance with what God has revealed or *fitna* (discord) away from what God has revealed ... Since democracy is not governance with what God has revealed, then in the eyes of God is *jahiliyya*.' According to Qutb, *jahiliyya* is

1   Hasan Abdullah Al-Ourabi, *Nazarat Fi Al-fikh assiyasi* (Glimpses of Political Jurisprudence), Khartoum, 1998, p. 72.
2   Radwan al-Sayyid, *Siyasat Alislam Almouaser: Morajaat wamoutabaat* (Politics of Contemporary Islam: Reviews and follow ups), Beirut, 1997, pp. 157–158.
3   Abdulsalam Yassine, *Hiwar ma Alfudalaa Aldemikratiyyeen (A Dialogue with the Deocratic Notables)*, Casablanca: Al-Mouallef, 1994, p. 46.
4   Sheikh Yusuf al-Qaradawi, *Min Fikh Addawlah Fi AlIslam*, (From The State – Fiqh In Islam), Cairo: Dar al-Shuruq, 1996, p. 33–58.

defined as 'the worship of people to people: since some people legislate and make laws for people, which are not in concordance with the orders of God.'[1]

According to Abu Ala'la al-Mawdudi, *hakimiyya* only originates from absolute political theocratic authority derived from God's delegation: 'It is not right to employ the concept of democracy and apply it to the Islamic state; rather, and more accurately, it is a divine government or theocracy.'[2] By this, al-Mawdudi is considered to be the first contemporary Muslim thinker who originated a shift in the understanding of politics and authority in Islam from a Sunni perspective, but in striking concordance with the Shi'i concept of Imamate, the doctrine of *wilayat al-faqih*, and the theory of divine right, which characterised the political ideology of theocratic states in Christian Europe before the Renaissance.

1. Is Shura a Democratic Practice?

In the Shi'i view, *shura* is most productive and efficient in the religious sphere of *wilayat al-faqih*. Everything that humanity needs to conduct its affairs and achieve felicity at the level of state and society is within that sphere.

There is no prohibition of adopting democracy or *shura* save the stipulation that this adoption should be based upon divine laws. The reason behind that is that *shura*, as stipulated and exercised in Islam, is not an institution of legislation or an electoral district in the sphere of *wilaya*; rather its role is confined to what the believers need to conduct their daily affairs. However, secular democracy in the West became an institution of legislation, law-interpretation and elections. Therefore secular democracy replaced divine laws with positive or man-made laws. From this perspective *shura* can never amount to secular democracy since the former is a true expression and embodiment of *wilaya*. Since secular democracy practises legislation according to the strict dichotomy between state and church and its duties are confined to supporting the existing rule, then it can never be synonymous with *shura*. For *shura* is based upon belief and is the distinguishing trait of the believers who have conducted prayers and performed alms giving. If the source of democracy is not prescribed from God's injunctions then it can never be one and the same thing as *shura*.

There are precepts that set apart *shura* from democracy. Dia'aeddine Al-Rayyis has boiled down these into three: the absence of the conception of the populace or the nation in the Western nationalistic dimension; the goals of 'Islamic democracy' are two-fold, in this world and the hereafter; and the authority of the nation state in Western democracy is absolute, while in Islam it is tied to abidance by the Shari'a. *Shura* in Islam is one of a kind and does not overlap with any other

---

1   Sayyid Qutb, *Maalem Fi Al-Tareeq* (Signposts on the path), Cairo: Dar al-Shuruq, 1997. p. 163.
2   Abu Alaala AlMawdudi, *Nazariyat Alislam Wahadyehi fi Assiyasah WalQanoun Waddoustour* (Islamic Theory: Guidance in Politics, Law and Constitution), Beirut 1980, p. 158.

system; that is why it is better to label it as 'an Islamic order' in order to distinguish it from other existing systems in the world.[1]

The natural historical stance of democracy as portrayed in reality makes it susceptible to *shura*, and as such to Islam. However, the *nass* (sacred text) has delineated all the processes pertaining to democratic choice, and allegiance. This process has led al-Mawdudi to vilify democracy as a perversion of reality and a form of waywardness from Abrahamic religions. He argued that democracy has nothing to do with Islam; from this perspective it is a grave error to label the Islamic order as democratic. Rather, he preferred to label the Islamic government as divine or theocratic.[2]

In turn, Muhammad Qutb and Sayyid Qutb launched vehement attacks on democracy. They contended that it is an un-Islamic concept because it stresses materialism, *jahiliyya*, and positive or man-made legislation instead of God's *hakimiyya* and legitimacy. Sayyid Qutb claimed that democracy is an imported concept that aims at conspiring against Islam and the *umma*.[3]

2. Democracy Is Not Shura

It is a blunder to assume that democracy is synonymous with *shura* even though there might be points of concordance between the two. Some authors claim that *shura* and democracy are one and the same from a practical and conceptual stance. This characterisation totally ignores the historical evolution of democracy, be it in the West or in other places, since they regard democracy as a mechanism of governance without any consideration to its essence and value. However, a better perspective is to look at its consequences since it is constrained by religious and ethical considerations. This might lead to the legislation of laws that run against the good of humanity.

For his part, Radwan al-Sayyid, in his discussion of *shura* as a concept wavering between theory and practice, has stressed that Sheikh al-Na'ini was clear when he labelled democracy as the antonym of despotism, and considered *shura* as democratic.[4]

It could be argued that Radwan al-Sayyid's interpretation of al-Na'ini's conception is one-sided at best, resulting from a misunderstanding of the text of Sheikh al-Na'ini. Al-Na'ini had spoken of democracy in the context of supporting the Constitutional Movement in Iran, not because democracy is something

---

1   Dia'aeddine Al-Rayyes, *Political Theories in Islam*, nd, np, 1953, pp. 227 ff.

2   Mawdudi, *Nazariyat* pp. 46 ff.

3   Ahmad Moussalli, *Al-Usuliyya Al-Islamiyya: Al-Khitab Al-'Aydiyuluji 'ind Sayyid Qutb* (Islamic Fundamentalism: The Ideological Discourse of Sayyid Qutb), Beirut 1992, pp. 168 ff.

4   Radwan al-Sayyid, *Masalat AshShura bein Annas wa Attajrobah At Tarekhiyyah Lil-Ummah* (The issue of Shura: Between the Religious and Historical Practice of The Ummah), first edn, Beirut 1997, pp. 262 ff.

un-Islamic; rather his discussion of democracy came in the context of the aboli-
tion of despotism and tyrants. In short, al-Na'ini was faced with a Machiavellian
choice, namely, 'choose the best evil among the set of evils available'. Al-Na'ini
was fully aware that democracy without *wilayat al-faqih* cannot prevent tyranny;
rather it constitutes the road to it. He considered that there is no problem in
using *shura* and democracy interchangeably as long as the desired effect is democratic governance in the domain of public deputies. However, the result was
the direct opposite: despotism. This reasoning is warranted by more than one
historical precedent from the Ottoman and Iranian milieus. What al-Na'ini
discussed on the opinion of the majority and the necessity of abiding by it was
interpreted as equating *shura* with democracy. However, al-Na'ini recommends
that the ingredients of *shura* has to take into account its wavering nature when
there is a seeming opposition with the majority, or when it is given an elaborate
consideration because it is one of the strongest mechanisms recommended by
the majority.[1]

3. Shura in Islam: The Intellectual and Jurisprudential Stance of Shura

Shura in Islam has special characteristics, the most important being that it should
be viewed in the sphere of *wilaya* and that the final say should be in the hands of
the Infallible Imam or the *faqih*. It is he who fulfils the stipulations of governance
as such, being a natural extension to Prophethood and the Imamate in the age of
Greater Occultation, such that the domain of *shura* and its context are in accordance with an unequivocal *nass*. The Prophet or the Imam or the *faqih* is the one
who has the final say in executive and legislative decisions rendering a legitimate
umbrella over *shura*. In short, the *faqih* is the one who renders legitimacy to the
umma to pursue its prescribed role and gives *shura* its legitimacy in accordance
with the Shari'a since he is aware of the vital interests of the *umma* when he takes
decisions and executes them.

From the aforementioned, it is not far-fetched that *shura* and democracy are
different concepts; each one has its specificity and particularity. Democracy has
been used as a mechanism of governance and a source of legislation, while *shura*
has not. Sheikh al-Na'ini stresses the necessity of the establishment of Islamic
government and the execution of Shari'a within the narrow confines of God's law.
He discussed the role and the mission of the *faqih* in the period of Occultation,
considering that he has the final say since he construes the word of God and
abides by it in order to fill the world with equity fairness and justice in order to
completely eliminate despotism.[2]

---

1 Al-Allamah Al-Na'ini, *Tanbih Al-Ummah Wa Tanzih Al-Mullah* (The Awakening of the Nation
   and the Purity of Religion), in *Al-Ghadir Journal*, pp. 57 ff.
2 Ibid., *Al-Ghadir Journal*, vols. 12 and 13, 1991.

Equating democracy with *shura* and attributing that to al-Na'ini as some scholars have done is a mistake, since al-Na'ini's text that discusses *shura* in the framework of *wilaya* – be it in the period of Occultation or during the presence of the Infallible Imam – does not support such a claim. Na'ini used the concept of democracy in opposition to tyranny and warned that democracy would degenerate into tyranny when it becomes the sole mechanism of producing law and governance.

Perhaps the imbalance in the search for democracy and the drive to recast it as an Islamic tenet could be attributed to the achievements in the West from the stance of institutionalism, absolute freedoms and other privileges that characterise Western societies.

4. Shura and Wilaya

Our understanding of *shura* is that it ought to be juxtaposed with the *wilaya*. Hence, a detachment between the two would necessarily lead to tyranny and the rule of the dictators, as the *wilaya* will always give the *shura* its moral and ethical content. Upon investigating history one can cite many examples, where the practice of the *shura* as a mere consultation with the people led to tyranny. The story of Pharaoh serves as a good example in this context: 'Thus, he incited his people and so they obeyed him. They were, indeed, a sinful people.' (43:54)

The aforementioned does not necessarily lead to the conclusion that *shura* contradicts and is diametrically opposed to democracy; rather this viewpoint necessitates that *shura* should be juxtaposed to its political and ethical value under the leadership of the appointed Imam in order to realise it in a faithful society under the guidance of the Prophet or the imam, where obedience is mandatory. In this regard, it is worth noting that scholars such as Rashid al-Ghanushi, Radwan al-Sayyid, Muhammad Abd al-Jabiri and others equate democracy to *shura* or regard *shura* and democracy as one and the same thing. They contend that the West has transformed the Islamic *shura* into a mechanism of governance after adapting and rationalising it through the principle of elections, electoral ballots, pluralism and elite rotation.[1] In turn, Sheikh Abu Zahra contended that governance in Islam is in itself *shura*; however, he claims that *shura* is not democracy because the Prophet or the Infallible Imam cannot be appointed by people's volition. People can choose their leaders if the Infallible Imam did not exist. However, since he is in existence, then the *umma* cannot elect him based on popular vote because he is divinely appointed. Abu Zahra affirms that in

---

1   See also Al-Ghanushi in his article entitled 'Political Jurisprudence', in: *Al-Muntalaq* vol. 110, 1995; Radwan al-Sayyid in his article entitled, 'Shura between Nass and Experience', in *Al-Muntalaq* vol. 98, 1993; and Muhammad Abed Al-Jaberi, *Democracy and Human Rights*, first edn, Beirut 1994, pp. 38–42.

all respects the *khalifa* should not be imposed based on hereditary succession because *shura* and hereditary succession are at loggerheads.[1]

The concepts of *shura* and democracy are not one and the same thing, even when the ruler assumes office by the way of election. *Shura* remains distinguished from democracy from the perspective of the nature of exercising authority; rather it has to do with the nature of choosing the ruler. The contention that the West has transformed *shura* into a mechanism of governance is a distortion of the true nature of *shura*.It is not known if *shura* is a mechanism of governance *per se*, but all its dimensions and premises ought to be exposed in order to be able to construe the differences between it and democracy.

However, taking this road is necessary but not sufficient, because *shura* supersedes democracy by its distinguishing trait, which is the philosophy of freedom that is governed by God's right. This freedom and these rights are possible through obedience to God, his Prophet and the believers in every epoch. If *shura* was only fulfilled through producing a set of norms, standards and mechanisms without attaching the essence of the concept to the *wilaya*, then we should cast every doubt on it and be very sceptical about its results and consequences, because this would strip the *shura* from its essence as demonstrated in the spiritual, religious and coalescent dimensions. In spite of that, a few contemporary thinkers argue otherwise, stressing the utility and the pragmatism of the concept of *maslaha* or interest. In this respect, al-Ansari argues that this is feasible if the *umma* finds that its *maslaha* dictates granting governance based on merit, and if people supported this, and if the interest of the *umma* found that the authority of the governor should be limited as sanctioned by *ahl al-shura* (the house or community of *shura*) or the majority of them.[2]

The Prophetic tradition suggests that *shura* did not continue with those who took power after the death of the Prophet since they have given themselves more stature than the Prophet himself and they considered themselves above the principle of *shura*. By neglecting *shura* the rulers aimed at keeping away the real Imam from conducting the affairs of the state. This resulted in confining the principle of *shura* to a practical dimension so that recourse to it is only from the ethical stance by the governor in order to obtain counsel and virtue, rather than obligation and right. As expressed by al-Jabiri, 'The Islamic jurisprudential vision of the Caliphate is based upon the idea that the Caliph is held responsible in front of God and God alone, and not in front of those who voluntarily or by coercion gave their allegiance to him.' Al-Jabiri adds that the contract between the people and the governor is theoretical in nature, and confined to the doctrine of *hakimiyya*

1   Sheikh Muhammad Abu Zahra, 'The History Of Islamic Mazaheb', in *Religious Trends*, vol. 1, Beirut 1985, pp. 93–94.
2   Abdul Hamid Ismail Al-Ansari, *Shura and its Impact in Democracy*, third edn, Beirut, p. 112.

or ruling by what God has ordained. As such, *hakimiyya* does not dictate the governor in any way to abide by people's opinion, whichever and whatever class or position they have in society.[1]

Based upon the philosophy of freedom confined to God's volition, some scholars contended that the Islamic Republic of Iran embraces this principle and its ramifications which some have dubbed as 'democracy'. This democracy could not have been forged from the beginning and flourished later on had not it been for the *wilaya*, because this fusion between the principle of *wilaya* and *shura* has led to the establishment of the Islamic Republic in Iran which, according to the morphological dissection of the name itself, puts Islam next to republicanism. In this respect, Rashid al-Ghanushi in his discussions on the Islamic Republic of Iran considers that the mechanism of government was not known to our tradition, that is, democracy, because Iran has had recourse to it after it rejected its secular implications. However, Ghanusi's drawback is that he turned a blind eye and a deaf ear to a very important truth, namely, that the mechanism was not a consequence of scientific progress. Rather, it was the result of the implementation of *wilaya* that is known and recognised as a sacred text since the concept of *wilaya* is clearly stipulated in the Qur'an. If we keep this in mind, then there is no problem in labelling this mechanism with any name such as 'Islamic *shura*' as a natural consequence to the concept of *wilaya* as argued by Imam Khomeini.[2]

Sayyid Muhammad Baqir al-Sadr stressed that the *faqih* is the one who grants legitimacy to the *umma* in exercising its vital role. He witnessed this process by emphasising that Islam has stipulated the general injunctions for the Marja' and left the issue of appointment to the satisfaction of the general conditions as dictated by the *umma* itself.[3] However, al-Sadr did not elaborate the aforementioned with the exception of his emphasis that pertaining to the role of the Marja' and his responsibilities which dictate rectifying any atonement in the process of implementation. Thus he unequivocally resigned himself to the principle of God's governance (*hakimiyyat Allah*) through the Marja'. Therefore, any *shura* that is not under the guidance of the *faqih* is denied any legitimacy; it could be equated to democracy in our current world. However, since the *faqih* is not infallible then he is susceptible to the ideas and opinions of other Marja's or *mujtahidin* with one basic difference: that the *faqih* has the full prerogative and right to preside over differences in light of the Islamic Shari'a, and he can give due credit to the sacred texts. Nevertheless, as pertains to the organisational and management circle (*tanzim wa tadbir*), the *faqih* is obliged to abide by the consequences of *shura*, as well as issues pertaining to war and peace. It is of prominent importance to note

1   Al-Jaberi, *Democracy and Human Rights*, pp. 38 ff.
2   Al-Ghanushi , 'Political Jurisprudence' in *Al-Muntalaq* vol. 110, p. 9.
3   Muhammad Baqir al-Sadr, *Islam Guides Life*, Beirut 1979, p. 133 ff.

that the capacity of the *faqih* dictates arbitrating the issue in light of the Islamic Shari'a, which distinguishes *shura* in principle from democracy. And this in turn leads in the final road to become a law for those who abide by it.

The contention is that *shura* without *wilaya* would inevitably lead to inculcate the materialistic dimension of people's movement in this life – that is if the Arab and Muslim world is allowed to have and practise *shura*. In all respects, the results of *shura* or democracy are not guaranteed if they were not practised under the guidance of God's *wilaya* and his Prophet's *wilaya*, and the believers' *wilaya*. The drastic consequences of that might be to prohibit what God has already sanctioned and subjugate people to laws that are contrary to God's *hakimiyya*. Centuries ago, Muslim religious leaders questioned what should be done if the ruler has asked the Muslims to be subjugated to a law contrary to Islam.[1]

Nonetheless, *shura* entails some democratic aspects in such a way that it is democracy from the stance of placing the choice in the hands of the *umma*. Certainly, *shura* is not equivalent to democracy from the stance of absolute freedom because *shura* insists on the *hakimiyya* of God, The Prophet and *ahl al-bayt*.[2] It insists that the Qur'an alone is not enough to guide man in order to achieve Islamic principles. This negative conception distorts the meaning of *shura* and confines it to the governance of a person who needs other people to teach him the Qur'an and the Sunna, and to guide him in the implementation of the Islamic principles. This could lead either to belittling people or to despotism, as was the case in *shura* or Pharonic democracy or *jahiliyya* despotism.

Based on the aforementioned, it could be argued that the political implication of *shura* is that it is a mechanism and an ethical value. If democracy nowadays is established on the level of political realism as a mechanism of governance that protects the rights of a lot of people and renders services to the institutions and organisations without any spiritual and religious dimension, then it is an empty structure that separates religion from politics (secularism) and that does not give due regard to ethical and humanistic values and does not exhort people to abide by them. Some democratic expressions stress that politics should not give due credit to ethics, because the credentials and ingredients of politics deal with the reality from the stance of interest (*maslaha*).[3]

Exercising the principle of *shura* in Islam dictates the inculcation of higher moral values in political work and prevents desires and inclinations to interfere in political decisions, thus leading to unethical politics. Unlike democracy, *shura* has insisted on the amalgamation of faith and ethical values as distinguishing

---

1   Farah Musa, *The Necessities of the Regimes and the Choices of the Ummah according to Sheikh Shamseddine*, first edn, Beirut 1995, pp. 75 ff.

2   Lit. people of the house [of the Prophet]; Shi'i Islam holds great store by the authority vested in the descendants of the family of the Prophet Muhammad.

3   Sheikh Muhammad Mahdi Shamseddine, *The Book on Secularism*, Beirut 1983, p. 99 ff.

features for the Muslims, since God has placed prayer and spending on the same par. 'Those who, if We established them firmly in the land, will perform the prayer, give the alms, command the good and prohibit the evil. To Allah belongs the outcome of all affairs.' (22:41) According to Hafiz Yusuf Ali, a renowned Islamic scholar, 'The justification of the righteous in resisting oppression when not only they put their Faith is persecuted and when they are led by a righteous imam, is that it is a form of self-sacrifice. They are not fighting for themselves, for land, power, or privilege. They are fighting for the right.'[1] God has dictated the heeding to the call from the stance of performing prayer, *shura* and expenditure.[2]

In short, democracy has been transformed into a mechanism of governance that adjusted reality and established substantial results; however, it appears not to abide by ethical, religious and humanistic values. In other words, it could be expedient to resort to democracy but if *shura* is stripped out of its religious and ethical dimensions then its application is not suitable to the Muslims; however, if democracy is fused with ethical and religious values along the lines of God's *hakimiyya* and *shura*, then the Muslims can abide by it. The nuance is that the ethical dimension is not enough to render true *shura*; there is a vital necessity to abide by an Islamic principle based on the sacred text – and not relying upon what has been established by Western democracy – in the direction of achieving coalescence and balance across private and public life in such a way that the human being connects to his past, present and future, since this connection remains a basic stipulation for the movement of the *umma* in the direction of its freedom. *Shura* is the trait par excellence for religious people and similar to the religious organisational injunctions, then the Muslims can transform it to a mechanism of governance under the supervision of the true jurist consult whose presence gives it an ethical and religious dimensions linked to obedience to God and his Prophet.

It has been demonstrated that the intellectual and jurisprudential stance from the principle of *shura* is a stance based upon independent reasoning (*ijtihad*) that has led to grave variations leading to either acceptance or rejection. Acceptance alternated between individual sanctioning and transforming it into basic political system or integrating it within *wilaya* so that the authority would be based upon two pillars: popularity and religion.

Nevertheless, in all respects, there is no innate value for *shura* in relation to the *nass* (sacred text), for *shura* cannot legitimise a *haram* (illicit), or prohibit *halal* (religiously sanctioned). Even if *shura* is absolutely accepted and if people

---

1   Yusuf Ali, *The Holy Qur'an: Translation and Commentary*, Lahore: Islamic Propagation Centre International, 1993, pp. 862–863.
2   Abdul Qadir Awdeh, *Islam and Our Political Situation*. Beirut, Mouassasat Al-Risalah, 2008, pp. 193.

seek to validate democracy by *shura*, these two do not have the same intellectual import since there is no prohibition on democracy except democracy itself, while religious injunctions (*ahkam*) have an important bearing on *shura*. That is why *shura* cannot constitute the mechanism of legislation outside the safeguards of religious text. Rather it falls within the domain of execution and management (*tanfiz wa tadbir*). In case it is employed as a framework of legislation, then it needs recourse to religious options employing independent reasoning (*ijtihadi-shar'i*), which could eventually lead to a variety of *ijtihadi* alternatives.

The Islamic vision agrees with legislative democracy if and only if it is in conformity with the religious text. However, there could be harmony between democracy and Islamic vision from the stance of seeking the dignity of the human being. Nevertheless, the variance in philosophical substantiation cannot be denied because freedom, including personal freedom, constitutes the spirit of democracy. Limitations on freedom from the stance of religion and religious thought are diversified.

5. Qur'anic Legitisation of Shura

The concept of *shura* in Islam is based on a host of Qur'anic verses, which present conclusive evidence (*adillah*): 'As to the believers, males and females. They are friends of one another. They enjoin what is good and forbid what is evil, perform the prayers, give the alms and obey Allah and His Apostle. It is those on whom Allah will have mercy. Allah is Mighty, Wise.' (9:71) 'And those who answer their Lord, perform the prayer, their affair being a counsel among themselves and of what We provided them with, they spend.' (42:38)

Other evidence can be found in the Traditions or Sunna: 'Only the believers are the protectors of each other aside from all other people.'[1]

As is known, the evidences of *shura* in the Qur'an were not absolute but were rather tied to *wilayat*: 'The Prophet is closer to the believers than their own selves.' (33:6) 'O believers, obey Allah and obey the Apostle and those in authority among you.' (4:59) 'It is not up to any believer, man or woman, when Allah and His Apostle have passed a judgment, to have any choice in their affairs.' (33:36)

Shura before Islam and the Prophetic revival was existing and employed by the Quraysh tribes,[2] and before them by the Pharaohs of Egypt. It is impossible that God has ordered the believers to employ *jahiliyya* (pre-Islamic period of ignorance) *shura* because it is based upon the strongest party who has the prerogative and the right to discriminate against others according to his authority,

---

1   Abdulsalam Haroun, *Tahzeeb Sirat Ibn Hisham*, (Compilation of the Biography of Ibn Hisham), tenth edn, Beirut 1984, p. 124.

2   The tribes who governed Mecca before the advent of Islam; the Prophet was a member of a minor branch of the Quraysh tribal confederation, yet he opposed their pagan ways.

wealth and statute. In other words, we can say that the *jahiliyya shura* was not the *shura* of the righteous, but rather the *shura* of private interests of this tribe or that. From this stance, the Islamic norms and regulations were distinct from what people have known before, since the Prophet himself was ordered by God to practise *shura* and he was appointed by Him as a governor of the Muslims. The implication of this is that *shura* became tied to *wilaya* and functions within its framework, because if *shura* was independent of *wilaya* then there would be an unequivocal setback and return to the *jahiliyya*.

If *shura* was practised during the time of the Prophet, then it goes without saying that after his death, and during the Greater Occultation, it is incumbent upon the *umma* to engage in *shura*, especially in the political sphere on the level of electing a governor, as well as in a host of administrative and organisational issues after the evidence was established that this issue was the prerogative of the *umma* even during the presence of the Infallible Imam himself.

Further, the Qur'an has unequivocally defended the dignity of the human being. 'We have honoured the Children of Adam and carried them on land and sea, provided them with good things and preferred them greatly over many of those We have created.' (17:70) According to Yusuf Ali, the distinction and honour conferred by God on man are recounted in order to enforce the corresponding duties and responsibilities of man. 'He is raised to acquisition of honour above the brut creation [of animals]; he has been granted talents by which he can transport himself from place to place by land, sea, and now by air; all the means of sustenance and growth of every part of his nature are provided by God; and his spiritual faculties (the greatest gift of God) raise him above the greater part of God's Creation. Should he not then realise his noble destiny and prepare for his real life in the Hereafter?'[1]

Also the Qur'an has mentioned pluralism as one of the customary practices of life: 'And Had your Lord willed, He would have made mankind a single nation; but they will continue to differ among themselves.' (11:118) According to Yusuf Ali, all mankind might have been one, but in God's plan man was to have a certain measure of free will, and this made differences inevitable. 'This would not have mattered if all had honestly sought God. But selfishness and moral wrong came in, and people's disputations became mixed up with hatred, jealousy, and sin ...'[2]

This theme also resonates in verses 10:19 and 2:213, among others. In 10:19: 'Mankind was a single nation; then they differed. Had it not been for a prior order of your Lord, the matter over which they had differed would have been settled.' According to Yusuf Ali, all mankind was created as one, and God's Message to mankind is in essence one, the Message of Unity and Truth. But as selfishness

---

1   Yusuf Ali, ibid, p. 714.
2   Yusuf Ali, ibid, p. 546.

and egoism got hold of man, as verse 2:213 expresses it, certain differences sprang up between individuals, races, and nations, and in His Infinite Mercy, He sends them messengers and messages to suit their varying mentality, to test them by His gifts and stir them up to emulation in virtue and piety,[1]

The Qur'an also stressed freedom and rejection of enforcing one's doctrine: 'Let there be no compulsion in religion: Truth stands out clear from error: whoever rejects evil and believes in God has grasped the most trustworthy hand-hold that never breaks. God is All Hearing and All Knowing.' (2:256) According to Yusuf Ali, 'Compulsion is incompatible with religion: because (1) religion depends upon faith and will, and these would be meaningless if induced by force; (2) truth and error have been so clearly shown up by the mercy of God that there should be no doubt in the minds of any persons of good will as to the fundamentals of face; (3) God's protection is continuous and His plan is always to lead us from the depth of darkness into the clearest light.' In commenting on the hand-hold, Yusuf Ali explains that it is 'something which the hands can grasp for safety in a moment of danger. It may be a loop or a handle, or anchor. If it is without flaw, so that there is no danger of breaking, our safety is absolutely assured so long as we hold fast to it. Our safety then depends on our own will and faith: God's help and protection will always be unfailing if we hold firmly to God and trust in Him.'[2] The Prophet used to address the 'People of the Book' with the following Qur'anic header: 'Say O People of the Book, come to an equitable word between you and us, that we worship none but Allah, do not associate anyone with Him and do not set up each other as lords besides Allah.' (3:64)

According to Yusuf Ali, 'In the abstract the People of the Book would agree to all three prepositions. In practice they fail. Apart from doctrinal lapses from the unity of the One True God, there is the question of a consecrated priesthood..., as if a mere human being ... could claim superiority apart from his learning and the purity of his life, or could stand between man and God in some special sense. The same remarks apply to the worship of saints. They may be pure and holy. But no one can protect us or claim Lordship over us except God. Abraham was a true man of God, but according to normative Muslim belief he could not be called a Jew or a Christian as he lived long before the Law of Moses or the Gospel of Jesus was revealed.'[3]

These Qur'anic values and teachings are not in disagreement with what democracy claims. However, what should be stressed is that the flexibility of democracy and its inability to be delineated in a clear-cut formula, as well as its great capacity to continuously accommodate to the values of society, makes of it a liberal democracy in the West. However, in the Islamic milieu, democracy has

---

1   Ibid., p. 488.
2   Ibid., p. 103.
3   Ibid., p. 138.

to abide by the values of this environment, which will ultimately result in Islamic democracy. This Islamic democracy abides by the holistic Islamic vision, while at the same time expressing the convictions and choices of the socio-Islamic milieu.

It is the responsibility of the religious elite (the Islamic movements and the clerics) to forge a marriage between the democratic choice and justice because the latter is the most salient principle in the religious vision, a thing which was overlooked in the liberal vision, and which prompted the emergence of a new trend in the West that calls for the adopting the communal democracy which in turn stresses the primacy of justice. This is the best way to achieve balance between individuals' rights and the society's rights and between the individual interest and the public interest.

6. Secularism and Democracy

The Islamic discourse on secularism since the 1920s has been of a negative nature, especially since its advent to the Arab and Islamic world was accompanied by Western colonialism and the spread of a wave of cultural liberalism and national fragmentation. However, this position has not been static; rather, it went through transformations as a better understanding of secularism emerged as time elapsed. At first, secularism was viewed as an adversary or in opposition to religion, and as a product of the Western life and its material civilisation and the socio-economical evolution of this civilisation which did not necessarily fit with the Arab and Islamic worlds. Added to this was the belief that Islam as a religion had everything that people needed to lead their life without any help from any source or system, especially if it is of a mundane origin. This was the predominant position of many Muslim scholars, especially during the 1970s. After the lapse of some time, in the beginning of the 1990s, secularism was viewed with a less negative approach, reaching a kind of reconciliation with Islam. The late Sheikh Muhammad Mahdi Shamseddine of Lebanon argued along similar lines; he rejected the idea of a religious state, and stressed the necessity of civil society and citizenship in secular societies. In turn, Hasan al-Turabi of Sudan accepted not only the application of Shari'a in Muslim majority countries, but also in Muslim minority countries. Finally, Rashid al-Ghanushi of Tunisia recommended that it was preferable to live under a Western secular state, rather than an Arab or Islamic state that was or is ruled by a dictator.

The juxtaposition of secularism and democracy has been the result of Western experience based upon sociopolitical circumstances that the West passed through as a reaction to church practices that cracked down on freedom of thought, impeded scientific progress and put a hold on the possibility of social progress. It seems that democracy in the West emerged in the course of confrontation with political and religious despotism, leaving room for a third party, the populace, to emerge.

The Middle Eastern socio-political milieu is different from that which was dominant in the West. The concordance between secularism and democracy is not a historical inevitability; rather, it is the result of specific Western experience. It does not sound scientifically valid to suppose that democracy in the Muslim world will take the same course and produce the same results that Western democracy passed through. The main point behind this difference is that ethical and religious values in both societies are drastically different.

The democratic endeavour finds solid ground outside the socio-political milieus that are characterised by religious and sectarian harmony; as such it becomes difficult for a political Islamic project to take root and to achieve its objectives by remaining pure and authentic.

An exception is the Islamic Republic of Iran, where governance is based upon *wilayat al-faqih*, which constitutes the epitome of religious governance that combines religious legitimacy with popular legitimacy. *Wilayat al-faqih* is based upon *shura* or consultation in its legitimate framework

The existence of a viable social entity capable of holding the reins of the populace and expressing its political convictions leads to socio-political democratic transformation. From this perspective, when moderate Islamic movements embrace the call for religio-democratic transformation, then this condition would have been fulfilled.

Islamic democracy implies a constitution that is in conformity with religion, a neutral state upholding the rights of all the citizens, and an authority governed by peaceful transactions. All of these boil down to an Islamic state based upon popular sovereignty through a fair and equitable political process. Both the populace and the state should accept the outcome of the electoral process even if it results in a non-Islamic party holding the reins of power.

As for freedom, equality and pluralism, there should be a consensus to broaden their horizons and constituents based upon religious injunctions that have the characteristic of being flexible in relation to social practices as opposed to rituals (*'ibadat*) characterised by rigidity. All of this is based upon the interest of Islam and the Muslims in this important phase of humanistic progress that gives centre stage to the values of freedom and pluralism as bases for socio-political stability.

However, this process has not been smooth. For instance, Algerian Islamists have paid a heavy and early price for their rejection of democracy,[1] a situation that frightened the other groups including wide societal segments and prompted them to integrate with the existing secular political structure. It was under these circumstances that the Islamists were accused of adopting democracy (only one time), and only when it serves them.

---

1   They defined democracy as *kuffar* (infidelity).

Democracy has become a persistent test as it became congruent with modernity and pluralism. In Islamic societies where sectarian and ethnic harmony exists, opponent democracy or *al-dimiqratiyya al-munawi'a* would be mild; but in the communities where sectarian pluralism exists, as is the case in Iraq and Lebanon, it would be almost impossible to islamise the political and social reality, and as such democracy becomes the only solution to these societies, though the experiments have not given enough guarantees for the anticipated outcomes.[1]

THE DILEMMA OF DEMOCRACY IN CONTEMPORARY ISLAMIC POLITICAL THOUGHT

Over the course of history, many jurisprudents have sanctioned controlling governance by force, by succession or by *nass* (sacred text), even against the will of the *umma* forcing people to obedience. In order to sanction this line of thought the Islamists have relied upon a host of primary sources attempting to substantiate their claims; the most salient are these two:

— The Prophet is reported to have said that: 'You will be ruled by leaders whom you know and whom you deny. Those who deny are exonerated, those who despise are sheltered, but those who accepted and given their vows of allegiance ...' Here he was interrupted and asked by fellow Muslims: 'Shall we fight them?' The Prophet said: 'No, as long as they held to their prayers.'
— If a ruler were to exercise despotism upon his subjects, then they should be patient since he will ultimately be held accountable in the end. If a person defies the ruler's authority, then that person will die a *jahiliyya* death.

The ambiguity of accepting or rejecting democracy usually happens when we investigate the *shura* concept in Islam, as such a concept was subject to many interpretations. Muslims have never had a single understanding of this concept, and the Shi'is in particular had a general sense of resentment towards the *shura* concept due to religious historical reasons, when this very concept was employed by the Sunnis versus the text or Hadith vis-à-vis the Caliphate of 'Ali Ibn Abi Talib.

According to the Shi'i doctrine, the succession of the Prophet should not be subject to *shura* or to any mundane authority, rather to a divine appointment by text (*t'ayin bi al-nass al-ilahi*). On the contrary, the Sunnis believe in the *shura* and *bay'a* (pledge of allegiance) as a mechanism of choosing the successor of the Prophet.

In contemporary and recent political thought, the Shi'i stand towards understanding the *shura* has varied immensely, as some clerics considered it obligatory

---

1 *Nazra Jadeedah fi wilayat Alfakeeh* (A New View of Wilayat al-faqih), pp. 22–23.

where other clerics considered it not obligatory. There was also discord over whether to make it a basis for the political system or to limit it to a mere general moral value in the intra-relations among the Muslims themselves; or whether it could be obligatory as a procedural tool but not obligatory in the results it produces.

Among those who staunchly reject the *shura* is Ayatollah Mahmud al-Hashimi Ashahrourdi, as he states that '*shura*, elections and choice on the basis of election is an innovation that came to us from the West and it represents the culture of anti-Shi'is in the *wilaya* issue and it has no trace in Islam.'

The Shi'i rejection in this regard has abundant occurrence in the Shi'i literature, as we can see also with Kadhim al-Ha'iri who clarifies that 'the problem exists in all the proofs (*barahin*) put forth as evidence that the principles of *shura*, voting and election should be adopted as a basis for state formation in Islam.' According to Ha'iri, 'had this been the Prophet's purpose to guide the *umma* to run their affairs after him through the *shura* principle, he should have explained the different aspects, articles and regulations of this principle.' He also adds, 'Had the Imams wanted to guide the Shi'is after the Ghayba period towards the *shura* and election, they should have explained to the Shi'is the different aspects, articles and regulations of the *shura*.'[1]

As for the many narrations attributed to the Imams about the *shura* and encouraging it – as is the situation with Imam 'Ali Ibn Abi Talib – the contemporary Shi'i stance would consider it a kind of *taqiyya*, or to commit the opponents to their standards to refute their positions.[2] The late Sayyid Muhammad Baqir al-Hakim of Iraq, the former head of the Supreme Council of the Islamic Revolution in Iraq (SCIRI), posed the same doubts on the *shura* concept vis-à-vis its ambiguity and the Prophet's reluctance to educate the *umma* according to this principle.[3] Nonetheless, al-Hakim concluded that it is a necessity to establish a merger between the *shura* principle and the *wilaya* principle. The late Mohammad Hussein al-Tabataba'i could be included in this category as well, as his position also fluctuated between accepting or rejecting the *shura*, and then approaching it without a clearcut position. According to him, 'it is not an Islamic standard in making a law or introducing a change to take the opinion of the majority of votes into consideration, though Islam does not neglect the *shura* in exercising power (*hukm*), or management (*idara*); still, the most important is to

1   Kadhim al-Ha'iri, '*Asas Alhoukomah AlIslamiyah, Dirasah Istidlaliya Mokaranah bein addimokratiyyah wal wilayat fi lislam* (The Foundations of Islamic Government: A Comparative Study Between Democracy and Wilaya in Islam) fifth edition, Beirut 1979, pp. 92–93.

2   *Nazra Jadeedah fi welayat Alfakeeh* (A New View of Wilayat al-faqih), pp. 95–96.

3   Mohamad Baqir Al-Hakeem, *Al-Alaqa bein Al-Shoura Wa Al-Eilayah Fi Al-Islam* (The relation between the Shura and the Welaya in Islam), Beirut 1993, pp. 17–30.

do and follow the right (*haq*).[1] But regardless of his negative position from the *shura* principle, al-Tabataba'i concludes that 'the regulations decided by the government should not be issued except after the *shura* (consulting the people) and after noticing the highest Islamic interest' (*al-maslaha al-islamiyya al-'ulyya*).[2]

1. Sayyid Muhammad Baqir al-Sadr

For his part, the late Sayyid Muhammad Baqir al-Sadr of Iraq nurtured his political theory through three transformations. The first transformation appeared in the 1960s through adopting the *shura* as a principle of power in Islam; the second took place most likely in the 1970s after being influenced by the writings of Imam Khomeini, who by then had adopted the general theory of *wilayat al-faqih*; and the third appeared in the late 1970s after the victory of the Islamic Revolution in Iran when he merged the general *wilayat al-faqih* and the *shura* theories; his research under the title 'The Caliphate of Man and the Martyrdom of the Prophets' would constitute the most expressive merging of these perspectives, as he gives the *umma* a pivotal role in establishing the power system upon two pillars: the caliphate system (*khalifa*) and the *shura*.

It is worth noting that al-Sadr mentioned in the first stage that it is clear that the form of power system currently has not been treated in any special Shi'i or Sunni text altogether. In other words, the *shura* in the Ghayba period represents an acceptable form of power system; upon this any *shura* system of power would be endorsed as correct as long as it observes the Islamic divine law (Shari'a),[3] as it is incumbent upon the *umma* when choosing the system and the apparatus of power to observe the Shari'a.[4] However, we would find a different perspective in al-Sadr's approach towards the *shura* concept in the second stage, which culminates towards a radical criticism of the *shura*. In his research, 'Around the Wilaya' (*hawl al-wilaya*), al-Sadr suggests that the Prophet did not start an awareness

---

1   Mohamad Hussein al-Tabataba'i, *Nazariyat Alhokm wa Siyasah fi al-Islam* (Views, Laws and Politics in Islam), third version, translated and introduced by Assefi Mohammd Mahdi, Tehran, 1402 AH (2003), p. 26.

2   Al-Tabatabi, p. 39.

3   According to Sunni Islam, shari'a is compiled from at least four sources: The Qur'an; Sunna or Hadith; *qiyas* (analogical reasoning), based upon comparison among the different hadiths in order to validate the resemblance (*mushabaha*); and *ijma* of the umma (consensus). According to Shi'i tradition, shari'a is based upon four sources: The Qur'an; The Sunna or Hadith of the Prophet and the Twelve Imams which according to devout Shi'is constitute the household of the Prophet; *al'aql*, the employment of human reasoning to sort out things and find solutions as it represents the ultimate principle that governs human behaviour; and *ijma*. However, unlike Sunnis, *ijma* is confined to the jurisprudents (*fuqaha*) and not the lay people who are not well versed in interpreting the ultimate Divine truth.

4   Muhammad Baqir al-Sadr, 'Usul Adostur Alislami' (Origin of Islamic Constitution), from Chibli Mallat, *Muhammad Baqir Al-Sadr - Between Najaf and the Shiites of the World*, first edn, Beirut, pp. 42–43.

campaign vis-à-vis the *shura* concept among the Muhajirun and the Ansar,[1] as this first generation of Muslims did not work according to the mentality of *shura*, and we therefore cannot imagine that the Prophet has established this 'system and defined its legislative and conceptual context, and in the same time refrained from educating the Muslims and raising their awareness about it. As such, this constitutes proof that the Prophet had not suggested the *shura* to be an alternative system to the *umma*'.[2]

By this radical criticism of the role of the *shura* in the Islamic political system, al-Sadr launched in his second stage a complete theoretical antithesis to the vision that he proposed later on, about the caliphate of the man and the Prophet. As he says: 'God has assigned the Prophet a duty (*wajib*) to consult the Muslims and make them feel their responsibilities in the caliphate issue through consultation, (3:159); '... Consult them in the conduct of affairs. Then, when you are resolved, trust in Allah; Allah indeed loves those who put their trust in Him'. This consultation issue by the impeccable leader is considered a preparation procedure of the people to the caliphate issue and an assertion of its importance. Al-Sadr notes that Prophet Muhammad was keen on the practical level to include the *umma* in the responsibilities of power that sometimes he would respect and carry the viewpoint of his supporters though he was personally convinced of its invalidity.[3]

We have to mention here that al-Sadr validated the *shura* principle in the legislative domain on the premises of the two verses of the Qur'an:

And those who answered their Lord, performed the prayer, their affair being a council among themselves, and of what We provided them with, they spent.

According to Yusuf Ali:

Their conduct in life is open and determined by mutual consultation between those who are entitled to a voice, e.g., in private domestic affairs, as between husband and wife, or other responsible members of the household; in affairs of business, as between partners or parties interested; and in state affairs, as between rulers and ruled or as between different departments

---

1   The Muhajirun are the earliest followers of Islam who joined the Prophet Mohammed on his hijra from Mecca to Medina. The Ansar, or 'helpers', were the earliest followers of Islam from Medina who helped the Prophet and Muhajirun upon their migration to the city.

2   Muhammad Baqir al-Sadr, *Bahth hawl Alwilayah* (A Research on the Wilaya), Beirut 1990, p. 25.

3   Muhammad Baqir al-Sadr, *Khilafat Alinsan Washahadat Alanbiyaa*, (The Caliphate of Man and the Martyrdom of Prophets), from series on 'Islam leads the life', Qom, Iran, 1399 (2003) pp. 43–44.

of administration, to preserve the unity of administration ...
Consultation is the key-word of the Sura and suggests the ideal
way in which a good man should conduct his affairs, so that, on
the one hand, he may not become too egoistical, and, on the
other, he may not lightly abandon the responsibilities which
devolve on him as a personality whose development counts in
the sight of God ... This principle was applied to its fullest extent
by the holy Prophet in his private and public life, and was fully
acted upon by the early rulers of Islam. Modern representative
government is an attempt – by no means perfect – to apply this
principle in state affairs.[1] (42:38)

And:

As to the believers, males and females, they are friends of one
another. They enjoin what is good and forbid what is evil, perform
the prayers, give the alms and obey Allah and His Apostle. It is
those on whom Allah will have mercy. Allah is Mighty. (9:71)

The first Qur'anic text entitles the *umma* to run its affairs through *shura* as
long as no other Qur'anic text contradicts this. The second verse talks about
the *wilayat* and that every believer is *wali* to the other believers, which seems
to imply the functionality of the *wilaya* among the believers, men and women,
equally; thus producing the validity of the *shura* principle and the opinion of
the majority upon conflict.[2] As such, popular legitimacy is based on religious
substantiation.[3]

The ultimate result is that al-Sadr's theoretical vision of power concludes the
fusion between the *shura* principle and the *wilaya* principle, which means the
attempt to reconcile between the religious and the popular legitimacy. In this
context, what is meant by *shura* is popular legitimacy.

2. Sheikh Muhammad Mahdi Shamseddine on Shura

The late Sheikh Muhammad Mahdi Shamseddine based his argument in legislating the *shura* on two Qur'anic verses. The first one indicated the necessity (*wujub*)
that the *umma* adopts the *shura*: 'their affair being a counsel among themselves'.
(42:36) According to Shamseddine, this verse is not a description of the believers

---

1   Yusuf Ali, pp. 1316–1317.
2   Ibid., p. 54.
3   According to Shi'i tradition, popular legitimacy should always be enshrined within the scope of
    the religious mandate because it cannot stand on its own.

in his opinion, rather it is an organisational and religious order to all the Muslims to apply and abide by in their life so they would have perfection in their being Muslims and believers. He argued that the verse below indicated the necessity (*wujub*) of adopting the *shura* principle for the ruler in exercising his power and authority: 'consult them in the conduct of affairs'. (3: 159)[1] Shamseddine reached an interesting conclusion when he argued that in the absence of the impeccable ruler 'there is no legitimacy to any disposition in the general affairs of the society unless it is based in the *shura* principle'.[2]

Shamseddine's perspective towards the *shura* led him to accept democracy, which is a rare position among the jurists, and he is considered to be a pioneer in this field. This breakthrough by Shamseddine in his approach to democracy came after a profound review of his own thinking in the introduction of the second edition of his renowned book.[3] He wrote: 'In the first edition of this book we considered that democracy is a complete antithesis to Islam without distinguishing whether it is a legislative tool or whether it is considered a tool for choosing the ruler or power rotation, and without making any distinction between the pre-Greater Occultation and the post-Greater Occultation. But now we can see the difference between the two so clearly, in the sense that in the pre-Greater Occultation period there is no legitimacy for the democratic style in choosing the ruler, and there is no legitimacy for whoever could be chosen as opposite to the Impeccable Imam; however, our opinion in the post-Greater Occultation period is based on our jurisprudential *fiqhi* principle of the *wilaya* of the *umma* on itself.'[4]

3. Imam Khomeini on Shura

As far as Imam Khomeini was concerned, and after reviewing two of his books which included his theory on *wilayat al-faqih*, one cannot find a treatment for the *shura* principle which clarifies his position vis-à-vis the issue of *wilayat al-faqih*. But the *wilaya* of the jurisconsult from the jurisprudence perspective stands on the religious legitimacy, which means a divine authorisation to the jurisconsult or *faqih* to exercise power through his deputyship to the impeccable, according to definite legitimate standards and regulations which take into consideration the public good of Islam and Muslims. In other words, this means that the *wali al-faqih* has comprehensive authority over the community, and although the

---

1 Muhammad Mahdi Shamseddine *Fil Ijtimaa Asiyasi Alislamiz Almojtama Asiyasi Alislami* (An attempt for a historical and jurisprudence validation), first edn, 1982 pp. 8–11.

2 Shamseddine, *Al-Ummah Wa Al-Dawlah Wa Al-Harakah Al-Islamiyyah*, (The Islamic Ummah, State and Movements), first edn, Lebanon 1994, p. 123.

3 Shamseddine, *Nizam Al-Hukum wa Al-Idara fi Al-Islam* (The system of power and management in Islam), fourth edn, Beirut 1995; from the introduction.

4 Ibid.

government is instrumentally subdued to the interest of the people, as one of its major tasks, its ultimate and conclusive reference is the *wali al-faqih* himself, as he represents the divine law.

In approaching Khomeini's thought one could find two levels of texts which include a definition of the role of the people in the frame of the general *wilayat al-faqih*. The first kind of texts are of a *fiqhi* or more strictly legalistic nature in which the texts give exclusive political legitimacy to the *wilayat al-faqih*. The second kind of texts could be derived from the daily discourses and speeches of Imam Khamina', where a crowd of concepts and notions which reflect Khomeini's genuine trust in the people's awareness and competence appears; and these concepts in turn give the people the right to exercise checks and balances over their rulers' actions. Khomeini in this sense makes the people the foundation of the system and the guarantors of its continuity. An attempted fusion between the two levels of texts shows that the people are an integral part of the power establishment, though they occupy a lesser rank compared to that of the *faqih*, the law, Shari'a, and the interests of Islam.

In any respect, it is worth mentioning that although Imam Khomeini declined adding the label of democracy to the Islamic Republic, the etymology of the word 'republic' conveys the populist nature of governance. Furthermore, in the first year of establishing the Islamic Republic four basic populist referenda were conducted, among which was a referendum on the declaration of the Islamic Republic, as well as another one on its constitution.

THE CONCEPT OF SHURA AND ITS POSITIONING IN THE ISLAMIC ORDER

Shura institutions constitute the body politic of the Islamic Republic because *shura*

> is the base and one of the two major pillars of the system, the first and foremost being *wilayat al-faqih*, which constitutes the apex of the pyramidical structure of Iran. The backbone of the Islamic political system are the authorities that emanate from the *shura* Council; these guarantee that the *umma* will take a constructive role in the affairs of the state as well as accommodating its potential power which is made up of human and material resources. The *umma* expresses its will through the *shura* institutions that are present in all the pillars of the system and its apparatus. It also manages the affairs of the state and has a say in decision making within the confines that Islam has stipulated. In other words, it has

a large margin to exercise its rights and freedoms within its *taklif shar'i* or the duties that religious commitment entails.[1]

The Islamic political system derives its legitimacy and justification from doctrinal religious norms in such a way as to activate the political system by resorting to the mechanism of *shura* and majority vote. This has led some Muslim political thinkers to consider *shura* as the source of legitimacy of the Islamic government and to compare it with democracy. What is construed by *shura* here is a mechanism to exercise authority through the various councils of supervision, planning, legislation, execution and judiciary.

---

1   Sheikh 'Abbas 'Ali 'Amid Zinjani, *Majalis Al-Shura Al 'amud Alfiqari Lilnizam Alsiyasi Al Islami* (Shura Councils: The Backbone for the Islamic Political System), from the proceedings of the Fourth Conference On Islamic Thought, Tehran, 1989. p. 130.

CHAPTER FOUR

Islamic Principles Applied in the Islamic Republic

Building on the discussion in the last chapter, this chapter will discuss how the concept of *shura* is applied in the Islamic Republic. The Islamic Republic ensures the central role of the populace and the individual through the application of the Islamic concepts of *shura* and *umma*, while simultaneously preserving the rights of the community, by applying the concept of *maslaha* in the system of governance, and giving centrality to the notion of pluralism (*ikhtilaf*). This unique combination of Islamic principles creates the basis of a system of governance that is both rich in character and flexible to adaptation.

THE CONCEPT OF SHURA AND ITS POSITIONING IN THE ISLAMIC ORDER

The Shura Council's authority guarantees that the *umma* will take a constructive role in the affairs of the state as well as accommodating its potential power which is made up of human and material resources. The *umma* expresses its will through the *shura* institutions; it also manages the affairs of the state and has a say in decision making within the confines that Islam has stipulated. So it has a large margin to exercise its rights and freedoms within its *taklif shar'i*, or the duties that religious commitment entails.[1]

By way of a close look at the nature of the functioning of the Islamic system in Iran it could be inferred that the *shura* which originates from the will of the *umma* is a salient feature from the apex of the system all the way down to its

---

1 Sheikh Zinjani, *Majalis Al-Shura Al 'amud Alfiqari Lilnizam Alsiyasi Al Islami*, p. 130.

base, passing through the different apparatuses.[1] For instance the Council of Experts is the direct product of the will of the *umma*, and it is incumbent upon it to choose the *wali al-faqih*, the *rahbar* of the regime. Based upon the rights that his station in office stipulates, the *rahbar* consults with the Expediency Council (*majm'a taskhis maslahat al-nizam*) in drawing up general policy statements of the state.

The Constitution of the Islamic Republic of Iran has stipulated that the drawing of the general policies of the system by the *wali al-faqih* should always be done in conjunction with the Expediency Council.[2] Also the Constitution has stipulated that the *faqih* holds the *wilayat* and all the responsibilities attached to it by choice of the Council of Experts, which is elected by the people.[3] This is the case in spite of the theory that the contemporary Islamic political system is based upon, which considers that the *faqih* holds the reins of the *wilayat* since he is considered the deputy of the Infallible Imam.

The relationship between the Iranian Islamic political system and *shura* is based upon the following. First, *shura* is a means of choosing the officials of the system by majority vote of the populace. From this comes the election of *wali al-faqih* by the Council of Experts and the election of the president and his cabinet as well as the speaker of the Shura Council (Parliament) and its members, the head of the Council of Experts and its members, and the head of the municipal council and its members.

Second, *shura* is a focal point for decision making on a popular scale by majority of votes through councils, committees and specialised departments, instead of individual decision making. This trend is applied by all executive, legislative and judicial powers especially in situations that do not require speedy decisions. The Expediency Council, the Islamic Shura Council, the Council of Experts, the Council of Guardians, the Higher Council of National Security, the Higher Council of National Defence, the State Security, the Higher Council of the Cultural Revolution, and others each take its decisions by recourse to *shura* based on majority decision.

Third, *shura* is a mechanism to consolidate authority by way of sustaining it by expert opinion and learned consultation. In this respect, *shura* is not in a position to take decisions; rather, the decisions are left to the incumbent in office by the right balance among the views of the advisors. This type of *shura* can be seen in its implementation by way of the relationship between the *rahbar* and the Expediency Council; the relationship between the president and the council

1   Sheikh Muhammad 'Ali Al Taskhiri, *Hawla Al-Dustur Al-Islami Fi Mawaddihi Al'Ammah* (On The Islamic Constitution in its General Articles), pp. 283–332.
2   The Constitution of the Islamic Republic, article 110, 68.
3   Ibid., article 107, 67.

of ministers; and the relationship between the head of the judiciary with the council of the judiciary.

SHURA COUNCILS IN THE ISLAMIC REPUBLIC OF IRAN

Most of the *shura* institutions are constitutional institutions, while the institutions that are not mentioned by the Constitution have been elected on the basis of laws and decisions emanating from the Islamic Shura Council. The fundamental *shura* institutions in the Islamic Republic are the following:

— *Expediency Council*: It is the highest Shura Council in the Islamic Republic, since the *faqih* draws up state policy based on its recommendations, and resolves any disputes that might arise between the Shura Council and the Council of Guardians. The Expediency Council is composed of the most prominent statesmen and leaders who either hold or have held public office, including the president of the republic, the president of the Shura Council, and the head of the judiciary. The *rahbar* nominates the head of the council as well as its permanent and temporary members. All issues that are open for discussion are debated by the council by way of *shura*, and then decisions are taken by a majority vote. From this perspective the Expediency Council is the equivalent of the people who bind and loose or the council of leadership of the state, but not from the perspective of executive leadership, rather by way of the higher leadership of planning that submits its decisions to the *rahbar* in order to ratify them. The Constitution did not bestow the Expediency Council with the right of legislation; rather it gained the right to solve basic disputes in the political system and ratify the final wording of the laws whenever the Council of Guardians and the Shura Council are in disagreement. All of this is done while maintaining state interest as the highest priority.[1]

— *Higher Council of National Security*: It is composed of the main leaders of the state such as the president of the republic who heads the council, the head of the Islamic Shura Council, the head of the judiciary, chief of general staff of the armed forces, the head of the Revolutionary Guards and the representatives of the *rahbar* and others. It is incumbent upon the council to come up with the defence and security policies of the state, and coordinate the security, social, cultural and economic policies that are concerned with general security, and invest in the country's actual and potential capabilities in order to face internal and external threats.[2]

---

1   The Constitution of the Islamic Republic of Iran, Article 112, 99–100; see also ʿAmid Zinjani, p. 59.
2   The Constitution of the Islamic Republic of Iran, Article 176.

— *Council of Experts*: It is incumbent upon the council to choose and remove the *wali al-faqih* who is the head of the state and the *rahbar*. The members of the council are directly elected by the people. The council studies and debates the issues on its agenda by way of *shura*, issuing its decisions by a majority vote.[1]

— *Islamic Shura Council*: It is the legislative authority in the system. The populace elects its members directly.

— *The Council of Guardians*: It is the *shar'i* constitutional council or the constitutional court that ratifies the laws of the Islamic Shura Council and its decisions.

— *Council of Ministers*: It is the executive authority of the cabinet. It is composed of the president who heads the council, and his first deputy, the ministers and the political aides of the president. The council delineates the general policies for state functioning and executes the laws; it also has the right of drafting legislation and executing administrative and governmental policies.[2]

— *Councils of State Security and Defence*: These two councils are headed by the president or someone nominated by him. The two councils are appended with and follow the direct orders of the National Security Council. Their mission is to plan security and defence policies and ratify them.

— *Council for Constitutional Amendments*: Its primary mission is to amend the articles of the Constitution, or to add to it or delete from it. The decisions of the council are ratified by the *rahbar*, and then put to a national referendum. If the absolute majority of the participants in the referendum agree to it then it becomes binding.[3] The council is composed of the leading state and judicial figures such as the members of the Council of Guardians, the president of the republic, the speaker of the Shura Council, the head of the judiciary, the permanent members of the Expediency Council, five members of the Council of Experts, ten members appointed by the *rahbar*, three members of the Council of Ministers, three members of the judiciary, ten members of the Islamic Shura Council and three university professors.[4]

— *Shura Council of the Head of Judiciary*: This council replaced the Higher Council of Judiciary, after the constitutional amendments of 1979. It is an advisory council and its decisions are binding if and only if the head of the judiciary approves. The council is composed of the leading figures in the judiciary such as the minister of justice, the state prosecutor, the head of the 'supreme court', the chief of the administrative courts, and the head of the general inspection agency.

---

1   Ibid., Articles 111, 99.
2   Ibid., Articles 134 and 138.
3   Ibid., Article 177.
4   Ibid.

— *Higher Council of the Cultural Revolution*: Its primary mission is to supervise higher education, scientific research and general cultural issues of the state. It is composed of the president of the republic who heads the council and the speaker of the Islamic Shura Council, the head of the judiciary, the minister of scientific research, the minister of culture, and a substantive number of ministers, presidents of universities, scientists and university professors.

— *Higher Council of Provinces*: It is made up of the representatives of the Shura Council for the provinces. Its mission is to ensure cooperation and coordination in the domain of urban planning, including entertainment facilities and their proper functioning supervision.[1] The council prepares plans and projects and submits them directly either to the cabinet or to the Islamic Shura Council.[2]

— *Municipal Councils*: These are directly elected by the people; they are found in every state administrative division, and their primary function is to elect the head of the municipality who foresees social, economic, cultural and educational and health services.[3]

— *Shura Council for Professional Vocations*: It is composed of the representatives of workers, peasants, professional vocations, and educational and administrative institutions. Its mission is to prepare and coordinate programmes dealing with industry, agriculture and production.[4]

There are also other subsidiary *shura* councils that foresee special tasks. Among these are the Higher Management Council, the Higher Economic Council, the General Culture Council and the Higher Council of Media. All of these councils are composed of a host of ministers and leading heads of institutions. Thus, the abundance of high-quality *shura* institutions testifies to the role of *shura* as the main backbone of the Islamic system in Iran.

THE ROLE OF THE UMMA IN THE ISLAMIC SYSTEM

The *umma* is one of the four pillars of the Islamic state, the others being the government, the land, and the law. The concept of *umma* is defined in a variety of ways, some of which highlight the doctrinal bases, while others focus on the political domain, and still others deal with legal implications of the concept. This richness in the connotative meaning of the *umma* positively reflects upon the

---

1   Ibid., Article 101.
2   Ibid., Article 102.
3   Ibid., Article 100.
4   Ibid., Article 104.

conception of citizenship (*muwatana*) and leadership (*wilayat*). What we are going to stress is the legal connotation of the conception of the *umma*.

The *umma* is an amalgamation of Muslims who live in a certain province of the Islamic state and bear its nationality; as such they are labelled as the populace or the citizens. In its positive or situational legal form this conception is dictated by the circumstance and place, especially by geography, politics, international law, and state security. This *umma* is part and parcel of the great classical Islamic *umma*; as such it is the *umma* of a specified Islamic order, rather than an overall inclusive Islamic *umma*. The conception witnessed a dramatic change after the drastic disintegration of the Islamic state throughout history. For instance, during the ascendant period of Islam and the few centuries that ensued, the *umma* lived on one land, which is the land of the Islamic state.

However, after the disintegration of the state, the disintegration of the *umma* ensued in such a way that every part of the *umma* lived on a certain portion of the Muslim land.[1] This phenomenon implied from then on common rights and duties among all the members of the *umma* in relation to each other and in relation to the state in which they live. This also implies rights and duties with respect to the leadership of the *umma* and its Marja's, even if the citizen lived in another state. Therefore, the Muslim has a variety of affiliations: s/he not only belongs to the Islamic *umma* but also to all the land that s/he lives in, the specific Muslim state where s/he dwells, the state that s/he bears its nationality, and most importantly to the leadership of the *umma* who may reside in another state. Also it could be that s/he resides in an Islamic state but does not bear its nationality or that s/he resides in a non-Islamic state but bears its nationality. These positive situational affiliations were imposed by a variety of external and internal factors.

We are concerned with the role of the *umma* that bears the nationality of the Islamic state or that could be expressed under the rhetoric of the rights and duties of the Islamic state, as delineated by a constitution. The expression of duties and rights could be construed as such: that this role is not a mere right for the *umma* to assume or be guaranteed to it, rather this right has a further dimension which has to do with the duty (*wajib*), that is the duty of the *umma* towards the Islamic system, which could be summed up by supporting this system, giving advice and counselling to it, and pledging support and loyalty to its officials. This duty has a religious and worship (*ibadi*) dimension as its intentions reveal. The most salient of these are responsibility, *shura*, enjoining the good and prohibiting the evil, and rendering advice to the leadership. These rights and duties materialise in two types in free participation: first, direct participation through electoral policies

---

1   Sheikh Muhammad Mahdi Shamseddine, *Fi al-Ijtim'a Al-Siyasi Al-Islami* (Studies in the Islamic Political Sociology), pp. 96–97.

and general referenda; and second, by way of people's representatives in the *shura* institutions of the state.

In reality, the *umma* in the Islamic order has only the right of voting and taking decisions in matters that are not decisively ascribed by the Shari'a. From this perspective the *umma* does not have the right to put forward issues that are not in harmony with the Islamic Shari'a and vote on these. Even if these issues receive a majority of votes from the populace of the *umma,* it is still considered non *shar'i.* It is precisely for this reason that the Islamic order has imposed safeguards in order to prevent such things from taking place.

The role of the *umma* that is guaranteed by the Islamic political system by way of constitutions and laws are general prescriptions specified by a host of Islamic poltical theories, whether those dealing with *wilayat al-faqih*; or *wilayat al-faqih* and *shura,* the political system that requires *wilayat al-faqih* to be elected; or *shura,* that is, the electoral political system or *wilayat* of the *umma* in its own right. As a case study we are going to indicate the degree of political participation of the *umma* by way of elections and the general free referenda that were conducted in the Islamic Republic of Iran between 1979 and 2006.

— A general referendum on the political system of the Islamic Republic was conducted on 30 and 31 March 1979 after the victory of the Islamic Revolution. This constituted a precedent since it was the first political and popular exercise that more than 20 million participated in, which amounted to more than 95 percent of the registered voters. The results were that 98.2 percent gave their total allegiance to the Islamic order that is based upon the elaboration of Imam Khomeini in his fiery speeches and as systematised in his book entitled *The Islamic Government.* That is why the establishment of the Islamic Republic is one of the best examples on the will of the people as expressed under the rubric of *taklif shar'i.* It is most likely that Imam Khomeini's aim behind the referendum was to fortify the Islamic system with a legal substantiation that encompassed both the modern contemporary world as well as the will of the *umma,* and to use these against any opposition. This referendum resulted in the founding of a new state whose Constitution and laws were guided by Islamic doctrines.

— The members of the Council of Experts were directly elected on 3 August 1979, which is legally dubbed as the 'founding association'. However, Imam Khomeini objected to this label by arguing that it denotes a written constitution based upon man-made or positive-situational laws while the truth of the matter is that a Council of Experts specifies its decisions in such a way that does not conflict with the doctrine and Islamic shari'a.

— A general referendum was conducted on the Constitution, on the 2 and 3 of December 1979, after it was ratified by the Council of Experts and Imam Khomeini. A total of 99.5 percent of the registered voters approved the

Constitution of the Islamic Republic. The draft of the Constitution was published in the newspapers and other media, and it was systematically debated by the different trends, organisations as well as political, religious and social personalities; it is also based upon the opinion of the common people. By way of the above-mentioned two referenda and election, it could be claimed that the institution of an Islamic order and the ratification of its Constitution was based on the choice of the populace. This represented a measure of choice, which could be lacking in traditional democracies, although these call for it on a theoretical basis and see in it a basis of legitimacy of the state and its political system.

— The president is always elected directly by the populace. The first presidential election in the Islamic Republic took place in 1980, and since then till 2006, the presidential elections were conducted nine times where six presidents were elected and three presidents were re-elected for two terms in office. In the presidential elections of 2001, around 90 percent of the registered voters took part. In the 2005 presidential elections that were conducted on two rounds President Ahmadinejad received an overwhelming majority of the votes. The tenure of the president is four years that can be extended once.

— The members of the Islamic Shura Council (the parliament) are always elected directly. The members of the Shura Council number 270 and the tenure of the parliament lasts for four years. Parliamentary elections were conducted between 1980 and 2006 a total of seven times.

— The members of the Council of Experts are elected directly. This council in turn directly elects the *wali al-faqih* or the *rahbar*. Between 1982 and 2006, the Council of Experts was elected five times. The tenure of the council is six years and it is composed of 74 *fuqaha* or jurists.

— The *wali al-faqih* is elected indirectly by way of the Council of Experts, which chooses one *faqih* from among the *fuqaha* who meet the qualifications of leadership. The Council of Experts in its second regular round in 1989 elected Sayyid 'Ali Khamina'i for the leadership. He was chosen because he satisfied all the qualifications of *wilaya* though he was not the highest-ranking *faqih*. This led to an amendment of the Constitution. From this perspective, the role of the *umma* is to choose the best among the incumbent *fuqaha*. A general referendum on amending the Constitution took place in 1989, to approve an amendment that created the Expediency Council.

— The members of the municipal councils are elected directly. Elections for the councils have take place at least twice since 1999.

— From the aforementioned, it is evident that the Iranian populace has participated during the span of twenty-four years (from 1979 to 2006) in three public referenda, twenty-five direct electoral processes and one indirect vote, which amounts to about one electoral process every year.

THE NECESSITY OF IKHTILAF[1]

Imam Khomeini stressed the necessity of *ikhtilaf* (pluralism): 'because people's temperaments are different, there should be two different intellectual ordinances. As such, *ikhtilaf* (differences) are necessary, however they should not amount to schisms and discords.'

Imam Khomeini conceded that people's desires are the main cause of conflict and hardships among human beings. However, he stressed that *ikhtilaf* among human beings is an inevitable reality that cannot be ignored. The Qur'an has highlighted this reality and regarded it as one of the basic foundations of human coalescence and progress in man's endeavour towards piety. 'And had your Lord willed, He would have made mankind a single nation; but they will continue to differ among themselves'. (11:118) Another Qur'anic verse stresses a similar theme: 'To each of you, we have laid down an ordinance and a clear path; and had Allah pleased, He would have made you one nation, but [He wanted] to test you concerning what He gave to you. Be, then, forward in good deeds. To Allah is the ultimate return of all of you that He may instruct you regarding that in which you differ'. (5:48)

These differences among people were thoroughly investigated by Imam Khomeini throughout his life as a leader of the masses. By this thorough understanding of human nature, he was capable of exercising a policy of openness (*infitah*) towards all the constituents of the *umma*, and he was able to invest this understanding in such a way as to promote the success of his revolution. After the victory of the revolution, at a time when colonial powers were employing the policy of divide and conquer by promoting a dichotomy between moderation and radicalism, Imam Khomeini stressed that both concepts are employed in the Muslim public sphere, highlighting that intellectual differences are a must in order to absorb people's temperaments and moods and channel these in a positive constructive manner.

In this regard, Imam Khomeini stressed the necessity of *ikhtilaf*, 'because people's temperaments are different, there should be two different intellectual ordinances. As such, *ikhtilaf* is necessary; however it should not amount to schisms and discords.'[2]

This thinking has become the backbone of modernity that is based on pluralism, public opinion and different points of view. This line of thinking is not alien to Islam, since this is the way education is conducted in the religious seminaries on the basis of the diversity of *ijtihad* in jurisprudence. This diversity has led to diversity in politics and orientation.

---

1   Mukhtar Al-Asadi, *Al-Thawra fi Fikr Al-Imam AlKhomeini* (Revolution in Imam Khomeini's Thought), third edn, Tehran 2003, pp. 42–45.

2   *Kayhan* (Iranian newspaper) in Arabic, issue of 8 June 1988.

In short, *ikhtilaf* according to Imam Khomeini is a necessary and indispensable tool to promote the nurturing, guidance and crystallisation of the *umma*, rather than rupturing it apart by divisions and partitions. The same point is highlighted by Imam 'Ali: 'Out of comparing different points of view, righteousness emerges.'

This line of thought was adopted by Imam Khomeini's followers and students; in this context his son Ahmad stated: 'Without the right to criticism, dictatorship will eventually return.' Ahmad al-Khomeini emphasised the necessity of the freedom to criticise all the state's institutions and personalities without exceptions.[1]

By this orientation, Imam Khomeini wanted to emphasise that tyranny is a disaster for people because it leaves no room for criticism and muffles dissident voices and strangulates the talented and gifted. As he saw it, some people reduce differences into conflict and other perspectives into strife and divisions, while it is meant to enrich the human experience, alleviate their sufferings by bringing them together via dialogue and constructive conversation. This is what the Qur'an kept warning mankind about: 'Had Allah pleased, He would have made you a single nation, but He leads whom He pleases astray and guides whom He pleases. And you surely will be questioned about what you did.' (16:93) In another verse: 'Had Allah wished, He would have made them a single nation, but He admits whom He wishes into his mercy. Yet, the wrongdoers have no protector or supporter.' (42:8)

THE CONCEPTION OF *MASLAHA*[2]

Linguistically, *maslaha* (interest) connotes *manf'a* (benefit, advantage, virtue) as opposed to *mafsada* (disadvantage, vice). According to Ibn Mandhur's famous *Lisan al-Arab* dictionary: 'Reform is the opposite of corruption, and *maslaha* is righteousness (*al-salah*).'[3]

According to Said Al-Khuri Al-Shartuni's dictionary, *maslaha* is the result of an action in the domain of righteousness. This is the view of the leader of the community on *maslaha*, the one who galvanises people to the path of righteousness.[4] This is the way *maslaha* has been employed in the Qur'an, the traditions, and books of jurisprudence. However, it was used in its extended sense to include the benefits of this world and the world to come. According to the

---

1   *Kayhan* in Arabic, November 1990.
2   *Dirasat fi Al-Fikr al-Siyasi 'ind Al-Imam Al-Khomeini*, Beirut 2002.
3   Ibn Madhur (1233-1312) was an Arabic lexicographer who penned the most comprehensive dictionary of the Arabic language. Ibn Mandhur, *Lisan Al-'Arab*, (the Tongue of Arabs), chapter on reform.
4   Said Al-Khuri Al-Shartuni *Aqrab Al-Mawarid fi Fusha al-Arabiyya*, (The closest cases in formal Arabic) Lebanon: Matbat Mursali al-Yasuiyya, 1889, Al, chapter on reform.

nineteenth-century marja' Al-Sheikh Muhammad Hassan al-Najafi, it is construed from the Qur'an: 'O believers, do not consume your wealth illegally,
unless there be trading by mutual agreement among you; and do not kill your-
selves. Allah is indeed merciful to you.'[1] (4:29) He added that the traditions, narrations, and all daily dealings (mu'amalat) have been legislated in the interest of
the people and their benefit in this world and the world to come.[2]

Based on that viewpoint, maslaha from an Islamic perspective guarantees felicity in the hereafter for humanity and achieving perfect semblance. From this perspective, moral maslaha has precedence over material maslaha as a prima facie duty
in case of conflict of priorities (tazahum). From the foregoing, the conception of
maslaha in Islam stands in direct opposition to the materialistic schools and ori-
entations. These schools limit its interpretation of maslaha and mafsada (virtues
and vices, advantages and disadvantages) to the material domain because they do
not acknowledge Allah's spiritual, metaphysical dimensions. Islam, however, does
not regard maslaha solely from its materialistic dimension. Advocating such a
view would strip maslaha of any religious dimension by contending that it could
be employed only in the domain of rationalistic theosophy ('irfan). As discussed
below, this had led them to speculate that Imam Khomeini's proposition of insti-
tuting the Expediency Council would lead to a dichotomy between religion and
state. However, Khomeini clarified that when the faqih interprets the principles
of jurisprudence he applies the concept of tazahum between two injunctions, one
dealing with a private good and the other dealing with a public good, in order to
choose the prima facie injunction. Then, the faqih chooses the public good, which
also deals with religious injunctions, over the private good.[3]

1. The Stance of Maslaha in Jurisprudence

Maslaha emanates from the spirit and essence of religion. Sunni jurisprudents
categorise it under 'unrestrained interests' (al-masalih al-mursala). Most of the
Sunni fuqaha or legal experts considered it as a source for the unchangeable and
changeable injunctions, which are not based upon shar'i evidence.

In turn, Shi'i jurisprudents have dabbled with two categories of injunctions and
interests (masalih). They came to the conclusion that there are immutable and
mutable injunctions as well as mutable and immutable masalih. Immutable injunctions have a fixed maslaha that is not relegated to a specific time or place; however,
in the case of mutable injunctions, the maslaha changes according to time and
place, which is why it is referred to as the wilayat injunctions (al-ahkam al-wilaiyya).

---

1 It worth mentioning that in some discussions it is often discussed with the purpose of shari'a
   (maqasid al-shari'a).
2 Al-Sheikh Muhammad Hasan Al-Najafi (d. 1849), Jawahir Al-Kalam (The Jewels of Discourse),
   vol. 22, Beirut, pp. 344 ff.
3 'The Repercussions of Secularizing the Shii Jurisprudence', in Kayhan, vol. 24.

All the injunctions that deal with revelation (*wahy*), that are transmitted by the Prophet to the *umma*, are characterised by immutable *masalih* unless the issue of concern changes or there is a conflict of priorities (*tazahum*) with other important prima facie duties.

2. Wilayat and Maslaha

Shi'i jurisprudence has always relegated to *wilaya* the concept of *maslaha*. As Imam Khomeini said, 'the primary foundation in every *wilaya* is abidance by *maslaha*.'[1] He added that the *wali al-faqih* ought to give primacy to *maslaha* in all his actions, rather than simply avoiding *mafsada*.[2]

Imam Khomeini accorded a salient place to *maslaha* in *wilayat al-faqih*: 'The *wali al-faqih* addresses the issues on the basis of righteousness to the Muslims. This should not be rendered as despotism since he follows the path of righteousness as a primary religious obligation.'[3] Imam Khomeini stressed that the governing prerogatives of the *faqih* are one and the same as the Prophet and the Imams. In this respect the concept of *maslaha* takes precedence as an organic entity, and not as an appendix to Islamic political thought and jurisprudence; rather the concept of *maslaha* is deeply rooted in the essence of religion. However, Shi'i jurisprudents did not elaborate on the concept of *maslaha*, especially in the domain of the expediency of the regime (*maslahat al-nizam*). It seems that the reason behind this shortcoming was that the political and administrative leadership of the society was not in the hands of the jurisprudents. One of the most important contributions of Imam Khomeini is that he was the pioneer in transforming the theoretical dimension of *maslaha* into a practical enforceable one.

4. The Expediency Council (Majlis Tashkhis Al-Maslaha)

The diagnosis of social interests is one of the main prerogatives of the Islamic governments, even though this issue does not exclusively pertain to *wilayat al-faqih* since this is the norm in most of the current political regimes. The Prophet, Imam 'Ali, and the rest of the Infallible Imams clearly delineated the injunctions that are based upon the concept of *maslaha*, in accordance with the requirements of that time in addition to promulgating the religious injunctions to the population.

The Expediency Council in the Islamic Republic of Iran is based upon the binding opinion of Imam Khomeini: 'Although determining the expedience (*tashkis al-maslaha*) of the Islamic Republic is the prerogative of the *wali al-faqih*, however, if need be, he consults with other jurists in determining the *maslaha*.'

---

1   Khomeini, *Kitab Al-Bay'*, 2:526, Ismailiyan.
2   Khomeini, *Tahrir al-wasila*, 1:514
3   Khomeini, *Kitab Al-Bay'*, 2:461

Imam Khomeini believed that *masalih* are administered by the Islamic Shura Council and the Council for Constitutional Ammendments. However, this did not always occur smoothly because in certain cases, especially those in which the law was promulgated on the basis of the expediency of the regime, discord emerged between the former (Islamic Shura Council) and the latter (Majlis Siyanat al-Dustur). This uneasy relationship led the leaders of the Islamic Republic to seek the guidance of Imam Khomeini; they wrote: 'the law undergoes thorough debates and evaluations in order to be ratified. If after ratification it is rejected by the Majlis Siyanat al-Dustur, what shall we do?'[1]

Imam Khomeini replied in a detailed letter prescribing the necessity and the raison d'etre of the formation of the Expediency Council: 'the main aim of the formation of the Expediency Council is to solve the dilemmas of the regime in consultation with the *rahbar*, in such a way that it cooperates in a smooth way with other authorities.'[2] In turn, and after much discussion and debate, the council incumbent with redrafting the constitution ratified the following article: 'The Expediency Council is composed by a direct order from the Islamic leadership for the purpose of determining the expediency in cases where the Majlis Siyanat Al-Dustur does not support the draft legislation enacted by the Islamic Shura Council because it does not abide by the Constitution or the *shar'i* laws. When the Shura Council does not support legislation – even after taking into consideration the interest of the regime, the opinion of the Expediency Council, in addition to its conciliatory function in issues that the *rahbar* bestows to it, as well as the other functions mentioned in the law – the *rahbar* is the one who appoints all the members of the Expediency Council.'[3]

The main purpose of establishing a Majlis Siyanat al-Dustur was to safeguard the Constitution and make sure that any law that does not accord with the Constitution or the *shar'i* injunctions is not ratified. However, the aim of founding the Expediency Council was to supervise and monitor this constitutional procedure.

The Expediency Council has to take into consideration the following five key injunctions:

— The community is the sphere where the governor exercises Islamic rule based upon the concept of *maslaha*.

— The necessity of the concordance of *maslaih* with the *shar'i* injunctions.

— Observing the purposes of the *shari'a* and its teachings.

— In the case of determining the actual duty among the prima facie duties, the

---

1 *Majmu'at Al-Qawanin Walmuqarrarat Almurtabita Bimajm'a TashKhis Maslahat Al-Nizam* (The Set of Laws and Deliberations dealing With the Expediency Council), 1: 1–3.
2 Khomeini, *Sahifat Nur*, 21:122.
3 The Constitution of The Islamic Republic Of Iran, after the amendments of the Council for Ammending the Constitution, Article 112.

following jurisprudential rule should be applied: '*taqdim al-aham ala al-muhim*', or 'choosing the most salient to the less salient'.
— Periodic consultations with experts and specialists in the areas and issues being debated.

5. Practical Dimension of Maslaha

According to Fuaʾd Ibrahim,[1] the conception of *maslaha* has been closely linked to a society based upon a communal nature of cooperation and interdependency to satisfy basic economic needs of food, shelter and clothing, both in the individual and communal dimensions. For instance, food, drink, sleep, marriage and vocation are individual *masalih* in the same nature as communal work, communal security and the reciprocation of benefits are *masalih* of a communal nature.

In order to ensure the biological and cultural survival of the community, then we are in grave need of a viable framework to regulate individual interest without favouring one over the other or posing a threat to other factions that comprise the community. Even state formation was based upon the instinctive need to regulate public interests.

In response to the question about the concept of *maslaha* in Shiite jurisprudence, Fuaʾd Ibrahim argues that the conception of *maslaha* from a theoretical perspective in Islam differs from the understanding of *maslaha* in the West. *Maslaha* in the West is individualistic and based upon personal benefit, the art of muddling through, the art of successful living and making a lot of profit without due regard to the source and the religious legitimacy of profit making. However, in Islam, *maslaha* is the opposite of *mafsada* or vice; it usually connotes public good. *Maslaha* is accorded a special stance in Shi'i jurisprudence, and it could be applied in an Islamic community as well as in a multi-confessional, multi-religious non-Islamic society or body politic.

He contends that the Western philosophical approach to the conception of *maslaha* (be it public good or national good) has the danger of the fusion of the individual with the community, which according to Western consciousness is the most perilous authority. Ibrahim adds that the dialectic between the 'I' and the 'we' has always had a bearing on the debates that are related to *maslaha*. He affirms that Islam, from an early stage, was aware of this dialectic in a meticulous act of balancing that clearly delineated what falls within the domain of the *masalih* of the individual and the *masalih* of the community without giving the upper hand to either of the two parties.

From a Qurʾanic perspective, the conception of *maslaha* in Islamic discourse is based upon a balancing act between individual needs and the *maslaha* of the community based upon the jurisprudential rule of the golden mean: '*la ifrata*

---

1   Fuaʾd Ibrahim, Saudi intellectual Shi'i dissident, interviewed by the author, 28 January 2007.

wa la tafrit, or 'neither too much nor too little'. Islam was revealed as a message to inculcate the deepening of the conception of the unity of the *umma*, which was torn apart by deadly tribal or territorial wars for the sake of narrow interests and gains. Thus the *umma* was based on the tenets of Islam, which have a communal connotation such as the following concepts: *takaful* (coalescence) based upon the Hadith, 'Me, and the provider for the orphan will go to heaven'; *t'awun* (cooperation) as stated in the Qur'an, 'cooperate on the grounds of piety and charity'; enjoining the good and forbidding the evil; peaceful coexistence as stated in the Qur'an when He ordered for the enjoinment of peace; religious tolerance as stated in the Qur'an: 'Say, everyone acts according to his belief, indeed Allah is the most knowledgeable about the mostly guided'; unity as stated in the Qur'an: 'Hold firmly to Allah's path'; and endeavouring for good as stated in the Qur'an: 'Be the forerunners to perform good deeds'.

The enhancement of the conception of the community as embodied in the *umma* sheds light on the individualistic dimension of *maslaha* in Islam, even though it is deeply rooted in Islamic discourse because it leads to a balancing act. Islam is neither an individualistic religion that calls for complete severing of the community from the life of the individual, nor a communal religion that compromises the individual personality. This balancing act guides the path of Islam in all its dimensions, especially the political, economic, social and educational.

Ibrahim stresses that when the Qur'an directs its discourse to the community of believers in the issues that deal with communal *maslaha*, the Qur'an also directs its discourse to the individual in the issues pertaining to individual *maslaha*, so it addresses her/him in a direct and personal manner: 'Do not forget to take your share of this world, and do good as Allah has done good to you'.[1]

Islamic legislation recognises this balancing act between the individualistic dimension and the communal one. In the practical treaties, Islam distinguished between *'ibadat* (ritual practices) and *m'uamalat* (daily dealings); the former deal with individual commitments, and the latter have a social dimension. The calibrations of *maslaha* in Islam are intended not only for Muslims, but rather for all of those who are governed under the umbrella of Islam, even if they belong to other religious denominations. For instance, Islamic legislation in the domain of *mu'amalat*, where the concept of *maslaha* is salient, does not dictate contractual safeguards on the concerned parties. Rather, in the first degree it is based upon legal litigation, which implies that *maslaha* in both the individualistic and communal dimension is conditioned upon equilibrium between communal and personal dimensions irrespective of the ideological orientation.

According to the contemporary Lebanese scholar Sheikh Muhammad

---

1   Ibid.

Shqayr,[1] etymologically, the concept of *maslaha* has to do with an action that is oriented towards reform. By way of introduction, he stresses that the concept of the *maslaha* in Shi'i jurisprudence falls within the domain of religious injunctions and legislation.

According to Imam Khomeini, the *wala'i* injunction[2] distinguishes between two modes of reasoning: (1) legislative reasoning, and (2) practical-specialised reasoning. The former reasoning is based upon Qur'anic verses and the Hadiths that constitute the legislative body of the religious tradition, while the latter deals with ongoing practical issues with their situational circumstances. Thus *maslaha* is more likely to fall within the domain of the latter reasoning, which is capable of diagnosing *maslaha* and reality in the domain of political sociology. In this respect, *maslaha* connotes the interest of Islam and the Muslims as well as the political system.

In dealing with *maslaha*, the juristconsult is well conversant in the mechanisms to come up with religious injunctions based upon Islamic law or Shari'a. The concept of *maslaha* does not only entail a here and now (mundane) dimension, but also a hereafter (divine), moral dimension. However, if there is a conflict between the mundane *maslaha* and the divine *maslaha*, then the latter has precedence over the former as an eternal prima facie duty.

Sheikh Shqayr distinguishes between two forms of governance: *wal'i* governance, which is endowed with the *wali al-faqih* as an Islamic ruler; and divine governance, which is endowed within the *wali al-faqih* as a jurist consult or *mujtahid*. The relation between the two is complementary, in the sense of interdependence.

Brushing aside the Shi'is who do not accept *wilayat al-faqih*, Sheikh Shuqayr distinguishes between two forms of governance: *wal'i* governance, which is endowed with the *wali al-faqih* as an Islamic ruler; and divine governance, which is endowed within the *wali al-faqih* as a jurist consult or *mujtahid*. The relation between the two is complementary, in the sense of interdependence.

From a Sunni perspective *maslaha* is being practised in the areas where there is no positive or negative *shar'i* evidence; the Islamic scholar has the liberty to legislate as he deems right. However, from a Shi'i perspective the concept of *maslaha* is construed within the framework of the *wali* governance that is enacted by the *wali al-faqih*. To elaborate, the Sunni religious scholars consider *maslaha* as a principal source of legislation in the case of the absence of *nass*, or sacred text. Yet Shi'i *fuqaha*, even though they insist on following the religious injunctions of vices and virtues (*mafased* and *maslalih*), believe that whatever is in the interest of man does not necessarily become the basis of divine governance unless it

---

1   Interview with the author in Beirut, 15 January 2007.
2   The injunction decreed by the *wali al-faqih* as a ruler and *wali* and not as a Marja' or a *mujtahid*.

is derived from the known sources of legislation. In other words, the concept of *maslaha* in its own right is not considered a source of *ijtihad* or independent reasoning.

The Sunni clergy do not seek recourse to unrestrained *maslaha* (*al-maslaha al-mursala*) unless analogical reasoning (*qiyas*) is not applicable in this case. In other words, the Sunni clergy do not employ the concept of *maslaha* in the presence of *qiyas*.[1] However, Shi'i jurisprudents do not give any consideration to *qiyas* because the latter is not a source of legislation to them and thus cannot substantiate the concept of *maslaha*.

Shi'i jurisprudents consider Islamic governance based upon the foundations of *maslaha* as an interim *wila'i* governance that ought to be followed on the basis of the duty of abiding by Islamic governance because it is not a primary binding religious injunction. However, the Sunni clergy consider this concept to be a primary binding religious injunction to the governor because they deemed the unrestrained *masalih* as a primary source of jurisprudence.

Shi'i jurisprudents consider that governance in the case of *maslaha* in political and social issues pertains strictly to the governor. However, the Sunni clergy deem that function as a prerogative for all the religious scholars. On the whole, they consider the governance of any ruler in these issues as God's governance, even if there are differences in opinion and justification.

Shi'i jurisprudents consider that the main purpose of the *wala'i* governance, or governance based on *wilayat al-faqih*, is safeguarding order in the Islamic community. However, Sunni clergy attribute a larger role to *masalih* (interests) that constitute the source of governance and independent reasoning. Most of the Sunni clergy who subscribe to this view stress the referential framework of the unrestrained *masalih* as apodictic proof, which does not pertain to the necessary *masalih*; rather it has a bearing on the everyday *masalih*.

6. Maslaha and Democratisation

Sheikh Muhammad Shuqayr[2] contends that there are essential differences between democracy and Islamic legislation. According to him, democracy was a result of a historical necessity that emerged in opposition to despotism. From a philosophical perspective, democracy does not rely on a religious dimension rather than a technical one which stresses the separation of powers and the rotation of authority. However, Islamic political thought relies on the political dimension, and does not only depend upon the technical dimension but also relies heavily upon the psychological factor as well.

---

1   Subhi Mahmasani, *Falsafat Al-Tashr'i fi Al-Islam* (Philosophy of Legislation in Islam), p. 160.
2   Shuqayr, Sheikh Muhammad, interviewed by author, Beirut, 15 January 2007.

According to Hasan Jaber, a professor of history at the Lebanese University,[1] the following Qur'anic verse is the most salient in expressing the concept of *maslaha*: 'The scum is cast away, but what profits mankind remains on earth'. (13:17) Although there are so many verses in the Qur'an that address the concept of *maslaha* and its related words of individual and public good, there has always been a juxtaposition between the believers and those who perform the good deeds. The aforementioned verse is appended to another verse by way of an explanation: 'But those who before them, had homes (in Medina) and had adopted the Faith, show their affection to such as came to them for refuge, and entertain no desire in their hearts for things given to the (latter), but give them preference over themselves, even though poverty was their (own lot). And those saved from the covetousness of their own souls, they are the ones that achieve prosperity.' (59:9)

The *faqih*, in interpreting the principles of jurisprudence, applies the concept of *tazahum* between two injunctions, one dealing with a private good and the other dealing with a public good, in order to choose the prima facie injunction. Then, the *faqih* chooses the public good over the private good.

---

1   Hasan Jaber, Professor of History at the Lebanese University, interviewed by the author, Beirut, 7 January 2007.

CHAPTER FIVE

Does *Wilayat al-Faqih* Lead to Tyranny?

BACKGROUND

Imam Khomeini asserted in his book on Islamic government, 'The issue of *Wilayat al-Faqih* is not something that could be founded by the Council of Experts. Since *wilayat al-faqih* is something decreed by God, do not be afraid of it. The *faqih* cannot treat people with force or power; if any *faqih* wanted to do so, he would be denied his *wilaya*.'

Though he represented the highest religious authority in Iran, Khomeini never encouraged the clergy to be involved in the executive affairs of the state. At an early stage of the Islamic Republic, he banned any *'alim* from running for the presidency. Later on, in 1986, he disbanded the Jumhuri Islami party, which was mainly the party of the *ulama*. Moreover, after he fulfilled his ambition of establishing a Shi'i religious state, Khomeini initially aimed to withdraw from the scene and to go to Qom to continue his job as a religious scholar and to indirectly supervise the system. However, the challenges that confronted the Iranian state, especially the Iraqi war against Iran, obliged him to stay in Tehran, and to closely monitor the affairs of his *wilaya*.

At an early stage, Imam Khomeini dabbled with the argumentative assumption that once the clergy achieved victory, they would confiscate the affairs of the state with all its bodies and apparatuses and hand them over to a new political leadership. So he paved the way for Mahdi Bazargan's liberal government to assume power and bestowed his legitimacy upon it; Khomeini did the same thing with Abu al-Hasan Bani Sadr. However, the failure of the liberal governments to maintain Khomeini's trust, as well as that of the populace, led him to support replacing those with the clergy, especially in the highest positions of the government and the state.

Although Khomeini had committed himself to the broad concept of *wilayat al-faqih*, nonetheless, he did not force that on the Iranian Constitution. This can be observed through an examination of the prerogatives and jobs of the different state institutions and activities. As such, the Iranian Constitution has not indicated, in any of its articles, the comprehensive *wilaya*; it also designated to the populace will as a final and ultimate choice to attain legitimacy. Choosing the leader (*rahbar*) or *wali al-faqih* is the responsibility of the Council of Experts, which is an elected body by way of periodic general elections.

WILAYAT AL-FAQIH: THE PROBLEM

During the last days of the life of Imam Khomeini, there appeared to be a kind of emerging problem vis-à-vis the prerogatives of the *wali al-faqih*. The then-president of the Islamic Republic, and the current *wali al-faqih*, Sayyid Ali Khamina'i, declared in a Friday prayer speech[1] his condemnation of the expanded prerogatives of the minister of labour, thus indirectly criticising the theory of the comprehensive authority of the *wali al-faqih*.

Khamina'i noted in his remarks that the comprehensive authority of the *wali al-faqih* is something separate from the function of the state. He added that it is still obscure and unknown even to those who were supposed to preach it, let alone to rule according to it. As such, Imam Khomeini's reaction was an angry one. The incident prompted him to write four refutations and to dedicate more time to clarify and defend his theory, thus introducing new prerogatives and indications about the space of authority the *faqih* has.[2] The text of Khomeini's fatwa runs as follows:

> It seems from your speech on Friday prayer that you do not believe that the government that stands for *hakimiyya*, or God's governance on earth, through the Prophet, has precedence over all secondary religious injunctions. Quoting me that 'the government's jurisdiction on the domain of religious injunctions' stands in complete contrast of what I said, I clarify that if the government's jurisdiction was confined to secondary religious

---

1   On 31 December 1987; 10 *Jumada* 1408 AH.

2   Imam Khomeini's letter to Sayyid Ali Khamina'i, the President of the Islamic Republic concerning the latter's Friday speech (on 31 December 1988) on the absoluteness of *wilayat al-faqih*. This became known as Khomeini's famous 1988 fatwa on absolute *wilaya*. Published in Farsi in *Kayhan* 13223 (16 *Jamadi Al-Awwal* 1409/ 6 January 1989).

ordinances, then the whole thesis on religious government and absolute *wilayat* delegated to the Prophet becomes stripped out of any substantial meaning.

Khomeini substantiated his argument by reference to the argument from analogy:

For instance, building a road that dictates confiscating a house or private property is not under the domain of secondary ordinances. Likewise, military conscriptions and sending the army to the front lines. Also, preventing the export or import of all goods and monopoly with the exception of three or two things which are the following: customs, taxes, and preventing overpricing and specifying consumer prices, prohibiting the consumption of drugs in any form or way, and bearing arms in any way. There are also so many other instances that fall outside the domain of the state's jurisdiction, according to your own interpretation.

Khomeini stressed:

It is incumbent upon me to clarify that government branches from the Prophet's absolute *wilaya* and is one of the primary injunctions in Islam, thus takes precedence over all secondary ordinances, even over prayer, pilgrimage, and fasting. The governor has the capacity, if need be, to destroy any mosque or house that stands in the way of the street, while rendering the due price of the house to its owner ... The governor could deactivate mosques if need be, destroy the mosque that is classified as a 'Dirar mosque'[1] that cannot be dealt with without destroying it and uprooting it. Likewise, the government can annul one-sidedly any religious (*shari'i*) treaties conducted with the populace, if the government deems these in opposition to the interests (*masalih*) of the country or Islam. Further, the government could obstruct or stand in the way of any religious or non-religious practice if it is detrimental to the interests of Islam or if it is deemed so. The government could temporarily prevent pilgrimage, which is a salient religious duty, in circumstances where it is in conflict with the interests of the Islamic nation.

---

1   This refers to a historical precedent based on the Prophetic tradition where the Prophet ordered the Muslims to destroy a mosque built by a man by the name of Dirar, who erected a mosque in Mecca, just to compete with the Prophet's mosque and to take away its followers and affiliate them with his mosque. It is worth mentioning that Dirar was not even a Muslim and was doing it to sow discord among the Muslims.

1. Discussions and Debates on Wilayat al-Faqih vis-à-vis Tyranny

Sheikh Shafic Jradi[1] mentions five points that he believes act as safety valves that would prevent the *wali al-faqih* from becoming a dictator or a despot. The first of these is the educational dimension which fosters internal scrutiny and self-monitoring. According to him, Islam emphasises the importance of education and bringing up people in a way to maintain their morality and support their integrity. He believes that no matter how efficient the checks and balances, safety valves or technical monitoring of any system, a leader would deviate if he did not have enough self-monitoring and discipline and fear of God which would prohibit him from committing vices; nothing else would stop him from pursuing his own interests.

The second point has to do with the community of *fuqaha* or juristconsults to which he belongs. The *wali al-faqih* is a *mujtahid*, and this puts him under the direct scrutiny of the community of the *mujtahidin*, and in the event that he deviated, this community would withdraw their support and thus force him to quit his position. The two aforementioned principles existed even before the Islamic system was established and continue to exist even after the formation of the Islamic government.

The third safety valve is the Council of Experts, which exercises a monitoring function and has the prerogative to oust the *wali al-faqih* if he deviates and violates their trust. Fourth, the *wali al-faqih* is bound by the constitution; he is under the law and if he breaches constitutional articles he can be held accountable and could lose his post. The fifth safety valve is a constitutional provision: the Iranian Constitution stipulates that the people are the guarantee to the proper functioning of the *wilayat al-faqih* system.

According to Ra'id Qasim,[2] a scholar of Islamic governance, absolute *wilaya* has positive trends from a theoretical perspective. It leads to the unification of Islamic movements since it will revert to one leadership, which is considered as a victory in its own right, since it consolidates the Muslim position vis-à-vis their enemies. It is also conducive to the unification of various trends in Islamic society, which is the dream of the pious and the loyal believers to their *umma* and their individual communities (cf. Khomeini's call for the unity of the Muslims every year in the week commemorating the birth of the Prophet).

From a practical perspective, Qasim says that *wilayat al-faqih* results in the interaction and commitment to the leadership, not only from a nationalistic or patriotic view but also from a religious-spiritual perspective. This unique centrality leads to uniformity and smoothness in decision making as well as speed in execution.

---

1   The director M'arif Hikamiya College, interview with the author, 6 June 2006.
2   *Ru'a fi Alqadaya Al-Shi'iyya Al Muasira*, Beirut 2006; specifically, chapter 4, analysis and criticism of the theories of Islamic governance, p. 82 ff.

Also, Qasim stresses negative trends from a practical perspective, since absolute *wilayat* is contested among the jurists (*fuqaha*). This has led to considerable debate among them, and has prompted some Marja's to openly oppose such a theory (such as Sayyid Fadlallah of Lebanon, Sheikh Husayn Ali Montazari of Iran and Sayid Ali Sistani of Iraq).

Qasim adds that *wilayat al-faqih* has both positive and negative trends. One of the positive aspects of the existence of the *wilaya* is the preservation of the Marja's and their right in assuming a leadership role. According to Qasim, this will lead to the advancement of Islam and Muslims through:

— A coalescence among the religio-political trends that will put their differences aside and direct their energy towards coordination, in spite of their differences in Marja's (this is the case of Hamas and Hizbullah who have placed their religio-political ideological differences aside and concentrated in furthering common ideological trends and interests such as the liberation of occupied territories).
— The maturity of vision within the council of the *fuqaha* in dealing with impediments and challenges.

According to Qasim, the negative trends of *wilayat al-faqih* comprise the following: divided loyalties among the various governing factions and institutions, and the possibility of discord among the ruling elite. These two points will ultimately affect the viability of the political system and threaten its institutions with paralysis.

A long procedure of decision making will jeopardise the political and economic stability of the system since those in power will not be capable of taking a swift rightful decision. On the other hand, when power is centralised, the head executive decrees decisions based upon a vision.

Qasim also asserts strong criticisms with regard to the absolute *wilayat*. According to him, the prerogatives of the *wali al-faqih* render his power not only above the Constitution but also above the political system; thus practically he is considered equivalent to the infallible Twelfth Imam. But Qasim's view here is based on a narrow reading of *wilayat al-faqih* that stresses the necessity of obedience to the *wali al-faqih* on the part of jurists and followers. But *wilayat* in Iran does not automatically translate itself into a kind of despotic use of power by the *wali al-faqih* since his mandate of power is confined within the limits stipulated by the Constitution. The mandate of power that the *wali al-faqih* wields does not entitle him to impose his religious will over the other *fuqaha*, since he cannot confiscate their role, nor coerce the lay people to follow his religious injunctions if they emulate another Marja' or juristconsult. His power only exists within the borders of the official governmental decrees that regulate the people's lives and preserve law and order in the same capacity as other senior officials in presidential democratic systems.

In turn, Abdulhalim Fadlallah[1] analysed the Islamic vision of the mandate of state authority. According to him, what necessitates the establishment and formation of the government in Islam is its role as the only tool in which the *wilayat* can be enforced. He stressed that the Western mind thinks along the lines of Lord Acton: 'Power tends to corrupt, and absolute power corrupts absolutely'(1883) and the Socratic tradition that no matter how clean you are, when you engage in politics you will dirty your hands. That is why he recommended that virtuous people should not engage in politics. According to him, this reasoning, as sound as it is, does not preclude Islamic movements from participating in governance. Fadlallah added that it is assumed that those who are in power will always be tempted to abuse it, even if they have a good reputation of probity, integrity, accountability, transparency, etc. That is why Islamist movements such as Hizbullah and Hamas are put to the test when they have the reins of the government. The West is very anxious to know if they can keep their probity while engaging in practical pluralistic politics that requires a lot of bargaining and compromise in order to get the affairs of the state done.

In addressing the question of how the absolute *wilayat* can avoid becoming despotic, Fadlallah stressed that for the Western mind, it is not enough that the *wali al-faqih* be virtuous, good and religious, because from what was said above, anybody could be tempted and easily corrupted by power. Now in the West, the chief executive of the state is bound by the law of the land or a constitution that is precisely written in such a way to make the abuse of power as hard as possible. Therefore there are safety valves and effective limitations to control the chief executive and keep his behaviour within the narrow confines of the law. Well, it seems that this cannot be applied to the *wali al-faqih*. Why? Because in absolute *wilayat*, the *wali al-faqih*, is not only above the Constitution, the executive legislative and judicial powers, on the one hand, but he is also above the law in the sense that he can even annul prayer and fasting.

Based on this, how does the so-called democratisation process in the Islamic Republic fare with republicanism (consensual representative democracy) and *shura* (consultative democracy)?

2. The Islamic System and the Stance from Despotism

Islam stipulates that the Shari'a (Islamic law) accomplishes the hopes of humanity to establish justice as well as to propagate charity and guarantee happiness in the here and the hereafter. The Shari'a upholds human rights, ethical values, the good, and freedom. Thus, it aims at uprooting all types of despotism and

---

1   Personal interview, 2 March 2006. Abdulhalim Fadlallah is the vice president of the Consultative Centre of Studies and Documentation, Hizbullah's think tank.

oppression. That is why it is a requirement for a political system that results from the Shari'a to bear the aforementioned characteristics.[1]

Imam Ali Khamina'i posed the rhetorical question of how a divine government could also be a popular one. He questions whether the term 'Islamic Republic' that combines Islamic government with popular government is a correct term, or if it is just apologetic. Khamina'i added that the contended opposition between Islamic government and popular government has historical precedence. According to him, most governments that were established in the name of the religion were despotic, since the populace and public opinion hardly had any role to play, as historical facts seem to imply.[2]

He added that the Islamic system is not only concerned with establishing public freedoms, but also its main aim is to foster justice and equity. By contrast with Western systems of government, where despotism is construed as the opposite of freedom, in Islamic systems the opposite of despotism is justice, or total justice as God wanted it for humanity, in all domains of life. Thus political justice cannot be separated from socio-economic justice. The system of justice that Islam aspires to is the basis of government and the essence of authority, 'to fit everything in its proper place'. Too much freedom is a dangerous thing, because it ultimately leads to aggression against the rights and freedom of other people, as well as to compartmentalising freedom and rights.

Imam Khomeini gave an example about the kind of justice that the Islamic system aspires to: 'If the president of the Islamic Republic slapped a poor person without due course, then his presidency is over and he should be ousted. Also, the aggressed upon person should come and slap him in turn.' This implies that justice, merit and people's satisfaction are the basic pillars for any official holding public office in the Islamic system. Any action that runs against justice means despotism and should lead to the downfall of any person holding public office in any position that he occupies.[3]

The modern Islamic political system in Iran is founded on two basic pillars: *wilayat al-faqih* and the *shura* of the *umma*. These two juxtaposed together act as a safety valve preventing Islamic governance from degenerating into despotic rule. It is incumbent upon the *wali al-faqih* to closely monitor the state apparatus and its leaders, making sure that no one of them exercises any kind of tyranny and any power confiscation. The *wali al-faqih* governs under certain stipulations, the most important of which are: *faqaha* (jurisprudence), *'adala* (justice) and *kafa'a*

---

1   'Ali Al-Mumin, *Qadaya Islamiyyah Mu'asira* (Contemporary Islamic Issues), Dar Al-Hadi, Beirut: 2004, pp. 172 ff.

2   Imam Khamina'i, *Government in Islam*, p. 32.

3   Taken from Imam Khomeini's speech, 19 November 1979. The speech can be found in *Sahifat Al-Nur* (Messages of Light), a collection of Khomeini's speeches, messages and writings, Tehran, 2006, vol 3, p. 141.

(competence). These tenets guarantee proper conduct of the *wali al-faqih* and prevent despotism since the jurisprudents 'who bind and loose' are constantly monitoring the *faqih* and can easily oust him if he practises any kind of oppression or despotism since he would have lost one of the major requirements for the *wilaya*, namely justice.[1]

Wilaya also denotes holding office, not a personification; this means that a *wali* is a *wali* because he is a jurisprudent who has qualified for this office. This is the basic difference between him and the Infallible Imam, since the person of the Infallible Imam and his office are one and the same. However, they are separated in the case of *wali al-faqih* since the *wali al-faqih* is not that different from others; as such in the elections he wields only one vote and is subject to the rule of law. Nevertheless, so long as he maintains his legal-religious character, the populace follows him to the letter in enjoining the good and forbidding the evil. He also has to act accordingly as evinced in his jurisprudent personality that is tied to administering justice and maintaining and conducting the affairs of the state, which are the functions of the *wilayat*, and not a product of his personality.[2]

The second pillar and guarantee for ensuring justice in the Islamic order is *shura*, construed as the *umma*'s contribution in the functioning of the Islamic order and its participation in decision making on all levels, as well as practising close monitoring of the government apparatus. As such, the *umma* constitutes the various *shura* councils, including the public, private, local and professional *shura* councils. This implies that *shura* is an important aspect in the Islamic order. The Islamic order is based on *shura* and pledge of allegiance (*bay'a*) and the delineated boundaries between those who are governed and those who govern, with the possibility of dismissing the governor while this is an impossible eventuality in despotic regimes.[3] That is why *shura*, as will be elaborated, precludes any authority, state apparatus, or any person holding responsibility in the Islamic order from becoming tyrannical, irrespective of the position he assumes, even if he is the ruling *faqih*, the president or the speaker of the parliament. These respectively correspond to the expediency (*takhtit*), executive and legislative authorities.

To elaborate, it has been stipulated that there should be a balanced allocation of powers in the Islamic political system, in which legal procedures are bound by the Islamic Shari'a, and the close monitoring of the *faqih*, *shura* councils and the *umma*. In addition to *shar'i* and ethical safeguards stipulated by the Shari'a,

1   Sayyid Khadim al-Hai'ri, *Asas Al-Hukuma Al-Islamiyyah* (The Foundation of Islamic Government), pp. 73–74.
2   Sheikh Abdullah Jawadi Amili, A lecture entitled 'Wilayat al-Faqih and Republicanism', in *Silsilat Al-Wilaya Al-Thaqafiyya*, vol. 35, 1998.
3   Abdul Qadir 'Awdeh, *Al-Islam wa Awda'una al-Siyasiya* (Islam and Our Political Affairs), Beirut: Mu'assasat Al-Risalah, 2008, p. 103.

the Constitution of the Islamic Republic has laid down these mechanisms in the domain of unequivocal legal safeguards.

Imam Khomeini corroborates the aforementioned by stressing that no one has the capacity to hold absolute governance, including the *faqih*. On the contrary, everyone works according to the law, and under the law, since they are only executors of it. The ruling *faqih* is required not only to be careful not to engage in any infringement but also to avoid imposing his will on the government; rather it is his duty to preclude the government from assuming any tyrannical or despotic role as was the case during the Shah's regime.[1]

Imam Khomeini clarifies that the Islamic government's primary duty is to eradicate despotism. The person whom Islam delegates the responsibility to govern opposes dictatorship from a religious perspective, as his religion orders him to do so.[2]

The Constitution of the Islamic Republic has laid down a meticulous system of checks and balances as well as constitutional prohibitions that are meant to bar any person in office from abusing his authority. The Constitution prescribes self-monitoring and external monitoring. Self-monitoring is based on the tenets and characteristics that the person in office should hold such as justice and piety, which are the opposite of despotism and inequity. This kind of self-monitoring prevents the person in office from committing despotism and inequity. However, if this monitoring fails for any reason, then external monitoring can intervene to uphold the Shari'a and the law, via the monitoring institutions such as the Shura Council, the Council of Guardians, and so on.[3]

The monitoring by the *umma* constitutes the backbone of this external monitoring process, and it is labelled by the jurisprudents under headings such as enjoining the good and forbidding the evil, as well as bestowing counsel to the Muslim clergy stressing allegiance to them and the rectification of opinion and behaviour (jihad of the self).[4] After Imam Khomeini established the Islamic Republic, he revived this concept by way of motivating the *umma* and its constitutional councils to perform such a duty.[5] In addressing the members of the Shura Council, Imam Khomeini admonished them that if in the course of their work, they come across perversion that allows for despotism and authoritarianism,

---

1   Imam Khomeini's speech, 25 September 1979, *Sahifat Al-Nur*, vol. 10, p. 53.
2   Imam Khomeini's speech, 17 December 1979, *Sahifat Al-Nur*, vol.1, p. 36.
3   See 'Amid Zanjani, *Al-Idara Al-Siyasiyyah wa-Al-Dusturiyya fi Al-Jumhuriyya Al-Islamiyya* (Political and Constitutional Adminstration in The Islamic Republic) in *Nizam Al-Idara Al-Hukumiyyah fi Al-Islam* (The Administrative System of Islamic Government), p. 61.
4   Sheikh Kulayni, 'What the Prophet has ordered of a counsel to the Muslim clergy', a chapter within the book *Usul Al-Kafi*, the book on *hujja*, vol.1, p. 403.
5   Muhammad Surush Mahallati, 'Nasihat A'immat Al-Muslim', (Advice for Islamic Leaders) in *Qadaya Islamiyya Muassira* (The Giving Council to the Muslim Clergy), vol. 1, 1996, p. 93.

which could be evident in the practice of corruption or embezzlement among the ministers and the president of the Republic, then it is their duty to stand up and face this situation ... The populace should judge one and closely monitor all of these practices.[1]

Imam Khomeini was not giving a political speech or a propaganda statement; rather he was expressing jurisprudence *(ta'asil)* on the issue of the monitoring of the *umma* and rendering counsel to those in power. He was also expressing the general orientation of the political system that stems from the Islamic Shari'a, which implies that the close monitoring by the *umma* prevents the system from diverging from its objectives in disseminating justice and equity. Imam Khomeini worked on transforming the *ta'asil fuqhi* into a general culture practised by the populace on a daily basis and on all levels. Imam Khomeini kept urging the populace to adopt this culture and to practise it, and by this he endeavoured to demonstrate the true picture and stance of the Islamic order, which is contrary to despotism. He also tried to ensure the well-being, stability and the future of the Islamic order, based upon divine stipulations, such as the following Hadith: 'Rule is sustained under *kufr* (non-belief), but it cannot continue to exist under oppression.'[2] Also, from this perspective, a maxim captures the same meaning: 'Justice is the foundation of rule.' In addressing the populace, Imam Khomeini stated that we all should bear responsibility not only on our deeds but also on the deeds of others: 'My responsibility is incumbent upon you and your responsibility is incumbent upon me, if I set my foot on the path of deflection then you are held responsible. You should not only say why did you set your foot on the path of perversion, but also you should take the initiative and prevent any perversion by questioning and holding me accountable for what I have done.'[3]

3. Constitutional Safeguards against Despotism

Many of the articles in the Constitution of the Islamic Republic were designed to act as safeguards and practical guarantees to prevent tyranny and dictatorship, as well as to ensure justice. The preamble of the Constitution provides that 'The Constitution guarantees the elimination of all kinds of intellectual and social dictatorship as well as economic monopoly, and endeavours to get rid of the tyrannical rule and to ensure the populace's right of self-determination.'[4]

Article 109 of the Constitution stipulates that justice and piety are very basic conditions that the ruling *faqih* should possess. It is worth mentioning that justice and piety have specific connotations in this regard. The latter signifies a

---

1   *Sahifat Al-Nur*, vol. 16, p. 30.
2   As cited by Al-Majlisi, in *Al-Bihar*, vol. 72, p. 331.
3   *Sahifat Al-Nur*, vol. 8, p. 47.
4   The Preamble of the Constitution of the Islamic Republic of Iran.

trait which prevents its holder from engaging in smaller sins and greater sins, and makes him observe all his religious duties. The former signifies a trait that acts as a bulwark against temptations and prevents man from committing sins or evil. However, it cannot hold against greater temptations. From this perspective, it is different from infallibility that can stand its ground against all the world's temptations and bestows upon its holder immunity against committing any misdeed.[1] In other words, according to this constitutional provision, the *faqih* loses his *wilayat* if the principle of justice is not upheld. The Constitution has stressed the importance of justice and put it on equal footing with the jurisprudential condition (*faqaha*). The justice stipulation is so stringently expressed in the Constitution that the utterance of a single lie by the *faqih* or the practice of any kind of tyranny, even against one member of the populace, would compromise his integrity and therefore should result in his permanent ouster from office.[2]

The Constitution empowered the Council of Experts, which is directly elected by the populace, with the prerogative to identify the loss of the trait of justice by the *faqih* and to oust him. Also it is incumbent upon the *umma* to perform a similar role if the justice stipulation of the *faqih* no longer holds, or if he exercises tyranny or oppression.[3]

There is a consensus among the Shi'i and Sunni political jurisprudential schools of law on the stipulation of justice as a basic criterion for the Islamic ruler; if he loses it then he is no longer viewed as fit to lead and should be ousted. The justice stipulation also applies to the members of the Council of Experts, who closely monitor the *rahbar* and can oust him. They exercise the Shari'a rule on the behaviour of the ruler because they rank among the *fuqaha al-'udul* (the *fuqaha* who acquire the *'adala* condition), and they express the stance of the *umma* as regards the ruler, since they are elected by the *umma*.[4] The same stipulations apply to the head of the judiciary; in addition to these, the stipulation of piety applies to the person who holds the office of the president.[5]

In contrast with other state offices, the Constitution of the Islamic Republic of Iran did not specify a limit for the tenure of the *wali al-faqih*. For instance, the tenure of the president is four years and can be extended only once; the same holds for the Shura Council. In turn, the head of the judiciary holds office for a five-year term, which can be extended. Thus, term limits apply to almost all state offices that are administrative executive or legislative; however, the office of the *wali al-faqih* has its own specificity because it is directly connected to the *shar'i*

---

1   See Khazim Al-Hairi, *Al-Imama Waqiyadat Al-Mujtama'* (The Imamate and the Leadership of the Community), p. 68.
2   Imam Khomeini speech, 19 December 1979, in *Sahifat Al-Nur*, vol.11, p. 133.
3   The Constitution of the Islamic Republic, Article 111.
4   Ibid., Articles 108 and 111.
5   Ibid., Articles 115, 157 and 158.

stance of the state, being the highest religious office in it. Any incumbent to this office by implication is the best and most-qualified person for the job among the *fuqaha al-'usul* in terms of merit, competence, and management as determined by the experts of the *umma*, the 'people who bound and loose'. As long as the *faqih* is in office, the Council of Experts closely and continuously monitors him to keep track of whether he abides by the stipulations mentioned above. Thus the *faqih* could either lose office in a very short period after his election or remain in the post for life. The loss of any one of the stipulations or the discovery by the Council of Experts that he was incompetent will, according to the law, lead to his dismissal from office, since he is deemed as illegitimate even if he is considered as a political and religious ruler. On the other hand, if the *faqih* proved to be well qualified to hold office in accordance with the stipulations of *wilayat*, and if the Council of Experts remains fully convinced that he is the right and best person for the job, then there is no justification to limit his tenure.

In addition, the *wali al-faqih* is subject to periodic reviews by the Council of Experts, usually every six months, depending on how often it holds its sessions. In this regard, the Council dispatches a special investigation committee whose duty is to determine whether the *wali al-faqih* should be allowed to keep his post. This special investigation committee, which is formed from among the Council of Experts, conducts periodic thorough investigations in order to assess the leadership role of the *faqih*, his exercise of authority, and his aptitude for *ijtihad* (independent reasoning). In other words, this special investigative committee closely monitors his jurisprudential qualifications, his exercise of justice, his competence and his management ability. Article 111 of the Islamic Republic's Constitution unequivocally stipulates a clause on the dismissal of the *rahbar* from office in the event that the following conditions were present: incompetence to exercise his legal duties or loss of one of the stipulations mentioned in Articles 105 and 109.[1] These two articles include the following eight points: (1) the lack of scientific competence due to the loss of the qualifications to be a *mujtahid*; (2) the exercise of oppressive or despotic behaviour that contradicts the notion of justice; (3) weakness in piety and religious commitment; (4) weakness in the capacity to exercise political wisdom; (5) weakness in his socio-economic competence; (6) bad management and administration; (7) weakness in courage; (8) and the dwindling of his ability to lead.

Moreover, the Constitution of the Islamic Republic of Iran has placed the biggest and most important consultative council in the service of the *wali al-faqih*. This council is known as the Expediency Council (*majma' tashkhis maslahat al-nizam*) and it initiates high-level state policy. Also, the Higher Council of National Security is tasked with deciding the security and defensive policies

---

1   The Constitution of the Islamic Republic, Articles 105 and 109.

of the state. It executes these policies after the *faqih* ratifies them. Both councils prevent the *faqih* from unilaterally governing and supervise the planning and execution of the state's higher policies.

The authority of the president of the republic is also confined by a host of constitutional safeguards that prevent him from exercising despotism, since the Shura Council, which is elected by the *umma*, can dismiss the president from office after the ruler or *faqih* ratifies the dismissal. Equally the *wali al-faqih* can dismiss the president, but only in the event that a judicial sentence has been handed upon him by the Supreme Court.[1]

The Shura Council can call for questioning the entire cabinet or each minister in his own capacity.[2] In this regard, Imam Khomeini stressed that what precludes the president from becoming a dictator and what prevents the head of the army, the internal security forces or the prime minister from practising despotism, is the *faqih* himself. The *faqih* has been appointed by the *umma* and he became its Imam; he is the one who is obliged to wholeheartedly strive for the removal of dictatorship or any of its manifestations. He is the one who leads everybody under the banner of Islam and founds a law-abiding government.[3]

The *faqih*, the president of the republic, and all other public officials are held accountable under the law as are any member of the populace; this includes full responsibility in case any of them committed any common crime.[4]

Moreover, the Constitution has vested the responsibility of investigating the financial matters of the *faqih*, president of the republic, and all his aides and the ministers and their wives and children before coming to office, as well as after finishing their tenure, in order to make sure that their financial resources do not increase by illegal means. The head of the judiciary conducts such a procedure.[5]

The Constitution has subjected the legislations of the Islamic Shura Council to jurisprudential and constitutional monitoring by the Council of Guardians,[6] in order to prevent despotism in its legislation and to preclude any legislation that runs against the spirit of the Shari'a and the Constitution, or what is known as the tyranny of the majority (as John Stuart Mill argued), especially if the parliamentary majority belongs to the same ruling party.[7] The decisions of the Council of Guardians are not final; rather, the final court of appeal is for the Shura Council that can rectify it. However, if both the Shura Council and the

---

1 The Constitution, Article 110 and Article 89.
2 Ibid., Article 89 and Article 81.
3 See Imam Khomeini's speech of 9 November 1989, *Sahifat al-Nur*, vol. 11, p.174.
4 The Constitution of the Islamic Republic in Iran, Article 107 and Article 140.
5 Ibid., Article 142.
6 Ibid., Articles 91 and 94.
7 This was the case with the second cabinet of Sheikh Hashemi Rafsanjani, as well as the first Khatami cabinet.

Council of Guardians hold firm to their opinion then the matter is raised to the Expediency Council in order to adjudicate.[1]

This acts as a guarantee against any transgression or tyrannical conduct by the Expediency Council. Another guarantee that should be considered as well has to do with the way the members of this council are selected. They are selected by the *wali al-faqih*, the head of the judiciary system and the Shura Council, which would in theory preclude them from turning into despots.

Although the head of the judiciary is entitled to wide prerogatives of authority that even include the *faqih*, any action that is not in conformity with the stipulation of justice leads to his dismissal from office by the *wali al-faqih*.[2] There is also a special tribunal for judges who are held accountable for any crime they might engage in, and there is also a special tribunal for government employees. Moreover, any citizen has the right to file a complaint to investigate any of the major state institutions such as the Shura Council, the executive and judicial authorities. The Constitution makes it incumbent upon the Shura Council to thoroughly investigate these complaints and come up with a satisfactory response to them. If the complaint has public nature then the populace should be informed about the results of the investigation.[3]

It is worth mentioning that the *fuqaha al-'udul*, who do not take part in office, exercise their monitoring role on the state in its execution of authority. They have the right to abrogate a sentence in any of the articles that have been questioned, especially if the outcome results in lessening the destructive impact of the error that the governor committed. If need be, disobeying the governor could be better than the repercussions of going along with his mistakes.[4] Many articles of the Constitution stipulate the exercise of close monitoring of the state agencies in order to prevent dictatorship through various mechanisms, the most salient of which are participation in elections and free expression of opinion in order to constructively criticise and rectify the performance of the state; both of these are carried out from the stance of the Qur'anic injunction to enjoin the good and prohibit the evil as has been previously elaborated upon.

4. Prerogatives of the Wali al-Faqih: A Comparison

Mas'ud Asadullahi[5] contends that the best way to study the duties and executive prerogatives of the *wali al-faqih* in the political system of the Islamic Republic is to resort to the argument from analogy. He compares the method of choosing the

---

1   The Constitution of the Islamic Republic of Iran, Article 112.
2   Ibid., Article 110.
3   Ibid., Article 90.
4   Al-Ha'iri, *Asas Al-Hukuma Al-Islamiyya* (The Foundations of Islamic Government) Beirut 1979.
5   Mas'ud Asadullahi, *Wilayat Al-Faqih wa Al-Dimuqratiyya: Darasa Muqaran* (Wilayat Al-Faqih and Democracy: A Comparative Approach), Beirut: Dar Al-Mahajja Al-Bayda'. 2007.

wali al-faqih, his necessary qualifications in relation to the selection process, and his duties and prerogatives, on the one hand, with those of the US and French presidents, as well as the British prime minister, on the other. The merit of this comparative approach is that it sheds light on six complementary domains from the following perspectives.

The first perspective deals with the qualifications and the ways of choosing the leaders in Iran, Britain, France and the US. The second perspective deals with the stipulations and mechanisms to depose or oust the aforementioned leaders. The third addresses the duties and prerogatives of the head executives in these countries. The fourth deals with the duties and prerogatives of the high echelons in the military and judicial domains. The fifth has to do with the duties and prerogatives of the high echelons in the legislative domain. The sixth and last perspective highlights the general nature of the duties and prerogatives of the high echelons in these countries.[1]

POPULACE AND ISLAM

According to Imam Khomeini,[2] the responsibility of governance is mutual and reciprocal between the government and populace.[3] From this perspective, Khomeini made religion and the populace the two most important pillars of the Islamic order. Although religion as a divine law has precedence over the people, the populace enjoys a large margin of freedom, free decision making and the right of self-determination. Since the populace voted for a religious order then they have chosen religion to be the law of the land. This occurred in Iran when the first referendum was conducted on the Islamic order in 1979, where more than 98 percent of the people voted in favour of the Islamic order.

Khomeini stressed that there are two parties to this human referendum: the first is God, the Divine Creator, and the second is the populace. When people accepted God's providence, it became incumbent upon them to abide by His sayings, decrees and injunctions, since acknowledging providence is a prologue to accepting His sayings and decrees. However, if the populace refused to acknowledge God's providence and did not recognise the Oneness of God, then there could not have been a covenant between the two. People abided by God's injunctions and laws by acknowledging that they are the subjects and the mechanism to execute this law. Put simply, there are two parties to the contract: the governor (God) and the governed (populace).

---

1   Mas'ud Asadullahi, 159–160.
2   Imam Khomeini speech, 19 December 1979, in *Sahifat Al-Nur*, vol. 11, p. 133.
3   This bears a striking resemblance to John Locke's concept of fiduciary trust.

From this perspective, any political system requires two parties: governor and governed. Imam Khomeini emphasised that the political system could not be established without these two parties; the political order loses its acceptability (*maqbuliyya*) if the populace is excluded. However, since the governor is divinely appointed, he does not lose his legitimacy and his post will remain preserved, even with the absence of the political order and state.

THE DEMOCRATIC NATURE OF ISLAM

The referendum on the Islamic content of the political system and people's endorsement of this system require abiding by the injunctions of Islam. Referenda or elections express the will of the people, and since democracy implies the people's rule, then the Islamic order is considered democratic from this perspective. In this respect, Imam Khomeini stressed: 'Democracy is embedded in Islam and people are free in conveying and practising their beliefs and convictions in total freedom, unless there are conspiracies or hidden hands that are doing their best to cause their future generations to become delinquent.'[1] Khomeini linked the concept of democracy to public opinion; he blasted Western-style democratic political systems even if they are covered with an Islamic garment. Khomeini considered characterising Islam as democratic as tantamount to insulting Islam, since in his view Islam is far more supreme than all democracies. Likewise, if somebody says that an Islamic republic guarantees justice, then this is also an insult to Islam because justice is part and parcel of Islam.[2] Khomeini considered democracy as the fulcrum of Islamic government: 'Islamic government is a government which is based upon justice and democracy, as well as the principles, decrees and injunctions of Islam.' He added that by stressing the concordance between the Islamic republic in its Islamic context, then on the level of implementation it would be a model to be emulated by all the countries of the world. Democracy in the Islamic republic thus assumes its full, heavily value-laden meaning.

This perspective gives the lie to Samuel Hungtington's theory of the clash of civilisations, which stresses that democracy is a product of the West and its brainchild par excellence.[3] Khomeini stressed that a genuine conception of democracy bestows on people the right to take part in decision making, as well as self-determination, which are parts of the Islamic doctrine, being integral to its injunctions and doctrine.

---

1   Khomeini, *Sahifat Al-Nur*, vol. 11, p. 133
2   Khomeini, *Al-Hukuma Al-Islamiyya*, p. 59.
3   Samuel Huntingdon, *The Clash of Civilizations and Remaking of World Order*, Touchstone First Edition: New York, 1997.

Khomeini added that many have fallen into the fallacy of comparing Islam, a divine religion, and democracy, a man-made political concept. One should compare two conceptions that are on the same level and of the same nature. A constructive comparison, he argued, is one that entails the democratic system and the Islamic system, because the Islamic system portrays the true nature of Islamic Shari'a in its interpretation.[1]

The Islamic order in Iran is based upon the concept of democracy, since through elections and referenda the populace has endorsed the Republic under the banner of Islam as a democratic system. This formulation furnished the ground for a solution to the problem of reconciling the concept of state with that of religion. The Islamic Republic in Iran has been a pioneer in this respect, since it was able to legislate an Islamic Constitution that proposed a practical solution to the dilemma of religious authority (marja's) and conveyed the possibility of trusting the populace by way of the ballot box. This has been done both for the protection of the national interest of the *umma*, on the one hand, and the stability of the system on the other. The Islamic Republic succeeded by separating and fusing the aforementioned concomitantly.[2]

The Islamic Republic distinguished between two sources of legitimacy which have been the two standing pillars of the system. First, Islamic legitimacy and second, a democratic legitimacy based upon elections where it is incumbent upon the parliament (*Majlis*) to safeguard the revolution on the basis of the aforementioned legitimate foundations. Thus, there are two complementary legitimacies and arenas. In issues where Islam does not provide direct and unequivocal opinions and stances, then the second arena, namely democracy, comes into the picture in order to guarantee: individual freedom; political pluralism; active civil society and institutions; the formation of local councils, and other aspects that are conducive to administering the affairs of the society and the state. In this regard, Imam Khomeini stressed: 'The main function of government is to serve people'[3] or 'the governor and governed are equal in front of the law'; 'Islamic government is rooted in justice, democracy and Islamic law'.[4] Then, it is a two-sided *wilayat*, that of the governor and that of the governed in accordance with the following Qur'anic injunction: 'As to the believers, males and females, they are friends to one another. They enjoin what is good and forbid what is evil ...' (9:71) This verse renders counsel to the Muslim religious scholars (*ulama*) where enjoining the good and prohibiting the evil[5] is equally incumbent upon the ruler and on the ruled.

---

1   Khomeini, *Al-Hukuma*, pp. 59–60.
2   Radwan al-Sayyid, *Siyasat Al-Islam Al-Mouaser: Morajaat wa Moutabat* (Politics of Contemporary Islam: Reviews and Follow-ups), Beirut: Dar Al-Kitab Al-Arabi, 1997. p. 43.
3   Khomeini, *Al-Hukuma*, p. 59.
4   Khomeini, *Al -Hukuma*, p. 38
5   The five pillars of Islam (*arkan*) are: 1. There is no God but Allah and Muhammad is His Prophet

Imam Khomeini clarified that the domain of democratic legitimacy is confined to personal matters and customary law, while the domain of Islamic legitimacy is confined to Islamic injunctions and laws.

People have the freedom to exercise their opinion as they see fit in personal matters, daily dealings, customary practices and the like. The former can never have precedence over the religious and Qur'anic injunctions even if this was the call of the majority. In this regard, Imam Khomeini stressed that: 'People's opinion as opposed to God's governance does not constitute a legal-religious opinion because it is considered wayward.'[1] Imam Khomeini added: 'God is the creator and people are his creation[2]; He is the originator and everything that emanates from Him is binding upon the people.'

This separation between individual matters and customary laws, on the one hand, and the *shar'i* issues, on the other, is not tantamount to secularism, since secularism is the separation of state and religion and it is people's rule where the parliament legislates laws. However, in Islam there is a fusion between politics and religion, and laws in Islam are divine laws and not positive laws (*wad'iyya*); it does not follow the Christian injunction 'render what is for Caesar to Caesar and render what is for God to God'; rather, it is God's governance of His people. In other words, since people are free to contract any conviction they choose, then they will choose Islamic governance, where this freedom is a divine gift from God, rather than a concession or a *sadaqa* from the governor or any other person who revokes it or gives it whenever he wills. Thus, people take part in decision making and self-determination from the perspective of this divine gift. If people choose Islam and they abide by its injunctions and laws, then they are first and foremost free in exercising their doctrines and beliefs. Secondly, they are free in

---

(*ashshahadatan*); 2. Prayer: five daily ritual prayers (*salat*); 3. Fasting during the month of Ramadan (*siam*); 4. Alms giving (*zakat*); 5. Pilgrimage to Mecca (*haj*). To these Shi'i Islam adds: One fifth tax on the profits to be given to the Imam or marja' (*khums*); enjoining the good and prohibiting the evil (*al-amr bi al-ma'ruf wa al-nahyi 'an al-munkar*); Struggle in the way of God (*jihad fi sabil Allah*). Parallel to the *arkan*, Twelver Shi'ism believes in *usul al-din* (the foundation of the faith), which consist of: divine unity (*tawhid*), prophethood (*nubuwwa*), Imama, justice ('*adl*) and resurrection (*al-ma'ad*). See: Muhammad Jawad Maghniyye, *Al-Shi'i wa Al-Hakimun* (The Shi'is and the Rulers), Beirut 1966, p. 7; Sheikh Muhammad Mahdi Shamsuddine, *Nizam Al-Hukum wa Al-Idara fi Al-Islam* (The Order of Governance and Administration in Islam), seventh edn, Beirut 2000, p. 105 and p. 382. See also Moojan Momen, *An Introduction to Shi'i Islam: The History and Doctrines of Twelver Shi'ism,* New Haven 1985, pp. 175–180.

1   Although both the Sunnis and Shi'is acknowledge consensus (*ijma'*) as a normative principle, for the Sunnis it is the consensus of the umma at large, while for the Shi'is it is the consensus of the Imams or the jurisprudents (*fuqaha*). This is substantiated by two Hadiths. For the Sunnis: 'My community will not confer upon an error' (*ma ijtama'i ummati 'ala dalala*); for the Shi'is: 'My imams will not confer upon an error' (*ma aijma'iImmati 'ala dalala*).

2   People cannot create anything and should always abide by God's injunctions.

choosing the ruler that they want,[1] and thirdly they enjoy the freedom to take their own decisions in customary and personal matters, by exercising the freedom that God has bestowed upon them.

Imam Khomeini was unequivocal when he insisted that the governor (*wali al-faqih*) should be endowed with certain qualifications that will render his governance efficient and strong only after people's consent. He has placed religion and the populace as the two most important pillars in his Islamic order: 'We want an Islamic Republic, and republic should be considered as the form of government, while Islamic has to do with the content of the government, or religious injunctions.' It is government based upon the decision of the majority, and it is an Islamic government that is totally based upon people's opinions.[2]

Imam Khomeini added that the form of government and the system of government are not people's prerogatives only; rather, taking crucial decisions is incumbent upon the people. Thus, the system gives way to the concept of consensus: 'In this Islamic state it is incumbent the rulers remain in continuous consultation with people's representatives in order to take decisions, and if the members of parliament do not agree, then the rulers can never take crucial decisions on their own.' Rather, Khomeini considered any encroachment upon the people's opinion completely barred: 'People's opinion has the supremacy and the ultimate sovereignty since they control the government through people's institutions.'[3]

This freedom in exercising the right of self-determination is a religious, inalienable right that cannot be taken away or given away as expressed in the Constitution of the Islamic Republic of Iran in Article 54: 'Absolute sovereignty on the universe and human beings is for God, He alone has given man the freedom to determine his social fate; no one has the right to confiscate this religious right or use it for personal gain. People exercise this divine right through the mechanisms established by the Constitution of the Islamic Republic.'

The aforementioned pinpoints the importance of people's opinions in executing laws and taking key decisions in the country and acts as a guarantee to ward off dictatorship and tyranny. It also ensures a smooth transition of power. In the event that the *wali al-faqih* becomes tyrannical, then the ruler loses the right to govern, and his religious legitimacy becomes questioned since he would have lost popular legitimacy by way of surrendering this right of the people to determine their destiny under the governance of another ruler.

---

1   According to Imam Khomeini, Islam is the best system of governance, and choosing any other system does not achieve justice, well-being and felicity.
2   Khomeini, *Al-Hukuma*, pp. 55–57.
3   Husayn Montazari, *Dirasat fi Wilayat al-Faqih wafikh Addawlah Al-Islamiyyah* (Studies in Wilayat al-Faqih and The Jurisprudence of The Islamic State), vol. 4, second edn, Beirut 1998, pp. 141–145.

SAFETY VALVES AND CONSTITUTIONAL PROHIBITIONS AGAINST
THE DICTATORSHIP OF THE RULER

Islam has placed safeguards and mechanisms in order to prevent despotism in the Islamic government. These mechanisms can lead to the downfall of a tyrannical ruler after he loses both divine and popular legitimacy and acceptability. Some of these safeguards are the following:

— Monitoring: The Council of Experts meets on a regular basis in order to monitor the *wali al-faqih*. The close monitoring of the Marja's in the religious seminaries (*hawzat*) is based upon their religious duty or the acts and deeds of the *wali al-faqih*. Thus the Marja's must still have the required qualifications to govern, the most salient being justice, extensive knowledge of the law and the Islamic injunctions or Shari'a.

— Constructive criticism: Islam necessitates constructive criticism, and holding the rulers accountable for their actions and decisions. This falls within the domain of the Islamic doctrine of enjoining the good and prohibiting the evil. This criticism is a *taklif* and a *shar'i* duty that entails those in power, even the *wali al-faqih*.

— Popular monitoring: Imam Khomeini argued that labelling *wilayat al-faqih* as despotic is the result of the inability of the critics to understand the real essence and meaning of *wilayat*. Khomeini asserted that *wilayat al-faqih* is the government of the populace; therefore, it stands in the way of despotism. In clarifying the meaning of dictatorship, he added that the absolute prerogatives, if granted to the president by the populace, would make him become a dictator. However, if he rejected these, then he could not be labelled as a dictator. Khomeini continued that Islam rejects dictatorship, and if the *faqih* entertained the idea of becoming a despot, then Islam would oust him. Khomeini posed the rhetorical question: 'Were the Prophet and Imam 'Ali practitioners of dictatorship? Definitely not, and no one can claim otherwise.'[1]

In addition, if the *wali al-faqih* objects to the opinion of the majority in domains other than religious obligations or religious prohibitions, then he loses his legitimacy, and this leads to his downfall from the stance of *wilayat*. Khomeini affirmed: 'There is no reason for anyone to be afraid of *wilayat al-faqih*, since the *faqih* does not want to impose any injunction by force. If he imposed an injunction by force, then his *wilayat* is immediately annulled and declared void. The

1   Husayn Montazari, *Dirasat fi Wilayat al-Faqih wafikh Addawlah Al-Islamiyyah* (Studies in Wilayat al-Faqih and The Jurisprudence of The Islamic State), vol. 4, second edn, Beirut 1998, pp. 313–331.

smooth running of *wilayat al-faqih* assumes shouldering the responsibility of people's well-being.'[1]

— Equality before the law: The *wali al-faqih*, like any other person, is under the law and must abide by the stipulations of the law. It is the right of any citizen to file a complaint to the chief magistrate in order to subpoena the *wali al-faqih* and he has to show up. In this regard, Imam Khomeini stated: 'All Muslims, including the Prophet, are equal before the law, and the Islamic and Qur'anic injunctions are binding upon all, without any exceptions whatsoever.'[2]

— The prohibition of assuming power by way of coercion and oppression: A smooth, peaceful transition to power is a distinguishing trait of the political school of Imam Khomeini; he never believed in oppression or coercion. He was not only against oppression and aggression against others, but he prohibited it: 'We neither have ambitions in any country nor do we have the right to do that. God Almighty does not sanction us to meddle in other countries' affairs, unless it was done in self defence.'[3] Imam Khomeini stipulated that the *wali al-faqih* does not enjoy one of the prerogatives of the Prophet and the infallible Imams, namely initiative jihad (*al-jihad al-ibtida'i*).[4]

— No religious, political or constitutional authority is immune to criticism: According to Imam Khomeini: 'Every member in the *umma* has the direct right to hold accountable Muslim rulers and governors, and he has the right to criticise them. The *wali al-faqih* must give convincing answers, and if he fails to do so and acted contrary to his Islamic duties, then he will be immediately ousted, and there are other mechanisms to solve this problem.'[5] However, the mechanisms of criticism and accountability are the most important since they are regarded as legal mechanisms guaranteed by the Constitution. In addition to that, there is the role of the close monitoring of the Council of Experts, which is a constitutional institution where its members hold regular sessions every six months in order to debate public Islamic policies as well as evaluate the behaviour of the *wali al-faqih*. If positively evaluated, then his tenure is extended; if negatively evaluated then he would be dismissed.

— The right to oppose the policies of *wali al-faqih*: Imam 'Ali stressed that it is incumbent upon the imam to rule by what God has revealed and to perform

---

1   Khomeini, *Sahifat al-Nur*, vol. 1, p. 27 and p. 29.
2   Khomeini, *Al-Hukuma*, p. 347.
3   Ibid., p. 446.
4   Ibid., p. 232. Although Shi'ism acknowledges the existence of religious authority alongside the political authority after the death of the Prophet to be present in the Imams, it does not endorse waging offensive or initiative jihad, which is the sole prerogative of the Prophet, and ceases to be permissible after his death.
5   Ibid., p. 332.

his duty (*amana*); if he does, then it is incumbent upon the people to listen and obey him, and to respond if called.[1] As long as the ruler is performing his duties, then the populace has to obey; however, if he neglects his duties and obligations, then the people have the right to object.

— Muffling public freedoms and the voice of opposition usually has to do with the despicable practices of the ruler which have been severely censored by Islam. The right to opposition should be granted to people and should be expressed directly or by way of the Shura Council or the Council of Experts. The members of these institutions are elected by the people, and these institutions assume the role of close monitoring and supervising the government's work as well as rendering advice to it or objecting to its work. It even supervises the *wali al-faqih* and his performance in order to ensure his actions are in accordance with the Islamic Shari'a and decrees.

— Political pluralism: The Islamic order leaves room for plurality of political forces and political parties, both of which are sanctioned in the Islamic order, on the condition that they do not encroach upon the public good or threaten national security. In this regard, Imam Khomeini stressed that any interest group or political party that does not jeopardise the interest of the populace is free to operate as it sees fit. It goes without saying that all political parties that work for public interest are free.[2] Elsewhere, Imam Khomeini affirmed that the political forces in the Islamic Republic are free to convey and exercise their doctrines.[3] Thus, Islam concedes to pluralism but according to specific safeguards, the fulcrum of which are people's interest. Also pluralism should neither be contradictory to established laws or Islamic Shari'a, nor give way to civil unrest.

— Legitimacy and acceptability: *Wilayat al-faqih* enjoys a divine legitimacy hence it is a divine position and a continuation of the Prophethood and the Imamate, but people's acceptance is a crucial precondition to its application; this is the true meaning of people's acceptance. If people refused to abide by the divine law (Shari'a) and chose another system, then the divine system would cease to exist and another political order would take its place, because 'there is no say for a person who is not obeyed' (*la ra'i liman la yuta'*).[4] It is incumbent upon the *wali al-faqih* to sustain people's acceptance of Islam and the Islamic order to preserve the continuation and the very existence of the Islamic government. In addition, the *wali al-faqih* is neither entitled nor allowed to impose the Shari'a on people by force or coercion. In the view

1   *Kanz Alummal*, vol. 5, p. 764. (What is this?)
2   Khomeini, *Al-Hukuma*, p. 713.
3   Ibid., p. 53.
4   Imam Ali, *Nahj Al-Balagha, Khutba*, p. 27. (Quoted in what book, volume?)

of Islam, people would be committing a grave sin (*kabira*) by rejecting the Shari'a after they had committed themselves to the Qur'an and its injunctions and the Prophet. But even so, with the absence of people who are the cornerstone of any government, the Islamic government would not be able to exist.

Imam Khomeini stressed that the legitimacy of any Islamic ruler emanates from his commitment to the Islamic regulations and its application; otherwise, he would definitely lose legitimacy and his *wilayat* and official status. He affirmed: 'A government which is appointed according to a legitimate *wilayat* is a legitimate government and not only a legal government; rather, it is a legitimate government that should be obeyed by all.'[1]

He further added that Islam bestows legitimacy upon any ruler: 'If the government exercises any action that is not sanctioned by Islam, then all its actions and affairs are rendered to be tyrannical and prohibited.'[2] In this context, Imam Khomeini believed that the *wali al-faqih* loses his legitimacy and his *wilayat* as well, if he forcefully imposes his *wilayat*. This reasoning is substantiated by reference to the Prophetic tradition where the Prophet advised Imam 'Ali upon assigning him the obligation of *wilayat*: 'You are assigned the *wilayat* over the *umma*. If the believers voluntarily and unanimously acknowledged your authority, then bear the reins of government; however, if they differed with you, then let them be'.

In line with the Prophetic tradition Imam Khomeini emphasised that the *faqih* does not aim to impose his will on the people, and if he does, his *wilayat* loses its legitimacy and falls apart. As previously discussed, the kernel of the argument is that the *wali al-faqih* will not impose Islam on his people by coercion; but if the populace has chosen Islam, then they have to abide by its regulations and the *wali al-faqih* has every right to apply Islamic injunctions, or else Islamic order can never be established in any society.

— Freedom and its connotations in Islam: Freedom is an inalienable, instinctual right, which is a divine gift from God to humanity. 'Freedom' is used in politics as an antonym to despotism; however, Islam regards it as salvation: 'And He relieves them of their heavy burden and the shackles that were upon them'. (7: 156)

Nowadays, freedom connotes an emotional and moral meaning; it has become the catch phrase of politicians, especially those who manipulate the term for political gains. Freedom also connotes the following: free will; individual freedom; freedom to seek education; freedom to abide by the laws and obey the ruler; freedom to legislate; and freedom of personal status.

---

1   Khomeini, *Sahifat Al-Nur*, vol. 4, p. 138.
2   Khomeini, *Al-Hukuma*, p. 54.

In discussing freedom in the Islamic polity, Imam Khomeini granted it legitimacy based upon the *wilayat al-faqih* doctrine where the *ulama* have a cardinal role in guiding the *umma* towards its salvation. In spite of that, Khomeini left a big margin for public freedom to the individual: he endeavoured to uphold difference in opinion; freedom of expression; separation of powers; transparency, accountability, and surveillance on the leadership and its institutions, which gives a political vitality to the system and guarantees its dynamism and stability.

From this perspective, the Constitution of the Islamic Republic of Iran, in Articles 19 and 31, stresses equal opportunity and equality under the law. Furthermore, Articles 23 and 27 emphasise rights and political freedom; Article 29 stresses social security; Articles 46 and 47 emphasise private ownership; the Constitution has guaranteed all political and social freedoms under the narrow confines of the law.

Some of the salient freedoms that Islam guarantees and that were embedded in the Constitution of the Islamic Republic are the following: freedom of belief; the right to form associations, groups, political parties, syndicates, etc, on condition that they do not conflict with national independence, sovereignty, national unity, Islamic values and the principles of the Islamic Republic (Article 26); freedom of the press and media as long as it does not infringe upon Islamic norms and public rights; freedom to demonstrate and the right to voice opposition as long as these activities are peaceful; and women's freedom in the sense that Iranian women have the right to fully engage in the political and social spheres.

According to Khomeini, these political and ideological conceptions that are derived from authentic Islam are considered the emblems of the Islamic government that is characterised by freedom and independence as well as conformity to God's injunctions: 'The Islamic government guarantees freedom and independence, and those who are striving to obtain freedom, independence, and establish a just government ... earn the respect of the populace and human institutions as well as God's grace.'[1] Islam from the basis of its principles of *tawhid* (oneness of God) stresses that every human being has the inalienable freedom of self-determination since it reflects the authentic human freedom which cannot be taken away.[2]

Imam Khomeini clarified that the main two functions of the Islamic government are: (1) to execute Islamic injunctions, legal judicial penalties and enforce the laws; and (2) uphold public freedom and prohibit oppression.

The Ayatollah distinguished between divine injunctions, on the one hand,

---

1   Ibid., p. 405.
2   Ibid., p. 204.

and civil freedoms on the other, where freedom is exercised within the narrow confines of the law and the law alone is the one that can limit freedom.

Khomeini placed great importance on the freedom of the populace and their presence in the political, social and economic spheres. Imam Khomeini considered that these values constituted a basic ingredient in the Islamic polity: 'We require an Islamic government, a just government, a government that safeguards people's interests (*maslaha*), and not one that steals from people or is incapable of ruling ... we require an Islamic government supported by the people and based on public opinion where the populace is free in voicing their opinion and exercising their self-determination.'[1] Khomeini considered the Islamic government to be the true voice of the people, in that it is obliged to do its utmost to earn their respect, love and backing to the extent that they consider it a reflection of their own will. In a speech addressed to the Islamic Republic's officials, Imam Khomeini said: 'Be loyal to the people and earn their trust; then you will receive God's grace and the people's content, and the authority as well as the power will remain with you and with the populace.'[2]

— Politics as a means to felicity: Imam Khomeini considered that politics, governance and legislations serve one goal, and that is the felicity of the human being and raising him/her to be knowledgeable of God: 'The establishment of the government to found justice is only a means, but the ultimate end is knowledge of God ... the Islamic government is a government of raising the human being and inculcating values, norms and teaching him/her self-discipline and self-control.'[3]

The main goal of the Islamic political system is to lead man towards his perfection and towards God: 'Those who upon being visited by adversity: "We are Allah's (servants) and to Him we shall return".' (2:155) Other objectives of the system include *hakimiyya* (God's governance); applying the divine laws to the community; carrying out religious injunctions; and establishing individual, political, economic, social, cultural and ethical security. All of these goals help people to reach the ultimate goal of seeking the true path of God: 'O man, you strive unto your Lord and you shall meet Him'. (84:6)

THE IMAMATE AS A CONTINUATION OF PROPHETHOOD

Prophet Muhammad established the Islamic state in Medina and the twelve Infallible Imams followed his footsteps by way of knowledge through divine

---

1 Khomeini, *Sahifat al-Nur*, vol. 5, p. 25.
2 Ibid., vol. 1, p. 180.
3 Khomeini, *Al- Hukuma*, p. 107.

revelation (*wahiy*), either directly or indirectly. The deputy of the Infallible Imam is the *wali al-faqih* who satisfies certain preconditions and qualifications. His knowledge is derived from the Shari'a and infallible Sunna; his aim is not confined to clarifying the injunctions, but rather its application with his capacity to draw these injunctions from jurisprudence and Shari'a.[1]

Thus, the theory of the imamate, especially from a political perspective, emanates from the idea of the continuation of the phenomenon of Prophethood in the esoteric sense of imamate and *wilayat*.

Sadreddinne al-Shirazi argued for the continuation in the phenomenon of Prophethood in the imamate and the *wilaya*: 'Although *al-wahiy* has been severed, Prophethood and the essence of the message were not severed ... that is why the *mujtahid* and the Imam do not bear the title of the Prophet or Messenger.'[2] Al-Shirazi considered that the *mujtahid* and the Imam are the divine heirs of *ahl al-bayt*.

From the aforementioned, it could be concluded that the background of the theory of Islamic government is rooted in and is an extension of the Prophethood and *wilaya*: 'The Islamic state is a Prophetic phenomenon, it is the culmination of the Prophetic world that has started in a certain era in human life; however, it is not a human creation, but only an understanding of the religious text from human perspective. Since man is in need of spiritual guidance and revelation, God sent his prophets to help actualise the potential of the people. That is why a necessary ingredient is the belief in the divine and prophetic leadership is conceived as divine intervention in the destiny of the community and people. Indeed, if God has sent all his messengers and prophets to a certain [same] place and time, then they would not have disagreed.'[3]

Jawadi Amili, in his book *Absolute Wilaya and Tyranny*, argued that when we talk about the comprehensive *wilayat* or absolute *wilaya* (*wilaya mutlaqa*) we mean that the *shar'* or religious consensus has endowed the *wali al-faqih* with the authority of explaining the divine laws as well as administering them and managing the affairs of the Islamic *umma*, so *wilayat* means the management and the implementation of the affairs of the *umma*. The comprehensiveness of the *wilayat* means that the *wali al-faqih* should be committed to the divine regulations to ensure their implementation during the period of the Great Occultation. However, it does not mean in any way that the absolute or comprehensive liberty of the *faqih* is elevated to becoming the embodiment of the law and its application, in the sense that the *wilayat* becomes a form of dictatorship. And the *wali* has neither the legal authority nor the prerogative to interfere in the personal affairs or private matters of the people.

---

1   Al- Khomeini, *Wilayat al-Faqih*, pp. 8–14.
2   Sadreddine al-Shirazi, *Al-Shawhid Al-Rabawiyya*, p. 823.
3   Trad Hamadeh, *Qital Al-Akhar,* p. 29.

The *wali al-faqih* is assigned with three basic official functions: (1) issuing religious injunctions and informing people about them (*ifta'*); (2) acting as a chief justice (*qadi*); (3) producing the injunctions (*wala'i ahkam*) that have to do with the mandate of his *wilaya* on political and administrative affairs. However, the mandate of the *wali al-faqih*, even under the *wala'i* injunctions, does not allow him to interfere in social affairs unless the matter directly pertains to the political sphere. The *fiqh* and the laws of Islam regulate the authority and the prerogatives of the *faqih*, and not the *faqih* himself.

Is the *wali al-faqih* above the law, or could he be held accountable for his actions before the people?

Every incumbent to political authority in the Islamic order has to be under the law and accountable before the people from the stance of the Qur'anic injunction of enjoining the good and prohibiting the evil, which is also applicable to the *faqih* himself. Assuming the function of general supervision, the Council of Experts has founded a committee called the 'Committee of Inspection' which supervises the work of the leadership and conveys the results of its work in an open session of the Council of Experts. The experts, who are considered the elected body from the people that has the function to elect the *rahbar* and supervise the affairs of the leadership, call upon the leader to clarify certain issues by way of question and answer session. If the *wali al-faqih* produces reliable and convincing answers then he remains in office, and if he fails to do so, then he is immediately deposed and the search begins for a new *faqih*.[1]

CONCLUSION

Although certain prerogatives of the *wali al-faqih* seem to be tyrannical, the majority of these prerogatives are curbed through checks and balances by way of strict constitutional and regulatory institutions where the populace is meant to have the final say. There is a strong mechanism of safety valves and effective limitations to the power of the *rahbar* guaranteed by the myriad leading authorities. This sophisticated institutional apparatus is composed of many councils with different prerogatives, yet all contain within them strong and cohesive mechanisms of accountability, transparency, probity and meritocracy, as opposed to the spoils system that is prevalent in so many Third World countries.

---

1 Ayatollah Javadi Amuli, *Wilayat al-Faqih: Wilayat al-Faqaha wal'adala* (The Governance of the Jurisprudent: Mandate and Justice),Beirut 2002, pp. 183 ff.

CHAPTER SIX

Islamism and Republicanism

BACKGROUND

There is a political debate in Iran that employs a religious jargon, whereby the processes of legitimisation are based upon religious foundations. This debate relates to the principles of legislation (*usul al-hukm*).

In March 1979, popular sovereignty was exercised in a public referendum whereby 98.2 percent of the Iranians had chosen the Islamic Republic as their preferred system of governance, which represents an overwhelming majority. The main bone of contention of that referendum was its incapability to reconcile the concepts of Islamism and republicanism; in the framework of a system of governance, a grey area remained between framework and content. As such, the Constitution, adopted by referendum in December 1979 and again in its amended form in August 1989, prepared the ground for establishing institutions based on elections, and at the same time founded parallel institutions based upon appointment (*tansib*).

For a while, the debate in the Iranian public sphere had been focused on three basic constitutional elements: the drafting of the Constitution; the Constitution in its own right; and the way of its exegesis.

THE DRAFTING OF THE CONSTITUTION

Perhaps the circumstances in which the Constitution was written would make the best introduction to a discussion about it. Shortly after the triumph of the Islamic Revolution in Iran, a committee formed under the interim administration of Mehdi Bazargan produced a draft constitution that was heavily modelled on the 1958 Constitution of the French Republic.[1] Hasan Habibi, a doctor of law and sociology, was a member of the committee and is considered the main author of this early version of the Constitution. The committee was comprised of mostly legal experts and professors of law, the most renowned of whom were Professors Abdol Karim Lahiji and Homayoun Katuzian.

Building on the Iranian constitutional history, this committee replaced the constitutional council existent in the French Constitution with the Council of Guardians. Likewise, the first Constitution in Iran's history in 1906 had introduced a similar body with the mission of revising the legislation of the parliament in order to study whether it tallied with Islamic legislation according to the Ja'fari doctrine. The same body would later be given another mission, which was to inspect the concordance of legislation with the Constitution. Some respected academics and scholars would attribute the ensuing disputes which ravaged Iran on the political level to this clause which gave the Council of Guardians extra prerogatives and enabled it to carry the two-fold mission of *shar'i* and constitutional inspection.

The Constitution that was produced by the committee of legal experts was thus a slightly modified version of a Western-style republican constitution. Its aim was to preserve the role of the *fuqaha* in supervising the *shar'i* perspective of the laws, and maintaining their significant stance among the people, rather than in the system of power. In other words, the logic of the draft Constitution was of a republican nature in the sense that it was a constitution that did not discriminate among the citizens as individuals, groups or classes, and did not allocate special privileges to any individual, group, or class of people.

Imam Khomeini was prepared to submit this version of the Constitution virtually unmodified to the public for referendum, but this procedure drew criticism from leftist groups, who demanded that the draft be submitted for review to a constitutional assembly. An election was therefore held to choose members of the first Assembly of Experts, a committee that would review and revise the draft constitution. Candidacy in the elections was open to any Iranian, provided that they had not been members SAVAK, the feared intelligence and security agency of the Shah's toppled regime. A group of seventy-three clerics and law experts was elected and convened on 18 August 1979 under the chairmanship of the late Ayatollah Hussein-Ali Montazeri and deputy chairmanship of Ayatollah Mohammad Behishti to review the draft.[2]

---

1   The provisional government published this early draft on 18 June 1979.
2   The election was held on 3 August 1979. The elected assembly was comprised of sixty-nine Muslims, while the remaining representatives were elected from Christian, Jewish and

The assembly considered the draft to be un-Islamic. While Imam Khomeini had earlier reviewed the draft and commented on it, he neither considered it un-Islamic, nor did he make any comment on *wilayat al-faqih* in particular. According to Khomeini's aides, he did not judge that it was the due time to install that *wilayat*. But it was the assembly that insisted on certain revisions, and thus the draft was ratified along with the extra prerogatives which were given to the Council of Guardians, the most salient of which was to have a say in supervising the elections. This mechanism was employed later as a policy tool to screen candidates in such a way so that the *rahbar*, and the state institutions over which he wields power, would remain dominant in the nascent republican system. (I will argue later that the mere presence of constitutional impediments acts as a safeguard and check and balance on the emerging process of democratisation in Iran).

After the assembly's revisions were incorporated, Khomeini lent his open support to the revised Constitution. Given the prevailing circumstances at the time, and taking into consideration the transcendental charisma of Imam Khomeini, and the widespread belief that everything the Imam said should be obeyed from his normative stance as deputy of the Hidden Imam who founded an Islamic state, it was difficult for anyone to give way to the opposition which was voicing objections to the suggested formula. Also, one should take into consideration the collective memory of the Iranian people that had been burdened for decades by the coercion of an autocratic regime that tried to weed out the democratic processes, which started taking shape after the seeds of the constitutional revolution of 1906 began to ferment. The subsequent regimes of the shahs used the iron fist of the state to curb religious institutions as well as civil institutions in civil society by the use of security forces, intelligence, and even the army.

From this perspective, Imami Shi'ism regarded the state as illegitimate in the age of the Greater Occultation. Against this backdrop, a new dawn emerged with the victory of the Islamic Revolution in 1979, and the euphoria as well as the ripple effect of the assumption of power of a theocratic-'democratic' regime.

THE ESTABLISHMENT OF THE CONSTITUTION IN ITS OWN RIGHT

The Iranian Constitution establishes two main types of bodies. The first are republican and based upon universal suffrage through the ballot box. This

---

Zoroastrian minorities. In terms of their educational background, 41 were mujtahid, 12 were hojetalislam, 10 were legal professors, 6 held master's degrees and 7 held bachelor's degrees. The Constitution produced by the assembly was completed on 15 November and later put to a referendum on 2 December 1979, when it passed by over 98 percent of the vote.

democratic process leads to the establishment of the institutions of the presidency, the Shura Council, the parliament, and the provincial as well as municipal *shura* councils. The second body assumes authority by way of appointment through state institutions, presided over by the *rahbar*, who is appointed by the Council of Experts. This latter body is elected by the people and has the full mandate over the institutions that are the product of this process. However, even the process of appointment embodies a democratic practice whereby the election of the Council of Experts and the way they elect the *rahbar* do not amount to mere appointment, which might be construed as a tyrannical practice. According to the text of the Constitution, the articles that deal with the number of the experts, the characteristics of the incumbents, and the way of electing them should be laid down by the jurists in the first session of the Council of Guardians. Here decisions are taken by majority vote, and in the end they are ratified by the *rahbar*. Also, the Constitution stipulates that any amendment, reconsideration of the law, and approval of decisions that relate to the duties of the experts are the sole prerogative of the Council of Experts. In other words, the Council of Experts operates according to a law that is not promulgated by the legislative branch. Rather, the Council of Guardians that issues the law is a monitoring body over the legislative authority, and the role of making draft legislation is incumbent upon half of its members, the six jurists who are appointed by the *rahbar*. The approval of their appointment is then granted through a majority vote, whereby the issuing of the law of electing the Council of Experts requires the approval of four of them. In spite of that, the Council of Experts has the sole prerogative of electing the *rahbar*.

Article 107 of the Constitution stipulates that the experts screen all the incumbents who satisfy the stringent qualifications of the *faqih* by way of consultations and careful deliberation. When they agree on the most knowledgeable in the jurisprudential issues, Islamic injunctions as well as political and social issues, they choose him to be the leader.

The *rahbar* who has been chosen has the prerogative of establishing general policy guidelines of the Islamic Republic, only after mandatory consultation with the Council of Expediency, an advisory body whose members he himself appoints. Also, the *rahbar* has the prerogative to appoint the head of judiciary, who in turn wields influence in electing the Council of Experts, which is elected by the people, since he nominates half the number of the incumbents to this council.

In brief, the two main elected bodies of the presidency and the Islamic Shura Council (parliament) are presided over by two other appointed bodies: the *rahbar*, and the Council of Expediency. The *rahbar* is the ultimate wielder of authority in the Islamic Republic, and the Council of Expediency is the body that judges any discord that might emerge between the parliament and the Council of

Guardians, which has the *shar'i* and constitutional right to voice its opposition to laws issued by the parliament.

As mentioned, from the inception of the Islamic Republic, intellectuals and members of the political community were preoccupied with a system and a mode of elected government compatible with and demonstrably derivative from the strictures of Islam. Historical studies have indicated that the concept of republicanism, as an imagined and cultural community, has penetrated the Iranian political culture for more than 150 years, as early as the Qajari period.[1] The Islamic Republic represents a new theory in the sphere of existing political systems, which were labelled as theocratic democracy. Establishing an Islamic Republic has to meticulously delineate the role of *wilayat al-faqih* as a bridge builder between republicanism and Islamism.[2]

The edifice of the Constitution of the Islamic Republic, like some old mixed constitutions, is an amalgamation of different theocratic elements of representative democracy, aristocratic or the rule of the elite (the *ulama*), and direct democracy, which is exercised in the election of the president and the parliament. In addition to these, the regime of the Islamic Republic has special ideological and structural traits of the state, such as the comprehensiveness of the authority, on the one hand, and some democratic notions on the other.[3] Scholars have addressed this apparent dilemma and their opinions are portrayed below.

According to Olivier Roy, the Islamic Republic of Iran, since its inception at the time of the revolution, has built upon an organic linkage between two kinds of legitimacy: religious and political, as conveyed through the conception of *wilayat al-faqih*. This implied that the higher authority of the Islamic Republic, the *rahbar*, has to be chosen from the highest religious authorities, so that he can also be the political leader. Roy contends that the amalgamation of *wilayat* and Islamism has led to serious complications in the political system.[4]

According to the Iranian political analyst Muhammad Husayn Hafizian, in his article, 'Theoretical approach to Republicanism and Islamism in Iran,'[5] the conception of the Islamic Republic and the interpretation of the meanings of republicanism and Islamism are some of the most hotly debated issues among religious scholars and politicians in contemporary Iran. In order to asses the viability of the concordance between republicanism and Islamism or their incompatibility,

---

1 Sa'id Hajarian, 'Republicanism as a Framework for Freedom', in *Sunlight Monthly*, vol. 13, March 2002, pp. 4 ff.
2 Habib Sa'i, 'Islamic Republic?', in *Iranian Echo Monthly*, 3.10, July/August 2002, pp. 10–11.
3 Husayn Bashiriyyeh, *A Contribution in Iranian Political Sociology: The Stage of the Islamic Republic*, Tehran 2002, pp. 50–51.
4 Olivier Roy, 'The Crisis of Religious Legitimacy in Iran', in *Middle East Journal*, 53.2, Spring 1999, p. 201.
5 *Iranian Arab Affairs Quarterly*, issues 10 and 11, Fall 2004 and Winter 2005, pp. 9–27.

the author begins by outlining the basic principles of the Islamic Republic, and discusses how the Islamic Republic came into being after the victory of the revolution. Two views seem prominent: the first stresses the incompatibility between republicanism and Islamism, while the other emphasises harmony and concordance between the two. Holders of the first view argue that the populace in a republican government controls its own destiny and decides on a certain way of life in society as well as legislating laws. However, in the Islamic government only God legislates, or the concept of *hakimiyya* is prominent, which results in granting very little sovereignty to the people. In contrast, holders of the second view argue that God's will is conveyed in the will of the *umma*. The author concludes that the relationship between republicanism and Islamism in Iran does not necessarily constitute concordance on a theoretical level, rather on a practical level.

As an interpolation, there seems to be an interesting concordance between Sunnism and Shi'ism on the issue of *wilayat al-umma*, although traditionally the expression of God's will through the will of the *umma* most likely informs the core point where Sunnism differs from Shi'ism. In the Sunni approach the will of the *umma* is expressed through the *ulama*, as most traditionalists would argue, or through some form of popular expression, for example, elections or referenda, as some modernists would suggest. The Shi'i approach is focused on the role of the Imam or his representative (e.g. Ayatollahs, marja's or *wilayat al-faqih*). That then suggests an interesting reflection about the *hakimiyya* (God's governance), as the idea was developed by Sunni scholars Mawdudi and Qutb, namely that at least on the surface this approach seems closer to Shi'i views than to traditional Sunni views.

According to Imam Khomeini, the Islamic government is the government that the populace longs for, but this does not amount to a civil government, rather a religious one that is chosen by the Muslim populace among other forms of government. Khomeini clarified this by characterising the government as a 'religious government', and 'in accordance with God's governance', and the government that he longs for, is 'governed by the righteous and the pious'.[1]

When Imam Khomeini called for the establishment of an Islamic Republic, he clarified that the concept of republicanism is a clear concept to the populace, and it entails the necessity of taking the public opinion into consideration. Islamism means commitment to Islamic principles. Khomeini posed the rhetorical question, 'Do you accept that the government be republican, and reject it being Islamic?' He concluded that as long as public opinion is Islamic, then the republican nature of the government does not contradict its Islamism.[2]

---

1   Khomeini, *Al-Kawthr*: A Collection Of Imam Khomeini's Speeches, vol. 3, Tehran 1996, pp. 12–13 and 339.
2   Ibid., 431.

THE CONCEPTS OF REPUBLICANISM AND ISLAMISM IN THE ISLAMIC REPUBLIC

The term 'republicanism' is used as a synonym of the 'state', as Plato entitled his book *The Republic*. Since the seventeenth century, republicanism came to imply a state without a king. Some definitions stress that only those countries that resort to direct or indirect elections for the state's pyramidal structures are labeled as republics. In spite of that, almost every country in the world that is not headed by a king labels itself as a republic.[1]

Republican government has been defined as: 'a government where people exercise direct sovereignty or elect their representatives in such a way that succession in the pyramid structure of the state is not hereditary. The terminology of the presidency should be confined to constitutional prohibitions, and the election of the president takes place from the stance of the public good.'[2]

Republicanism has been defined as: 'the personal conviction of the citizen that his or her country should be republican and not kingship',[3] or that republicanism entails 'buttressing republican government as opposed to hereditary or tyrannical governments'. By republican government it is meant that people decide their destiny in such a way that the running of state authorities by the populace and their representatives emanates from the sovereignty of the people.

According to Sayyid Muhammad Hashimi what distinguishes republicanism from monarchy are the following principles: first, a government that is directly elected from the populace (direct republican democracy) or indirectly through the parliament (representative republican democracy). Second, the tenure of the president is limited to a few years and his reelection for more than two consecutive terms is not feasible. Third, the ruler does not enjoy special prerogatives and privileges as compared to others; he is under the law like any other citizen and held fully accountable for all his actions. Fourth, the ruler entails dual legal and political responsibilities, as opposed to monarchy.'[4]

Other principles of republican government are that it is a government where people have the right of self-determination; where the state's power is governed by the people or their representatives; and where all higher authorities originate from people's interests (*masalih*). In this government, an incumbent cannot assume official responsibility unless he/she has an official delegation from the people, who will hold him responsible and accountable for his actions. As such, republican government does not allow any person to obtain a special authority or

---

1   Ian McLane, ed., *Oxford Political Dictionary*, Oxford 1996, pp. 428–429.
2   Ali Agha Bahkshi, *The Dictionary of Political Science*, Tehran 1995, p. 291.
3   McLane, *Oxford Political Dictionary*, p. 429.
4   Sayyid Muhammad Hashimi, *The Constitutional Law for The Islamic Republic Of Iran: General Principles and The Pillar of The System*, vol. 1, Tehran 1995, pp. 54 ff.

prerogative, even if he/she belongs to a certain governing elite; all people are free and equal in a republican society.[1]

In other words, Islamism needs elaboration, but not on the basis of defining Islamic government or Islamism as a religious trend. Rather, Islamic government has been defined as a government that executes the administrative affairs of the state and the community based upon the laws and stipulations of Islam: 'In the Islamic Republic, the authority over the people and the community is only for God (*hakimiyyat*). It is not allowed for any individual or community to govern people. From an Islamic perspective, governance does not emanate from an ascribed status or the hegemony of a certain group or people. Rather, governance is the embodiment of a political cause for the community of believers, which organises itself in order to pave the way towards the ultimate goal, the ultimate principle, God Almighty. It includes the basic principles that the Islamic government aims to achieve: the principle of *tawhid* and the rejection of paganism; establishing justice; weeding out oppression; enforcing the tenets of Islam and the spiritual purity and guidance of the populace; equality before the law; and establishing independence in all cultural, political, economical and military spheres.'[2]

The Islamic Republic entails a republican government based on Islam. Republicanism encompasses all the populace, and republican government implies that all people have a say in establishing the government that has a leading role in the administration of the community and the government by electing the ministers and participating in parliamentary life and referenda. The Islamism of government implies that all the political, cultural, military laws and legislations should be based upon Islamic principles.[3]

According to Hashimi, the basic principles of the Islamic Republic are the following:

— Article 6 of the Constitution stipulates that governance and administration of the country are based upon popular vote. Article 114 stipulates the election of the *rahbar* indirectly, and the election of the president by the populace. Article 123 advises that the formation of the cabinet has to pass a vote of confidence by the Shura Council.

— Article 114 adds that the tenure of the *rahbar* is unlimited, while that of the president is four years, subject to one term renewal, and the cabinet serves the same period.

— Article 107 stresses that the *rahbar* is under the law and it emphasises a separation of powers and checks and balances: 'The leader is equal with the rest of the people of the country in the eyes of the law.'

---

1   Mustapha Rahimi, *The Principles of Republican Government*, Tehran 1979, pp. 70–80.
2   Ibid., pp. 173 ff.
3   Ibid., p. 174.

— The Constitution is stringent in terms of political accountability, such that any incriminating evidence of negligence could prompt prosecution in a court of law. This applies not only to the ministers (as stipulated in Articles 137 and 142), and to the president (Articles 110, 122, 134, 140 and142), but also the *rahbar* (Articles 111 and 142). The aforementioned conveys that the Iranian political system embeds, in principle, the major pillars of republicanism.[1]

1. The Background to the Formation of the Islamic Republic

After the victory of the Islamic Revolution, heated debates centred on the drafting of the Constitution in such a way as to fuse the concepts of Islamism and republicanism. Other debates dealt with the issue of supreme authority in this nascent republic. In turn, social forces found expression in communicating their viewpoints in the domain of governance, and voiced their intellectual perspectives on the abstract conception of the Islamic Republic. However, after the referendum on the Islamic Republic, two basic principles became salient:

— The government should be republican from the following three perspectives: its basic formation, administrative organisation, and secondary governmental ordinances.

— The republic should be established within the basic Islamic framework, in such a way that it should be in complete harmony with Islamic conceptions.

The differences in interpreting these conceptions and basic principles result in different versions of republicanism in our contemporary world.[2]

After the advent of the Islamic Revolution, the nature of the would-be established government was not clear to the populace, even to some of the *ulama*. Also, the basic principles were lacking in clarity, and so were the norms that make up the founding pillars of Islamic republicanism, as preached by Imam Khomeini. In this respect, legal expert Homayoun Katuzian wrote, 'Republicanism is not an alien concept to the people, and Islam was the official state religion for centuries. It is unjust to claim that the populace aspires for something totally new that needs explanation.'[3] In spite of that, the aforementioned two conceptions were fused to the extent that some argued that republicanism stands in opposition to Islamic government, and that the Islamic Republic is built upon an internal contradiction. In order to circumvent this ambiguity, critics suggested that it would be better for the revolution to choose another slogan instead of republicanism. Others have voiced their preference to call it a 'democratic republic'. These are not semantic discords; rather, those who see that Islamism is an added word to

---

1   Hashimi, *Constitutional Law*, etc., pp. 54–55.
2   Nasir Katuzian, *The Principles of Public Law,* Tehran 1998, pp. 203 ff.
3   The Safavid Dynasty (1502-1722) adopted Islam as its official religion.

republicanism support a republic from a Western perspective, while those who support a democratic republic, imply a socialist republic based on the Eastern model. From here, the misunderstanding springs.[1]

2. Is there any Contradiction between the Two Concepts of 'Republicanism' and 'Islamism', or Is It Possible to Fuse them together?

A few months before the advent of the Islamic Revolution, and under the impact of Imam Khomeini, the Iranian people's quest shifted from an Islamic government to an Islamic Republic. An intellectual debate has ensued ever since the revolutionary movement in Iran was formed during the years 1978–9. The discussion centred on establishing an Islamic government as an alternative to the monarchy. However, the arrival of Imam Khomeini in France on 12 October 1978 and his subsequent return to Tehran on 1 February 1979 put an end to the ongoing debate by identifying the Islamic government as the Islamic Republic.[2]

The success of the Islamic Revolution and the establishment of the Islamic Republic and the Islamic government, as envisaged by the Shi'i legislation, have all made the Shi'i political legislation undergo a profound transformation in both politics and the state's affairs.[3]

In spite of all the other traits that characterise the Islamic Republic in Iran, the mere idea of establishing a political system under the banner of the Islamic Republic constituted a pioneering experience in the modern world.

A few months before the revolution, Imam Khomeini presented some significant points through his dialogue with the French press:

— The Islamic Republic is a government based upon Islamic principles and Islam is the main foundation of its constitution.
— The Islamic government is a government based upon popular vote. Republicanism means relying upon the voices of the majority of the people.
— The form of government is republican, as is known everywhere.
— The Islamic Republic is an independent country, especially in formulating its foreign policy.
— The Islamic Republic is a government based upon social justice.
— Islamic Republic is a government based upon freedom and is in complete opposition to autocratic government.
— It is incumbent upon the *ulama* to safeguard the laws in the Islamic Republic.[4]

---

1   Nasir Katuzian, *The Principles of Public Law,* Tehran 1998, pp. 203 ff.
2   Khomeini, *Sahifat Al-Nur,* vol. 2, Tehran 1995, p. 36.
3   Muhsen Kadivar, *Nazariyyat al-Dawla fi al-Tashri' al-shi'i* (Theories of State in the Shi'i Legislation), Tehran: Nay Publications, 1997, pp. 25–26.
4   Muhsin Kadivar, *The Government of Wilayat Al-Faqih,* Tehran 1998, pp. 171–174.

Imam Khomeini clarified that 'republicanism implies majority vote by the populace, and Islamism denotes a governmental order based upon the Shari'a.'[1] He
also stressed that 'Islamic government is based completely upon the votes of the
umma in such a way that every Iranian exercises self-determination for himself
and for his country by going to the ballot box.'[2]

And since the absolute majority of this *umma* are Muslims then the laws and
Islamic norms should be abided by, in all respects.'[3] He also added, 'The govern-
ment of the Islamic Republic is republican like other republics, but its law is
Islamic law.'[4]

From the aforementioned and other Khomeini declarations, it could be
deduced that, 'The opinion of the *shar'i* Imam is the participation of the people
in bestowing legitimacy to the Islamic government. The Islamic Republic is based
upon this foundation, as its Islamic Constitution conveys.'[5]

In the wake of the Islamic Revolution, and in an attempt to extrapolate why
the future government should be Islamic, Katuzian argued that 'Because people
longed for that from the beginning, the revolution was labelled as such, and the
revolutionary government requires that.'

Katuzian contends that Islam is compatible with republicanism. The Iranian
umma longs for justice and for changing its life, and this requires a well-thought
out economic and political plan. However, this plan is lacking in the conception of republicanism. Islam is the main trait and vigour of a future cultural and
economic revolution. Alienating Islam from republicanism would gradually lead
to deterioration in the spiritual and revolutionary notions of the government.[6]

According to Sa'id Hajarian,[7] the Islamic Republic blends Islamism with
republicanism without distorting any of Islam's basic principles. According to
Hajarian, Imam Khomeini considered the Islamic Republic similar to all other
republics; however, the functions that emanate from the legitimacy that governs
it are Islamic. Hajarian believes that the Islamic Republic constitutes a social contract between the government and the governed based upon establishing mutual
recognition and the rights and duties of every party to the contract. However, if
any party fails to deliver, then the contract is no longer binding.[8]

---

1   Khomeini, *Sahifat Al-Nur*, vol. 2, p. 545.
2   This seems like the Rousseauian notion of 'By giving yourself to all you give yourself to none'. See
    Rousseau's social contract.
3   Khomeini, *Sahifat Al-Nur*, vol. 3, pp. 70–71.
4   Khomeini, *Sahifat Al-Nur*, vol. 2, p. 351.
5   Mahmud Barakishian, 'Republicanism from Imam Khomeini's Perspective', in *Sunlight
    Monthly*, vol. 19, October 2002, p. 57.
6   Katuzian, *Principles*, p. 121.
7   A reformist intellectual and former advisor to Khatami.
8   Hajarian, 'Republicanism as a Framework for Freedom', in *Sunlight Monthly* 13, March 2002.
    The previous analysis bears a striking resemblance to the Lockian concept of fiduciary trust in his

3. Republicanism and Islamism in the Constitution of the Islamic Republic

In most constitutions of the world there is a special section dedicated to the rights of the nation in terms of sovereignty. Irrespective of how the state abides by Islamic concepts, in the Constitution of the Islamic Republic in Iran, the *umma* is more than qualified to uphold the rights by which the state should abide. Article 56 of the Constitution states the following: 'Absolute sovereignty over the world and the people is for God, Who made incumbent upon the people to control their social destiny, without allowing anyone from depriving the people from this holy right or exploiting this right in order to favour personal interest and gain. The *umma* executes this right that is bestowed upon it from God by means specified in other articles.' It is worth mentioning that this article contrasts with liberal theories that characterise Western political systems where sovereignty is for the people; the theoretical basis of the sovereignty for the people in the Islamic Republic is different. It is absolute sovereignty to God. It is natural to have safeguards, so that people should act and behave according to the Islamic injunctions of the Shari'a and in ways that are in harmony with the Islamic laws.

The stipulations that are present in the aforementioned article rule out any individual or autocratic authority, since sovereignty belongs to the *umma*, and no single individual or group can appropriate it, divide it, [1] or confiscate any part of it.

Article 107 of the Constitution stipulates that the *rahbar* is equal to others before the law, and is under the law. However, Article 57 which stipulates absolute trusteeship should be interpreted in the light of Articles 56, 58, and 59, so that there will not be any contradiction between the absolute nature of trusteeship of *wilayat al-faqih* and people's sovereignty as bestowed by God upon his people. *Wilayat al-faqih* is bound by four constitutional safeguards:
— Article 4: The Islamic principles and commandments.
— Article107: Legislated laws.
— Article 156: People's sovereignty and social destiny as bestowed by God.
— The republican requirements for a government supported by the people.

Bearing the aforementioned in mind, it is a mistake to conflate *wilayat al-faqih* and absolute sovereignty as is the case with the tyrannical and totalitarian theories. In other words, *wilayat* does not amount to sovereignty. Advocates of absolute rule consider that everything depends upon the ruler's whims. Iran's post-revolutionary Constitution does not represent a constitution of a

---

social contract, where government as a trustee has duties, and people as truster and beneficiary have rights. See John Locke's *Two Treaties on Civil Government*.

1 Katuzian, *Principles*, p. 201. This seems similar to Jean Boudin's concept of sovereignty that is 'absolute, perpetual and indivisible'.

republican government that has been accommodated to Shi'i Islam; rather, it seems that it is a genuine or authentic Islamic constitution in which the principles of Shi'i Islam have been fused. Also, in this institution national sovereignty and parliamentary representation were not mentioned as fundamental features of the Islamic Republic; probably that is why the republican nature of the regime was less manifest than its Islamic character.[1]

4. The Apparent Contradiction between Republicanism and Islamism

Some social scientists consider that the relationship between republicanism and Islamism is inevitably one of opposition. According to Katuzian, these scholars consider that in a republican government the people has the final say in terms of their way of life in the community, and by way of legislating rules and regulations. However, in the Islamic government, God is the ultimate legislator and sovereign. People are governed by divine ordinances and they do not have the authority to legislate laws. Katuzian questions how the government could be both republican and Islamic at the same time. How could it fuse these two diametrically opposed conceptions together? This reasoning is based upon Aristotelean logic which clearly states the impossibility of merging two opposites or contradictions. Upholders of this theory aim at depicting an unequivocal distinction between the conceptions of republicanism and Islamism, presenting them as opposing entities, which are contrary to independent analysis.[2]

Sayyid Muhammad Hashimi considers that republicanism is based upon people's participation, private and public freedoms, and decision making by the majority. This kind of participation and freedoms requires respecting the beliefs of all the incumbents; and the real chance to establish constructive relationships and harmonisation of different beliefs. In most societies, adherents of different religions and holders of variant political ideals are clearly distinguished from each other. However, the common traits among these are tolerance, coexistence, mutual cooperation among intellectuals, and freedom to found parties and associations. Everything that is not in conformity with the aforementioned might contradict republicanism. From this perspective, it seems that the distinguishing trait of Islamic ideology upholds popular participation in decision making and administration by majority vote, which is one of the basic pillars of republicanism that is incompatible with dictatorship.[3]

---

1   Sai'd Amir Arjomand, 'The Constitution of the Islamic Republic', in *Encyclopedia Iranica*, vol. 6, 1993, pp. 152–154.
2   Katuzian, pp. 108 ff.
3   Hashimi, pp. 55–56.

5. Divergence between Wilayat al-Faqih and Republican Government
Muhsin Kadivar lists the points of divergence between *wilayat al-faqih* and republican government as follows:
— In republican government, people are all equal in the public domain. Nevertheless, people are unequal with their superiors in the government of *wilayat*.
— In republicanism, people have inalienable rights and they are active in the public domain. In the government of *wilayat*, people have a lower status and they are barred from administering their affairs directly.
— In republicanism, the governor is on an equal par with the populace. However, in the government of *wilayat*, the governor is the trustee of the people.
— In republicanism, the governor is elected by the people, while the governor in the government of *wilayat* is appointed by God Almighty.
— Governance in republicanism is temporary and for a certain period, while in the government of *wilayat*, governance is for life, except in the case of resignation or loss of qualifications.
— In republicanism, the governor is held accountable before the people, while in a government of *wilayat*, the governor is not responsible before the people.
— In republicanism, the governor's authority is bound by the law; in the government of *wilayat*, the governor is above the law.
— In republicanism, the *shar'i* law is not a basic principle for administering society. However, in the government of *wilayat*, the governor is indispensable for governance.
— Republican government is a covenant and a social contract between the ruler and his subjects; however, the government of *wilayat* does not entail a covenant, rather a basic principle and the will issued by the divine legislator.
— In republicanism, the general will of the populace is the basis of administering society, while the government of *wilayat* is based upon the administration of society by the whimsical and personal vision of the governor.[1]

Yet another social scientist by the name of Hossein Bashiriyeh also believes in the opposition between republicanism and democracy, on the one hand, and Islamism on the other. However, he bases his argument upon the conduct of the Islamic Republic and not on theoretical aspects. Bashiriyeh adumbrates the factors that played a leading role in the alteration and demise of national sovereignty. He considers that the Constitution has relegated sovereignty and law-making to God, in spite of the apparent contradiction between this concept and the democratic aspects of the Constitution, which, as he claims, was not preconceived in the beginning of the revolution. As time elapsed, the practical drawbacks

---

1   Kadivar, *The Government of Wilayat Al Faqih*, Tehran: Nay Publications, 1998, pp. 207–208.

to this opposition started to gradually ripen, leading to dualism in sovereignty in the Islamic Republic. Because of this, the possibility for establishing people's sovereignty became limited within the narrow confines of the Constitution of the Islamic Republic and the structure of the existing political system.[1]

6. The Concordance between Islamism and Republicanism

Katuzian stressed the possibility of solving the apparent contradiction between the conception of republicanism and Islamism. He argued that republicanism stipulates the form of government while the concept of Islamism is an existential contextualisation because the Muslim does not ignore his religious duties and does not sacrifice the truth for the sake of benefit.[2]

From another perspective, it seems that there is a need for a legislative body and a consultative body in order to debate public issues in the republican government to which every framework might belong. Moreover, the avoidance of despotism is the main stipulation to accept the form of this government. After Islam has accepted the concept of consultation, it accompanied that by the establishment of an independent legislative body.

It might be that the person who is entrusted with all creatures might turn aside to enjoy the pleasures of the here and now, as tyrants tend to do. In that case, the etymology of the Islamic Republic might imply that the deputies are not free in conducting consultations and legislating laws in this republic since they are tied to the content of the republic that is Islam. Further, the deputies would not take any decision that does not conform with Islamic concepts.[3]

Another contention advanced by those who are arguing for opposition between republicanism and Islamism is that if the parliament in a republican government cannot legislate any law in opposition to the principles of Shari'a, does not that imply a breakdown of national sovereignty and an opposition to the republic? And does not the Islamic conception distort the notion of sovereignty and the foundation of the republic? Theocratic authority neither encroaches upon the general notions of Islam nor is it in opposition to the conception of republicanism, because God's will, in the final stage, will be epitomised by the umma's satisfaction. God is strongly with the community without any need for intercession. The Prophet destroyed all the statues and pagan worship in order to completely obliterate intercession, in such a way, so that there would not be any barrier between the creator and the creature. That is why it is not feasible for a person or a group of persons to govern people in the name of sanctified

---

1   Husayn Bashiriyyeh, *A Contribution in Iranian Political Sociology: The Stage of the Islamic Republic*, Tehran: Contemporary Outlook Publication, 2002, pp. 60–62.
2   Katuzian, pp. 108 ff.
3   Katuzian, pp. 108–109.

sovereignty and consider himself an existential necessity to the consultation and opinion of the *umma*. Thus, sovereignty is a gift and a divine deposition bestowed upon people, so that they can exercise self-determination through consultation in conformity with Islamic teachings. Katuzian refutes those who claim that Islamism and republicanism stand in contradiction to each other, by posing the following two rhetorical questions: 'Why is the absence of legislation barring human rights violations and the preclusion of Marxist-Leninist ideology in the constitutions of Western countries not considered a violation to the fundamentals of the republican government or national sovereignty? However, when it comes to certain Islamic concepts, then the contradiction becomes evident under the pretext that the concepts of Islamism and republicanism cannot merge. And why are the Americans and the French allowed to put specific safeguards in their constitutions and it precludes the parliament from encroaching upon these principles, while the Iranians are not allowed to adopt similar measures?'[1]

Concerning the concept of the Islamic Republic, Ayatollah Murtada Muttahari stated: 'The Islamic Republic implies a government whose head executive is elected by the populace for a certain tenure and its content is Islamic. However, the mistake that some people commit by claiming that this conception is vague, originates from a blunder in conflating the right of national sovereignty as an equivalent to a lack in ideology, intellectual thinking ... However, the expression of republicanism cannot be a real source of change. In addition, it does not result in opposition when another concept such as Islamism is added to republicanism. The Islamic characterisation does not by itself render the republic class-oriented.'[2]

Further evidence of the concordance between republicanism and Islamism could be displayed as follows: 'Although the principles of democracy and republicanism are adopted through people's participation, general freedoms and equality among people, the execution of democracy through consensus seem impossible. That is why reaching a decision through majority vote is introduced as a standard to preserve people's rights and interests. Even though it is necessary to abide by the decisions of the majority, the rights of the minority will be respected. In a country characterised by different religious traditions, where adherents of a certain religion compromise the majority, then the decision of the majority concerning the public ballot will receive the majority's approval. Applying this to Iran, where Muslims compromise the majority, it does not seem that the concepts of republicanism and Islamism are mutually exclusive; rather, they are complementary since the absolute majority of the population participated in deciding on a suitable political system of the country. In spite of the apparent contradiction between republicanism and Islamism, it could be inferred that republicanism

---

1   Katuzian, p. 119.
2   Soroush, p. 5.

points to the form of government and the Islamic characterisation is based upon the content, building upon the fact that the majority of the people who believe in Islam have chosen the Islamic content of sovereignty under the banner of an Islamic republic. From this stance, the free public will, coupled with Islamism that is characterised by public participation in deciding the political system of the country, has resulted in the Islamic Republic as an end product.'[1]

In response to what appears like a contradiction between *wilayat al-faqih* and the republic of the nation state, it could be noticed that Articles 1, 3, 6, 7, 56 and 107 of the Constitution of the Islamic Republic of Iran stress that the doctrine of *wilayat al-faqih* could be conceived within the framework of national sovereignty. In addition, the authority of the *rahbar* has been clearly delineated in Article 110. In turn, Article 9 stipulates the non-existence of an appointed authority to curb *shar'i* freedoms under the pretext of upholding the independence and territorial integrity of Iran, even if this prohibition came out as a result of legislating laws, rules and regulations. Thus, the execution of absolute *wilayat* by a leader endowed with a constitutional legitimacy within the framework of legitimate rights (*al-huquk al-shar'iyya*), which are inalienable rights, along with the freedoms that people enjoy.[2]

Concerning the concordance between Islamism and republicanism, it is worth noting that in Shi'i legislation the *marj'a al-taqlidin* can communicate their opinions in order to evaluate if the approved law is contradictory to Islam. If it is the case, then they order their followers not to execute these laws. However, this task has been accorded to Majlis Al-Wisaya or the Custodianship Council as a legislative body in the Islamic Republic, in order to ensure that the national will is reflected in the laws. Another concern is that the president, as a symbol of republicanism, assumes his presidency only after the *rahbar*, the symbol and upholder of Islamism, receives his credentials. This is a symbolic issue that stresses that the elected president by the populace is also supported by the symbol of the Islamic system. This suggests concordance between Islamism and republicanism.

7. How Can We Reconcile Islamism and Republicanism?

Sheikh Shafic Jradi[3] claims that, contrary to the West which establishes a dichotomy between the divine and the mundane, Islam does not believe in this dualism because it is not present in the principles of Islamic political thought. Islam encompasses the two. The late leader of the Islamic Revolution, Imam Khomeini, believed that there was no problem for the system of power to be republican or

---

1   Sayyid Muhammad Hashimi, *The Constitutional Law for The Islamic Republic Of Iran: General Principles and The Pillar of The System*, vol. 1, Tehran 1995, pp. 56–57.
2   Sayyid Muhammad Hashimi, *The Constitutional Law of the Islamic Republic of Iran: Sovereignty and Political Institutions*, volume 2, Tehran Qom 1996, pp. 73–75.
3   Director of M'arif Hikamiya College, interview with the author, 6 June 2006.

to take any other form, as long as it was sanctioned by the people, and originated from the purely divine values. In this perspective, religion renders legitimacy since it is part and parcel of religious norms.

In elaborating on religious authority from the perspective of Imam Khomeini, Rahim Pur Azeghdi[1] considers that the concept of theocratic democracy, as well as the fusion between republicanism and Islamism, is a new phenomenon that has ruptured the delineated boundaries in philosophy and political science. Imam Khomeini neither divided the right to *hakimiyya* (divine governance) into equal or unequal parts between God and man, nor did he forcefully reconcile Islamism and republicanism from a pragmatic perspective. Rather, his pioneering contribution was his conviction that people's right derives from God's right.[2] He claimed that republicanism is one of the modes of God's governance in such a way that renders democracy and republicanism inseparable from its Islamic goals and content, and inseparable from religious legitimacy; that is why it cannot be juxtaposed in opposition to religion. Since Imam Khomeini stresses that man's governance is in conformity to and under the umbrella of God's governance, then the characteristics of democracy and theocracy are not only in perfect harmony, but are almost identical, even if conceived from the Western understanding of the terms.

Building upon Imam Khomeini's theory, Azeghdi argues that the points of concordance between the conception of republicanism, which is linked to Islamism, and other conceptions, which are circulated in a non-Islamic perspective, are not equivocal. Rather, he contends that what needs to be stressed, in this regard, are the differences between Islamism, or theocracy, in relation to the conception of republicanism and Western secular democracy.

According to Azeghdi, the Islamisation of the concept of republicanism serves as a guarantee against demagogy and hypocrisy. At the same time, it guarantees that the populace remains active in the political domain, especially in exercising their right in the ballot box, thus satisfying both the democratic populace and the Islamic nature of the regime. *Wilayat al-faqih* is surrounded by many institutions such as the Council of Experts and the Council of Expediency (*Siyanat Al-Dustur*), which are not only conducive to the smooth running and functioning of the social and political issues in relation to Islamic rule, but are also in conformity with the right of the populace in choosing their rulers, governors and those who run the affairs of the state at large. Popular sovereignty is exercised because all of the effective institutions of the Islamic Republic are elected by the people through the Council of Experts, which in turn is directly elected by the parliament and the president of the republic. This is also the case of the *wali*

---

1   Interview with Dr Rahim Pur Azeghdi, Iranian intellectual, 6 May 2006.
2   Cf. John Locke's conception of natural law.

al-faqih, who is also elected by the elected Council of Experts. Azeghdi called for the acceptance of theocratic democracy within the framework of *wilayat al-faqih* and the Shari'a.

However, according to Azeghdi, when democracy is approached from an ideological perspective, which is closely related to liberalism and secularism, then there will not be a concordance between democracy and Islam. In other words, when we assume a certain level of morality; the separation between politics and ethics; the separation between these concepts and the concepts of justice or secularism or other non-religious concepts that are considered as ingredients to democracy; then the concept of theocratic democracy is considered unacceptable and untenable.

According to Dr Habib Fayyad, a theology professor at Tehran University, the concept of the Islamic Republic in Iran has at least two dimensions. The first is a republican (*jumahiri*) or populace dimension, which is evinced in the popular will and participation in the elections. The second is a religious dimension inculcated in a leadership endowed with 'divine' qualifications under the doctrine of *wilayat al-faqih*. The question then is what gives the system legitimacy: is it the popular dimension or the Islamic one? It seems that there is a dialectic between two opposing theories among Iranian intellectuals or religious thinkers. The first theory is labelled as revelation (*kashf*) and the second one as appointment (*nasb*). In the constitutional and legal dimension of *wilayat al-faqih*, there is an ongoing intellectual debate in Iranian circles. The first view reflects that of the clergy in the religious seminary, which falls within the theory of *kashf*, namely, that God has blessed the *umma* with *al-wali al-faqih*, who by way of God's All-Gracefulness, serves as a natural extension to the Infallible Imam, being his general deputy. From this perspective, the role of the Council of Experts comes to prominence as a representative or on behalf of the *umma* in order to reveal or uncover the *faqih*, and not to appoint him (*nasb*). Consequently, the Council of Experts does not render legitimacy to the *wali al-faqih*, rather it chooses him. The second theory, which in general expresses the opinion of the religious intellectuals, emphasises that *wali al-faqih* is chosen by way of *nasb* (appointment). The Council of Experts chooses and follows up closely the office of *wilayat al-faqih* on behalf of the *umma*. Consequently, putting aside the choice of the people for the *faqih*, the person who is elected for this post has no innate legitimacy. Rather, his legitimacy comes by way of elections since the opinion of the people is represented by the Council of Experts.

Aside from legal and constitutional dimensions, this debate also has a deep cultural dimension, which stipulates that *al-wali al-faqih* is elected and could be dismissed by the Council of Experts. One could question if the opinion of the people is a precondition for the legitimacy of the state. Debates over two contentions ensue. The first is propagated by the Iranian reformers who argued that there is no legitimacy of the state without popular support, this being the case since the state has been founded on public referendum, which resulted in overwhelming support from the populace to the Islamic Republic. As a result, if people's support diminishes then the state loses its legitimacy. However, the conservatives hold to a different contention and explicitly distinguish between acceptability (*maqbuliyya*) and legitimacy (*shariyya*). Acceptability reflects the agreement of the populace on the system, and is related to the concept of 'instating' (*tamkin*), that is, the ability of the state to perpetuate itself without recourse to legitimacy, as legitimacy is a divine grace that can only be bestowed by God. As such, the founding of the state is based upon both God's legitimacy and people's acceptance. This reasoning is substantiated by the Prophetic tradition where the Muslims gave a pledge of allegiance to the Prophet in order to instate him, and not to render to him Prophetic legitimacy and Prophetic leadership of the *umma*.

On face value, it seems that there is a problem that is overlooked by the Iranian Constitution, namely that the *wali al-faqih* has absolute prerogatives in line with those of the infallible Imam. The problem is whether the prerogatives of the *wali al-faqih* allow him to dissolve the Council of Experts, knowing that it has the right to dismiss the *wali al-faqih*. Keeping in mind that the *faqih* has absolute and multidimensional prerogatives, one could question whether the decisions of *wali al-faqih* are binding to the Council of Experts, which elected him in the first place. However, like the head executive in many countries, he too is subject to the rule of law, and as such is under the law. More discussion around this topic is deferred till the next chapter.

In all respects, the interconnection between the theory of revelation and the theory of appointment comes to the fore. As stipulated in the Constitution, the populace is the one that chooses the *wali al-faqih* and can dismiss him, since the mechanism of electing the *wali al-faqih* is based upon an indirect election where the populace elects the Council of Experts. Afterwards, the people delegate to the leading *ulama* the task of choosing the *wali al-faqih* or the leader, in case these are not able to delineate the qualifications of the *wali*.

CONCLUSION

In the Islamic Republic, the existence of constitutional safeguards and the supervision of the *rahbar* by the Council of Experts directly, which is elected by the people, lead to the possibility of transforming the leader into an individual governor. If the leader loses his senses, the Council of Experts in Iran has the right to isolate the leader if he transgresses against the Constitution, abuses his authority, or loses the necessary qualifications of *wilaya*. That is why it is possible for the leader to remain in office as long as he abides by the Constitution, does not take advantage of his authority, and continues to enjoy the necessary quali-fications. Therefore from a constitutional perspective there does not seem to be an existential contradiction between republicanism and Islamism in the politi-cal system of the Islamic Republic. What determines the republican or Islamic nature of the system has to do with a specific mechanism to execute the principles of the Constitution and the institutionalisation of democracy in the regime. This applies to a lot of Third World countries where republicanism and democracy are lacking, and where despotism reigns, in spite of the fact that these countries may possess democratic constitutions. In contrast, Britain is democratically adminis-tered, though it does not have a written constitution.

The balance between social forces that support democracy and republican-ism in Iran, as opposed to those forces which stress the limitation of national sovereignty, determine the existence or non-existence of republicanism and democracy. It seems that the Constitution, as such, or the philosophy of the public government in Iran, do not lend support to a concordance or contradic-tion between republicanism and Islamism. Basically, it seems the issue is of a political nature. That is, the practical arena is where one determines whether influential institutions (such as the Custodianship Council and the judicial system, for example) function in the context of supporting republicanism and democracy, and whether they work in a completely independent and unbiased way to ensure and guarantee the protection of the rights and freedoms, as stipu-lated in the Constitution.

As such, one can deduce that the concepts of republicanism and Islamism in the Iranian Islamic system seem to be complementary, at least on the theoreti-cal level. However, this issue depends, to a great extent, on our understanding and interpretation of the aforementioned concepts, and on the articles of the Constitution. A fair judgement of whether the two concepts are in concord-ance or opposition depends on the performance of the political system and the resulting consequences of this performance. In addition, the institutionalisation of democratic ideals has a lot of bearing on the concordance between the afore-mentioned two concepts.

Final Word: Practical Application

Interestingly, the debate over whether Islamism and republicanism are con-cordant or in opposition to each other is one that takes place even within Iran. This fact suggests that the system itself is flexible enough to allow for introspec-tion, adaptation and modification. The ongoing debate between those who say the two concepts are opposed and those who argue that they are in concord-ance produces a vivid and lively polemic, thus enriching Iranian political and cultural life.

Adherents of the theory of opposition between Islamism and republicanism have put their finger on the performance of the Islamic Republic in the previous two decades, which had led to weakening the republicanism of the regime, as they claim. On the contrary, adherents of the concordance theory, although they partially concede their adversaries' claim concerning the weak performance of the regime, relegate that to the implementation of a special system of governance after an ongoing political, social and cultural revolution. Immediately after that the regime was confronted with a demanding war with Iraq, with a devastating magnitude that continued for eight years. This led to the nascent necessities of reconstruction and building a viable economy at the expense of a viable political system in the second decade. These factors have snowballed to not giving due course to the debates on republicanism, and to weakening the efforts to conclusively attain it. Concomitantly, social scientists consider that the election of President Muhammad Rida Khatami in 1997 by an absolute majority of the people was a strong and salient indicator of republicanism. Similarly, the election of President Mahmud Ahmadinejad in 2005 by an unprecedented overwhelming majority of the Iranian people (60 million people participated in the two election rounds to elect the first non-clerical president since Muhammad Ali Raja'i in 1981) can be perceived as an expression of popular will within the context of republicanism.

Building on the aforementioned, the special role of the Council of Guardians in the elaborate Iranian political system becomes salient, since the council is officially entitled to interpret the Constitution. As such its interpretation of the ambiguous articles of the Constitution towards a republican or Islamic nature will determine to a great extent the course of the present debate. In addition, this Council of Guardians has a mandate over the Shura Council or the parliament in order to decide whether its legislations are in conformity with Islamic laws and the Constitution. Further, the Council of Guardians interprets what is suitable and beneficiary to the concordance between public administration and Shari'a. The third role of the Council of Guardians is its supervision of the electoral process pertaining to presidency, parliament, and the Council of Experts. Because of the leading role of the Council of Guardians, the presence of democracy, or its demise, depends on it, since the so-called opposition or concordance between republicanism and Islamism in Iran depends upon the interpretations of the Council of Guardians, its performance and its ideological vision.

Furthermore, reading through the Iranian Constitution and inspecting the building up of the check and balance institutions in Iran, even those which supervise the performance of the leader, would not lead to a clear-cut conclusion about the supremacy of either of the two concepts. The only umpire in this ongoing debate is the performance of the regime, which is limited not only to what the top officials deem appropriate, but to the way the regime adopts to the pressure of the different influential actors. This vivid ongoing debate within the Iranian society, among the various movements and intellectuals, has dictated a kind of paradigm shift within the Islamic Republic. The ensuing results will usher in a new era of reconciliation of the two concepts and consolidate the advances that have been made so far.

CHAPTER SEVEN

Democratisation in the Islamic Republic of Iran and the Emergence of the Iranian Reform Movement

Debates about the exact nature and form of the system of governance in the Islamic Republic began at its very inception. After the triumph of the Islamic Revolution, the newly established leadership did not set out to restore an Islamic caliphate, nor did they erect an Imamate, but rather they proceeded to establish an Islamic Republic. This was a new and somewhat ambiguous concept of governance that was as open to diverse interpretation as were its political and religious underpinnings.

A public discussion soon emerged on the question of what to call the nascent Islamic state, and among the most popular suggestions was the name, 'Islamic Democratic Republic'. However, Imam Khomeini declared in one of his speeches that he would only lend his support to the name 'Islamic Republic' because adding the word 'democratic' would imply that Islam is an inherently undemocratic religion, a view that he utterly rejected.[1]

Khomeini's view was adopted by a number of prominent intellectuals and clerics, who echoed the opinion that democracy was a key foundational principle of the Islamic Republic. Among them was Ayatollah Murtada Muttahari, who during a television interview stressed that Imam Khomeini had affirmed that individual freedom and democracy are not only compatible with Islam, but rather are inherent in it. Therefore the addition of the word 'democratic' to the name Islamic Republic was unnecessary.[2] Muttahari further elaborated

---

1 Ervard Abrahamian, *Khomeinism: Essays on the Islamic Republic*, London, 1993.
2 Interview with Sheikh Muhammad Shqayr, Beirut, 15 January 2007.

that democracy can manifest itself in a multiplicity of forms in myriad political systems, and that democracy and freedom in the Islamic Republic were based on an Islamic outlook, as opposed to a Western perspective.

It is important to note, however, that while a number of intellectuals and religious authorities conceded that the word 'democratic' did not need to be introduced to the Islamic Republic's name, not even Khomeini himself suggested that democracy was antithetical to the Islamic Republic. Rather, Khomeini and others publicly acknowledged that democracy and democratic concepts were underlying precepts of the system.

Therefore from the outset, Iranians were able to conceive of a version of democracy that could be fused with *wilayat al-faqih*. By envisioning democracy as an integral part of the system, along with Islam, the founders of the Islamic Republic opened the door to an organic process of democratisation. In the debate over the 'identity' and the name of the nascent Islamic entity, one might question the insistence of Khomeini to include the word 'republic' rather than 'state' for instance. Why was the word needed if democracy is inherent and it is well known to be the choice of the people? Unlike the Sunnis who consider the golden age of Islam to be the ten-year rule of the Prophet in Medina from 622 to 632 CE, when he supposedly founded the ideal Islamic state, the Shi'is believe that the Prophet as well as Imam Ali played a pivotal role towards the realisation of such process; however, according to Shi'i doctrine the ideal Islamic state will not unfold till the advent of Imam Mahdi at the end of time and will eventually find such a state through the process of restoring and upholding the rights and justice in place of oppression and injustice, as a Hadith stipulates.[1] This seems to be an important point because it links the theoretical dimension to the practical dimension, i.e. the case study. The concept of dual legitimacy seems to bridge the apparent problem.

THE DUAL LEGITIMACY OF THE ISLAMIC REPUBLIC

According to Dr Habib Fayyad,[2] the concept of Islamic Republic in Iran has at least two dimensions. The first is a republican (*jumhuri*) or populace dimension, which is evidenced in the popular will and participation in the election, and the second is a religious dimension inculcated in a leadership endowed with 'divine'

---

1 The above is based on the following Prophetic Hadith: *'yazharu fi akhr al-zaman al-Mahdi min wildi, ismahu ismi, kinyatahu kinyati, laqabahu laqabi, yamla'u al-arda qistan wa 'adlan, b'da an muli'at zulman wa juran.'* (There comes at the end of time, the last of my descendants, whose name is my name; his title is my title; whose epithet is my epithet, will fill the earth with justice and fairness, after injustice and oppression reigned.)

2 Personal interview, 23 May 2006. Fayyad is a professor of theology at Tehran University.

qualifications under the doctrine of *wilayat al-faqih*. The political system in Iran was therefore based on the fusion of two legitimacies, religious and popular. Indeed, Olivier Roy refers to the system of governance as a 'constitutionalist theocracy', or a mixture of theocracy and electoral democracy.[1]

On the one hand, the system is Islamic, and reflects Khomeini's view of government that is itself inoculated with democratic procedures and principles, such as *shura*, *maslaha* and *umma*. Keeping in mind that religious legitimacy is always synonymous with Shari'a, which is in turn equal to constitutional legitimacy, governance is conducted in light of the Qur'an and the Traditions, the two primary sources of the Shari'a. Furthermore the Constitution tasks Muslim scholars who are endowed with piety, justice and commitment with guiding and supervising the community. From this stance, the founders of the Iranian Constitution incorporated the concept of the perpetuity of the Imamate ruled under the guidance of the *wali al-faqih* who satisfies all the qualifications thus engendering recognition and obedience from the people in his capacity as a leader. The *wali al-faqih* derives his legitimacy from the stance of being a continuation of the governance of Imam al-Mahdi. In this capacity the *wali al-faqih* is the supreme authority who supervises other authorities from the stance of ensuring that the various apparatuses do not deviate from their original Islamic functions.

On the other hand, the Iranian system of governance is republican, and draws heavily from democratic principles such as consensus, popular participation, accountability and the rule of law. It incorporates democratic practices such as regular elections in which a wide array of political parties participate, as well as modern institutions such as a parliament (where lively debate takes place), a presidency, a council of ministers, and so on. Indeed, the Iranian Constitution, which is remarkably similar to the 1958 French Constitution (de Gaulle's Fifth Republic), guarantees the types of rights advocated in the Universal Declaration of Human Rights. It also allocates independent authority and responsibilities in an arrangement that bears resemblance to Montesquieu's and Locke's notion of a separation of powers.

Thus the system relies simultaneously upon theocratic and democratic mechanisms, with both sets of principles enshrined in the Iranian Constitution. Although some scholars have employed a reductive approach to describe the system of governance in Iran as a 'religious tyranny',[2] it is necessary to note that the populace dimension, along with the religious, has played a prominent role in the Iranian state since the dawn of the Islamic Republic. Indeed, Khomeini's theories on *wilayat al-faqih* emphasised the central importance of both. As Ayubi notes: 'It is now [at the outset of the Islamic Republic] the government that is

---

1   Nazih Ayubi, *Political Islam: Religion and Politics in the Arab World*, London 1991.
2   Michael Ledeen of the American Enterprise Institute has frequently used this term.

supreme, not the Shari'a; the state, not the ideology.'¹ In fact, by shifting the emphasis from the Shari'a to the jurisconsult, 'precedence has been given to the political, blending both religious and secular concepts and practices in a way that can still claim an Islamic legitimacy.'²

It is also important to note that the concept of *wilayat al-faqih*, from which the state draws its religious legitimacy, has proven to be adaptable and dynamic in accordance with changing circumstances. Indeed, as Abrahamian points out, during the latter days of his life, Khomeini, anticipating a succession problem, began to modify his *wilayat al-faqih* concept, 'in March 1989, three months before his death ... arguing that the political clergy should be the ultimate authority, and not those who were the most knowledgeable about religious scholarship ...'³

During the 'first republic', or the first ten years of the Islamic Republic, the fusion of popular and religious legitimacies did not pose a major problem or generate much internal debate, largely because of the added legitimacy lent to the system by Khomeini's broad charismatic appeal. Very few people at that time criticised the fact that both religious and political authority had been put in the hands of one person, since Khomeini's status as a symbol of the revolution had earned him an almost mythical stature.

However, Khomeini's death in 1989 sparked fresh ideological battles about the future of the Islamic Republic, and new debates that brought the state's dual legitimacy under critical focus. Much of the debate was touched off by the decision of the Council of Experts to elect 'Ali Khamina'i to succeed Khomeini as the *rahbar*. This decision generated controversy at the time because Khamina'i was only an *hojatoleslam wal Muslimeen*,⁴ or one well versed in Islam and Muslims, not a leading religious authority (*marja' al-taqlid*), although he later acquired the ranking. Khamina'i's election thus initially posed a problem because constitutionally, he lacked one of the two qualifications to be the *rahbar* of the nation. This dilemma was initially diverted by temporarily upgrading Khaminai'i's clerical ranking to *marja al-taqlid* shortly after his appointment. Ultimately, however, the problem was neatly resolved with a revision to the Constitution allowing lower-ranking clerics to become the supreme leader, an amendment that was put to a popular vote in a referendum on 28 July 1989. This modification of the Constitution was hugely significant: the leader no longer needed to be a *marja' al-taqlid*, meaning that the position of *faqih* was essentially reduced to a political office. The same constitutional amendment abolished the post of prime minister and granted more executive powers to the president, a post occupied at that time by Hashemi Rafsanjani.

1 Ayubi, *Political Islam*, p. 151.
2 Ibid., p. 149.
3 Ervard Abrahamian, *Khomeinism: Essays on the Islamic Republic*, London, 1993, p. 35.
4 See Roy, *The Failure of Political Islam*, for an overview of the Shi'i clerical ranking system.

This adaptation marked an important early step in the political transformation of the Iranian system of governance. This is not to suggest that the Iranians were beginning to embark on a process of 'de-Islamisation' or a marked departure from Islamic principles. Rather, it represents a kind of pragmatic evaluation of the system's underlying anomalies and attempts to correct them. This readjustment process continued during Rafsanjani's presidency, which lasted for eight years, a period that is called the 'Second Republic' (1989–1997), and continued to accelerate afterward.

Asef Bayat, a professor of sociology and Middle East studies, currently at Leiden University in the Netherlands, describes the start of this metamorphosis, which began with the end of the war with Iraq in 1988, the death of Khomeini in 1989 and the implementation of reconstruction policies after the eight-year long war with Iraq, as the onset of 'post-Islamism' in the Islamic Republic. By post-Islamism, he means both a political and social *condition* in which Islamists became aware of their system's inadequacies and were thus compelled to reinvent it, and also a *project* or conscious attempt 'to turn the underlying principles of Islamism on its head by emphasising rights instead of duties, plurality in place of singular authoritative voice, historicity rather than fixed scriptures, and the future instead of the past'.[1] In short, post-Islamist Iranian society has engaged in pragmatic attempts to construct an 'alternative modernity' that incorporates both modern democratic and religious principles. As we shall see, this pragmatic introspection and willingness to experiment with incremental adjustments in post-Islamist Iran has rendered the system of governance more conducive to democratisation.

One reason for this transformation that cannot be overlooked is the fact that Shi'i jurisprudence has proven to be dynamic and progressive, leaving ample space for flexibility in interpretation and compromise as long as it does not encroach upon the immutable set of principles (*thawabt*). Shi'ism holds that Islam leaves room for two things: an immutable space that cannot be changed regardless of the prevailing developments and circumstances and a second mutable space which is closely related to the changing circumstances and the prevailing objective conditions, on the one hand, and the principles of religious legislation on the other. This reasoning has been dubbed by the late Muhammad Baqir al-Sadr of Iraq (1935–80) as the general indicatives (*muashshirat 'amma*).[2]

The wide room for diverse interpretations in this mutable space has allowed for the emergence of new interpretations in Shi'i jurisprudence and new discourses in

---

1   Asef Bayat, *Islamism and Democracy: What is the Real Question?*, International Institute for the Study of Islam in the Modern World (ISIM) Paper, Amsterdam University Press, Amsterdam, 2007, pp. 18–19. Also see: Bayat 'The Coming of a Post-Islamist Society', in *Critique: Critical Middle East Studies*, no. 9, Fall 1996, pp. 43–52.
2   Interview with Shaykh Muhammad Shqayr, Beirut, 15 January 2007

politics, both representing a strong force in favour of democratisation as the following presentation of the debates seems to convey. In this chapter, the concept of dual legitimacy is conveyed through the following aspects: new discourses on the state's Islamic legitimacy, *wilayat al-faqih*, the Council of Guardians, women's rights, outlook of the Islamic Republic and the battle lines between the reformists and conservatives.

NEW DISCOURSES ON THE STATE'S ISLAMIC LEGITIMACY

As mentioned earlier, the Islamic Republic is built upon two legitimacies, popular and religious. But Dr Habib Fayyad[1] points out that *wilayat al-faqih* has become the subject of lively intellectual debate in Iranian circles. According to Fayyad, a key question that has arisen is whether *wilayat al-faqih* itself is based on popular or Islamic legitimacy. Fayyad says that two opposing theories have been embraced by Iranian intellectuals and religious thinkers: the first theory is based on revelation (*kashif*) and the second one on appointment (*nasib*). The first view reflects that of the conservative clergy in the religious seminary, who espouse the theory of *kashif*, namely, that God has blessed the *umma* with the *wali al-faqih* by way of His All-Gracefulness, the *wali al-faqih* being a natural extension to the Infallible Imam and his general deputy. From this perspective, the role of the Council of Experts comes into play as a representative on behalf of the *umma* in order to reveal or uncover the *faqih* and not to appoint him (*tansib*). Consequently, the Council of Experts does not render legitimacy to the *wali al-faqih*; rather his legitimacy comes from God, and the Council of Experts merely chooses him through a process of revelation.

According to Fayyad, the second theory, which in general expresses the opinion of the liberal religious intellectuals, emphasises that the *wali al-faqih* is chosen by way of appointment (*nasib*). The Council of Experts chooses and follows up closely the office of *wali al-faqih* on behalf of the *umma*; consequently, putting aside the choice of the people for the *faqih*, the person who is elected for this post has no innate legitimacy. Rather, his legitimacy comes by way of elections since the opinion of the people is represented by way of the Council of Experts.

This debate also has deep political implications, aside from legal and constitutional dimensions, which stipulate that the *wali al-faqih* is elected and could be dismissed by the Council of Experts. One could question if the opinion of the people is a precondition for the legitimacy of the state. According to Fayyad, two debates ensue: the first has been propagated by the Iranian reformers, who argued that there is no legitimacy of the state without popular support. They

---

1   From author's interview with Fayyad.

have argued that this is the case since the state has been founded on public referenda which resulted in overwhelming support from the populace to the Islamic Republic. As a result, if the people's support diminishes, then the state loses its legitimacy. However, the conservatives have explicitly distinguished between acceptability (*maqbuliya*) and Islamic legitimacy (*shar'iyya*). Acceptability reflects the agreement of the populace on the system and is related to the concept of 'instating' (*tamkin*), i.e. the ability of the state to perpetuate itself without recourse to legitimacy, as legitimacy is a divine grace that can only be bestowed by God. As such, the founding of the state is based upon both God's legitimacy and the people's acceptance.

This reasoning is substantiated by the prophetic tradition where the Muslims gave a pledge of allegiance to the Prophet in order to instate him, and not to render him prophetic legitimacy and prophetic leadership of the *umma*. This central concept stresses the sovereign role of the people in formulating the governance of Islamic Republic. It is precisely this fusion that makes Islamic democracy and gives it its defining features. Thus Shari'a is considered a natural law to Muslims; it enshrines the basic rights, the duties, and the obligations of an individual. As such, it is not considered a constraint on democracy, rather a guarantee of it.

The kernel of the argument then is that there is a problem not discussed by the Iranian Constitution, namely whether the *wali al-faqih* has absolute prerogatives in line with those of the Infallible Imam. This ambiguity in the Constitution raises important questions, such as whether the prerogatives of the *wali al-faqih* allow him to dissolve the Council of Experts, knowing that the Council of Experts has the right to dismiss the *wali al-faqih*. Bearing in mind that the *wali al-faqih* has absolute and multidimensional prerogatives, one could question whether the decisions of *wali al-faqih* are binding to the Council of Experts which elected him in the first place.

In all respects, the intertwinement of the theory of revelation and the theory of appointment reveals itself as stipulated in the Constitution: the populace is the one that chooses the *wali al-faqih* and can dismiss him because the mechanism of electing the *wali al-faqih* is based upon an indirect election whereby the populace elects the Council of Experts. In this case the people delegate to the leading *ulama* the task of choosing the *wali al-faqih* or the leader on their behalf, because they are not able to assess his qualifications.

Thus the philosophy of governance in the Islamic Republic of Iran hinges upon two basic dimensions: the public dimension and the Islamic religious dimension or what they call in Iran the religious populace governance. As such, the continuation of the Islamic state is reliant upon continued public support.

NEW DISCOURSES ON *WILAYAT AL-FAQIH*

Iran has in recent years witnessed an emerging debate on the mandate of *wilayat al-faqih*, previously a taboo topic. Interestingly, a number of the Islamist revolutionaries are among those who have taken part in this public discussion. One of the most prominent of these is Ayatollah Husayn Ali Montazeri (1922–2009), who was the heir apparent to the leadership of the revolution until he fell from grace shortly before Khomeini's death in 1989. Montazari did not oppose the concept of *wilayat al-faqih*, but rather he cited Islamic law in defence of his stance that the *wali al-faqih* should be directly elected and that his powers should not be absolute. He also argued that the *faqih* should be a leading *mujtahid* (or *ayatollah al-'uzma*, 'grand ayatollah'), thus posing a direct challenge to Khamina'i's legitimacy. Olivier Roy points out that a number of Montazari's colleagues, most of whom are 'grand ayatollahs', have *never* accepted Khomeini's doctrine of *wilayat al-faqih*, even if they did not oppose the Islamic Revolution.[1]

Among the many outspoken Iranian intellectuals is the political philosopher and theologian Abdolkarim Soroush, born in 1945, and one of the boldest social critics of post-revolutionary Iran. Soroush has openly questioned the theological, philosophical, and political underpinnings of the regime and has remained critical of the dominance of the 'clerocracy'. Because he has been such a vocal advocate of the evolution of an Iran that is both democratic and religious, he is often referred to as the 'Luther of Islam'. In a sense, Soroush embodies the spirit of post-Islamism, as he argues that while sacred text does not change, interpretation of the Qur'an and the Shari'a is always in a state of flux. He thus draws a distinction between 'religion' and 'interpretation of religion'.

Soroush also introduces the concept of 'religious democracy', which has become a widespread subject of study in Iranian intellectual circles. He also advocates the view that in Islamic democracy there is no *a priori* right for the clergy to rule; rather the state should be governed by officials who are popularly elected on the basis of equal rights under law. Soroush also speaks openly about secularism, a word he is not afraid to use. On this subject, he draws a distinction between what he terms 'objective' and 'subjective' secularisation. The former refers to the institutional separation of church and state, while the latter (also called 'profanation') implies a separation of religion from culture and conscience. Soroush favours the 'secularisation' of Islamic society without the profanation of its culture.

In the past two decades, a number of intellectuals have begun to demand

---

1   Olivier Roy, *The Failure of Political Islam*, 1994, p. 173. So it is a misnomer to call the Iranian system the 'regime of the ayatollahs', as many journalists do, since so many ayatollahs do not support it. Today there is not a single grand ayatollah apart from Khamein'i in power and most do not play a prominent role in politics.

fundamental constitutional reforms that would redefine the role of the *wali al-faqih*, including the direct election by the people of the *rahbar*, or supreme leader, who would hold office for a limited term and have only clearly defined powers.

NEW DISCOURSES ON THE COUNCIL OF GUARDIANS

The mandate of Council of Guardians, one of the most prominent institutions of governance in Iran, is outlined in the Constitution, in chapter VI, Articles 91 through 99, which delineate its way of functioning and the cases that fall under its jurisdiction. The Council is composed of twelve members, half of whom are clergy appointed by the *rahbar*, and the other half of whom are judges with different legal specialisations who are elected by the Iranian Parliament through an open process of selection based on the merit of the candidates, who are nominated by the Chief Justice, Mahmud Shahrawardi, who is in turn appointed by the *rahbar*. However, the Council of Guardians does not have the prerogative to enact laws or legislation; rather, all the laws that are voted by the parliament should be ratified by the Council in order to ensure the compliance of the laws with Islamic Shari'a on the one hand, and its conformity to the Iranian Constitution on the other.

The twelve members of the Council of Guardians have to vote on all the laws that pertain to the Constitution; however, only the six clergy have the right to vote on laws dealing with the Shari'a. In order to ensure the proper functioning of the democratic process, when the Council of Guardians finds a problem with a certain law it refers it to the parliament for amendment. But if disagreement persists between the Council of Guardians, on the one hand, and the parliament on the other, then the Expediency Council is charged with arbitration (*tahkim*) in order to settle the dispute.

In addition, one of the primary responsibilities of the Council of Guardians, according to Article 99 of the Constitution, is the 'supervising of the elections'. Reform-minded Iranians have publicly questioned the Council of Guardians' liberal interpretation of 'supervision', arguing that the Council of Guardians has incorrectly viewed this as licence to 'supervise the *candidates*', often preventing many of them from running in elections. The Council, after carefully studying the candidates' profiles, takes the decision of whether to allow them to officially nominate themselves. This precise issue constitutes the major bone of contention between the Council and many Iranian reformists. The Council of Guardians defines its role by its prerogative to accept or reject nominations, albeit on the basis of merit, while the reformists contend that this is not the proper role of the Council, which they say should only survey the list of candidates, register them and approve them. Thus it seems that the main conflict between the two parties centres on the interpretations of the Iranian Constitution which specify the pre-rogatives of the Council of Guardians.

As such, the Council of Guardians has been considered as the enemy number one of the reformists. The 2004 parliamentary vote saw the conservatives over-whelmingly sweep most of the seats after the Council of Guardians had rejected the applications of around 2,500 candidates, the majority of whom are from the reformist camp, including around eighty members of parliament whose tenure expired because of the lack of competency. Because of this, Mohammad-Reza Khatami, brother of former President Mohammad Khatami and former head of the Islamic Iran Participation Front, described the Council of Guardians as the 'killer of the reformist movement' in Iran. He propagated this statement on the eve of the 2004 parliamentary elections, which his party boycotted after he was barred from running, saying that 'the Council of Guardians has killed any chance to reach a solution.'[1]

However, Hojatoleslam Mehdi Karrubi, the former Speaker of the House during Khatami's presidency, took a more introspective approach on the matter, placing the blame for the reformists' decline upon those reformists who had unnecessarily fuelled problems with the Council of Guardians. Paradoxically, Karrubi emerged as a prominent reformist candidate himself in the 2009 presidential elections.

NEW DISCOURSES ON WOMEN'S RIGHTS IN THE ISLAMIC REPUBLIC

To illustrate the progressive nature of Shi'i jurisprudence, *wilayat al-faqih*, for example, legitimises the right of women to lead prayer – even in the holy semi-nary of Qom Ayatullah Sanei'i. One of the most prominent Marja's in the religious seminary in Qom,[2] Sanei'i has earned the title of the 'mufti of women' because of his fatwas, since he has argued for the permissibility of women to lead men in prayer. Not only that, he has issued fatwas to ease the constraint on the posts of *wali*

1   Talal 'Atrisi, *Al-Jumhuriyya Al-Sa'ba: Iran fi Tahawulatiha Al-Dakhiliyya wa Siyasatiha Al-Iqlimiyya,* (The Difficult Republic : Iran in its Domestic Changes and Regional Politics), Beirut, 2006, p. 42.

2   Sanei'i was born in 1937 in Nik Abad, near Isfahan. He signed the declaration 'deposing the shah', which was also signed by many leading clergy in the religious seminary shortly before ousting the shah. He received his religious studies at the hands of Imam Khomeini, Ayatollah al-Brujurdi, Ayatollah al-'Uzma Al-Damad and Ayatulla al-'Uzma Al-Araki. He was one of the pioneering clergy who went with Imam Khomeini to Tehran and served as a member of the Council of Trustees, and also represented Tehran in the Council of Experts in 1982. Imam Khomeini was very pleased with him to the extent that he said, 'I have raised Ayatollah Sanei'i as I am raising my son'. However, he resigned from all of these political posts in 1984 and headed to the religious seminary in Qom, dedicating his life to study and research ever since. *Al-Sharq Al-Awsat*, 17 March 2007, vol. 29, 10336, p. 6.

al-faqih, presidency and judiciary. He has also argued for the equality of women's blood money to that of a man as well as the right of a woman to travel alone in order to acquire a decent education. He has stressed that men and women stand on an equal par in all rights, save two issues, inheritance and divorce. He unequivocally stated that according to the Qur'an, the inheritance of a male is twice that of a female; and that men can divorce their wives, while the opposite does not happen.

As such, he sanctioned the right of women to be chief justices (judges). He based his argument on three main apodictic proofs:

(1) There is no *shar'i* evidence to prohibit women from assuming this role and serving in this post; (2) the apodictic proof, in this regard, is of a comprehensive nature, and thus cannot be only limited to male incumbents; (3) the Infallible Imams have bestowed this right to women as well as to men; thus it is not the sole prerogative of men.[1]

Sanei'i earned his main reputation among women since he was always adamant in defending their rights. It is worth mentioning that he was instrumental in passing legislation in the Shura Council (parliament) which allows women to travel for the purpose of study without being accompanied by any of their relatives, and also issued a fatwa in this regard.[2] One has to keep in mind that legislation in Iran cannot be ratified except when sanctioned by the Council of Guardains, which comprises twelve of the leading jurists and clergy who ensure that these laws are in conformity with the Constitution and Islamic Shari'a. Thus, women have a difficult task in making their voice heard through constitutional mechanisms, which is why they are very pleased to find an open-minded cleric like Sanei'i, who is more than willing, out of conviction, to lobby for their views and present fatwas which are binding as legislation.

Sanei'i's philosophy in the way of issuing fatwas is a tolerant one in the sense of avoiding complex and sophisticated methodology. His apodictic proof (*hujja*) is that Islamic Shari'a is built upon simplicity and comprehensiveness, thus enjoining the *fuqaha*, or religious jurists, 'to ease their reluctance in issuing fatwas since the Shari'a is built upon ease of approach'.

Concerning his views on *wilayat al-faqih*, Sanei'i has sanctioned any *mujtahid*, who meets the necessary requirements, incuding women, to be a *wali al-faqih*, since the only two conditions to be satisfied are piety and jurisprudential knowledge. He has further asserted that when Islam does not give a specific opinion about any affair that has to do with the public interest (*maslaha 'amma*), then the legitimacy to rule in this case derives from the people and the majority's consensus to the proposed solution.[3]

---

1   *Al-Sharq Al Awsat*, 17 March 2007, vol 29, No. 10336, p. 6.
2   Ibid.
3   For example, Sanei'i extends his *fiqhi* (jurisprudential) opinion into areas that are still considered a

In spite of all of the efforts of Sanei'i and others to place women on the same par as men at least from a legal and jurisprudential standpoint, Shirin Ebadi,[1] a human rights lawyer and Nobel laureate, argues that Iranian women still face considerable discrimination in the Islamic Republic. Although 65 percent of college students are females, and 30 percent of the job market is occupied by women, Iranian women are still lobbying to do away with discriminatory laws. One campaign aimed to collect one million signatures in order to lobby parliament to amend some discriminatory laws and enhance equality, for instance between the blood money of women and men as well as custody of children. They also argued in favour of recognising the testimony of women as on the same par with that of a man, even though such a demand is in clear contradiction with the tenets of the Qur'an.

Ebadi clarifies that the campaign behind the million signature aims at conveying Iranian women's rejection of these discriminatory laws; Ebadi has purported that a full thirty-one years after the Islamic Revolution, Iranian women cannot elect their representatives in political institutions.[2]

However, even Ebadi has admitted that Iran has witnessed limited but tangible developments. Previously the women's movement was an unacceptable taboo in Iranian conscience; now it has become a reality that the Iranian public sphere has to reckon with. These and similar trends have informed Iranian society, leading to a new phenomenon of raising the age of marriage among women from twenty-five years to thirty years, and increasing the number of women entering the workforce. However, this is not enough, Ebadi contends, because women aspire for more respect and better treatment from a patriarchal society.

NEW DISCOURSES ON THE OUTLOOK OF THE ISLAMIC REPUBLIC

The new discourses that have emerged in the Islamic Republic in recent years have not been confined to the domestic sphere. Indeed, Iran has witnessed a related metamorphosis in terms of its Islamist outlook toward the rest of the world. While the revolutionary Islamism had emphasised transnational solidarities and exporting the Islamist model of governance, recent years have seen new discourses arise.

Just as ideas about religious leadership, governance and the role of women have changed, a related phenomenon that has taken place is the localisation of Shi'ism

---

closed circle in the religious seminaries (*hawzas*). He has a very advanced *fiqhi* stance vis-à-vis music and signing: he sanctions them as long as they do not lead to deviation from or distortion to Islam.

1   *Al-Sharq Al-Awsat*, 17 March 2007, vol 29, 10342, pp. 1; 6.

2   Compared to Western standards of democracy, especially in Scandinavian countries, most notably Finland where the latest government was composed of fourteen women and eight men, not only Iran stands low on the scale of democracy, but so do long established democracies such as those in the UK and the US.

in Iran, a trend we can refer to as 'Iranisation'. In fact this phenomenon is not limited to the Islamic Republic, but rather is taking place across Muslim societies as Islam is reinterpreted in a local context.[1] Oliver Roy describes this development as the emergence of 'Islamo-nationalism' at the expense of the supra-national clergy. It is the logic of the *Iranian* state, with its *Iranian* geostrategic interests, that prevails as Islam is reinterpreted in the local context. Roy argues that Iranian strategic alignments have less and less to do with Islam, and even with Shi'ism.[2]

During his presidency, for example, Khatami called for regional détente and openness (*infitah*) toward the outside world as well as neighbouring countries, promoting cooperation and coordination in order to ward off violence. It seems that during Khatami's first tenure from 1997 to 2001 this détente, more or less, materialised. Iran was able to consolidate its ties with Arab and international countries as well as receiving support for his reformist trend from abroad, most notably from neighbouring Arab countries which saw in Khatami's *infitah* the new face of Iran. Khatami's other calls struck a resounding chord as well in Europe, which boosted its economic and commercial ties with Iran. In fact, the only country with which Khatami did not manage to make noticeable gains was the United States.

Mehdi Karrubi, who is also a middle-ranking cleric, has added his voice to this debate. He has contended that impromptu and ill-conceived declarations and speeches on the nuclear issue had led to increasing tensions surrounding the Islamic Republic's nuclear file. Karrubi also contended that the goal of the Islamic Republic is not working on exporting the revolution; however, he stressed that the Iranian leadership cannot prevent the dissemination of its influence. In the domain of regional foreign policy, Karrubi argued that Iranian policy in Iraq is based upon *infitah* (opening up) to all the multi-confessional, multi-religious, multiethnic constituents of the Iraqi mosaic Yet he contended that some 'Shi'i fanatics', as he calls them, refuse to do that.[3]

BATTLE LINES BETWEEN REFORMISTS AND CONSERVATIVES

During the 'first' and 'second' republics', the paradigmatic shifts taking place in Iran did not translate into a political crisis. Rather, these periods saw what can be described as a 'crisis of the clergy'. However, an acute political crisis came to the

---

1 See for example, Reinhard Schulze, 'The Ethnisation of Islamic Cultures in the Late 20th Century or From Political Islam to Post-Islamism', in George Stauth, ed., *Islam: Motor or Challenge of Modernity*, Yearbook of the Sociology of Islam, no. 1, 1998, pp. 187–98.

2 See Olivier Roy, 'The Crisis of Religious Legitimacy in Iran', in *Middle East Journal*, 53. 2, Spring 1999, p. 211.

3 'Atrisi, *Al-Jumhuriyya Al-Sa'ba*, p. 198.

fore during the run-up to the presidential elections in May of 1997, and arguably also in 2009.

Prior to 1997, a relatively homogenous group of ruling elite dominated Iranian politics, emerging victorious in successive elections. The 1997 vote, however, saw the triumph of a relative newcomer, Mohammad Khatami, against the wishes of the leader Khamina'i, who openly favoured his rival Ali Akbar Nateq-Nuri. This development brought the two legitimacies of the state under scrutiny: the supreme guide, who already lacked key religious credentials, was now also losing popular backing and authority in the public sphere. Furthermore, Khatami undeniably won popular legitimacy with his landslide victory in the polls, with almost 70 percent of the vote and over 80 percent of voters participating.[1] This begged the question of what remains of the guide's functions and how his role in Iranian governance might continue to evolve.[2]

In 1997, Khatami rode to power on a wave of public support by employing the slogans that had become increasingly popularised in post-Islamist Iranian society. These slogans – which championed concepts such as democracy, the rule of law, freedom, transparency and accountability – were part of the newly emerging discourse in post-revolutionary Iran. This discourse stood in sharp contrast with that of the previous generation of Islamic revolutionaries, who had employed slogans that called for defending Islam against a global onslaught and rallying calls such as 'death to America, the hypocrites, and the enemies of *wilayat al-faqih*'.

Khatami used this new discourse in his presidential campaigns, assuring the voters that he was going to deliver on his promises during his tenure. Thus he managed to gain broad popular support, particularly among the youth, who were very much attracted to his pledges to deliver change and a better future. On the other hand, these same slogans earned him the ire of the conservatives, who publicly criticised him for giving away the concepts of the revolution and making Iran amenable to cultural penetration.

The main differences between the reformists and the conservatives centred on their interpretation of Islamic principles, since the vast majority of Iranians, even the reformists, aim to initiate changes from within the confines of the Islamic Republic. Thus their aim was not to completely abolish the system, but rather to modernise it, while upholding its Islamic character.

---

1   According to Iranian Interior Ministry statistics released after the 1997 elections, Khatami won 69 percent of the vote, with 83 percent of voters participating.

2   Some scholars have suggested that the guide's function might be redefined. For example, Roy argues: 'A solution could be to acknowledge the purely political nature of the function of his office, as Ayatollah Ali Meshkini, the head of the Assembly of Experts, sometimes hints. The guide, in this sense, could become a 'constitutional *faqih*', as there are 'constitutional monarchs' in other countries, and Iran would openly become what it is already, according to its own constitution, a constitutional theocracy' (Roy, 1999: p. 214).

These differences in Islamic interpretation extended to virtually every aspect of political life in the Islamic Republic. The conservatives were very rigid in observing the centrality of the *wali al-faqih* and recognising his ultimate absolute power as the wielder of authority in society. On the other hand, the reformists tried to remove the halo of the *wali al-faqih*; they called for reducing his powers in favour of the institution of the presidency. They also stressed the salient role of the people in decision making as opposed to *wali al-faqih*.[1]

Similarly, the conservatives rejected the Western lifestyle and strove to fight off what they termed 'cultural invasion', while the reformists believed in constructive cultural interaction with the Western world, seeing many positive aspects in Western civilisation that could be incorporated into Iranian culture.[2] The conservatives stressed the importance of upholding law and order even if that meant imposing restrictions on the media and the press, while the reformists advocated public freedoms, especially the freedom of press, media, speech and expression, even the use of satellite dishes. The conservatives tried to centralise cultural ideology, especially in foreign policy and in dealing with the United States. The reformists stressed the saliency of promulgated standing laws that apply equally well to all people. Furthermore, a number of reformists openly called for a separation between religion and politics, but not to the extent of accepting full secularism since they generally upheld the principles of the Islamic Republic.

Khatami's 1997 election was a victory for the reformist camp in Iran, but it also had other important implications. First, it represented a victory for the 'Islamic Yuppies', i.e. those Iranians, mainly young but not necessarily, belonging mostly to the middle class, who in an era of globalisation seek to modernise Iran, but not Westernise it.[3] Second, it represented a victory for Iranian civil society, albeit within an Islamic context.[4] Third, Khatami's victory marked a manifestation of the startling transformations that were taking place in Iranian society.

These transformations continued to take place during Khatami's presidency: concepts such as civil society and the rule of law became the subject of public discourse, even in the right-wing press; hundreds of new cultural associations and non-governmental organisations were formed; censorship was eased, paving the

---

1   Fayyad, personal interview with author, 23 May 2006.
2   Khatami, for example, introduced the concept of 'Dialogue among Civilisations', a theory that was broadly circulated and accepted within the international community.
3   See Farhang Rajaee, 'A Thermidor of "Islamic Yuppies"? Conflict and Compromise in Iran's Politics', in *Middle East Journal*, Spring 1999, vol. 53, no. 2, pp. 217–231.
4   Many scholars have argued that 'civil society' plays a central role in democratisation. See, for example, Augustus Richard Norton, ed., *Civil Society in the Middle East*, vols. 1 and 2, Leiden, 1995, 1996.

way for the emergence of a vibrant press and allowing for the release of numerous books and films long in the censors' hands; and dozens of new newspapers and magazines were granted licences to launch (the combined circulation of Iranian newspapers and magazines reached 2,750,000, double that of the years prior to Khatami's election).

This societal mood of liberalism was further demonstrated by the outcome of the 17 February 2000 parliamentary elections, in which the reformist camp again triumphed. The vote made plain that the question was no longer whether or not to implement democratic reforms, but rather how far-reaching and comprehensive reforms should be.

THE LIMITS TO KHATAMI'S REFORMS

The reformist trend experienced a landslide victory in the first presidential election in which more than 20 million people voted for Khatami.[1] However, Khatami failed to invest this broad popular support and sweep clean the institutions that the reformists controlled, by using the strategy of pressure from the base of the pyramid and negotiations with the top. Had he done so he would have wisely pressurised the conservatives to bend to the demands of the reform-minded public, or at least offer some concessions. One of the main obstacles that he faced was the fact that all of the 'key opener' state institutions remained in the hands of the conservatives, such as the institutions of the judiciary, the Council of Experts, and the Expediency Council, to name but a few.

Khatami's failure to make practical gains in the face of conservative opposition translated itself into violent and serious confrontations in the streets on 9 July 1999, which were unprecedented since the victory of the revolution, most notably between the students and the security forces in and around the campus of Tehran University. This prompted analysts to hope for an oppositional revolution to the current regime led by the student movements as was the case during the Shah's reign. However, fearing discord and civil strife, President Khatami took strong measures to retain law and order and even dissuade opposition newspapers from attacking the system and the institution of the *wali al-faqih*. Many Iranians viewed this as a form of backtracking on reformist demands, and therefore Khatami began to fall out of favour, both among the reform-minded youth of Iran, and among Western countries that had embraced the unrealistic hope for a counter-revolution that would uproot the clerical system that had been in place since 1979.

The main threat to Khatami's reforms during his first tenure, however, came from the state institutions, which were predominantly controlled by the

---

1   Interior Ministry statistics.

conservatives, thus putting Khatami in a bottleneck and hampering many of his efforts to initiate change. The conservatives cracked down on the reformist icons, silencing many of these by threats, house arrests or imprisonment. The charges levelled against the reformists centred mainly upon 'insulting *wilayat al-faqih*' and 'rebelling against the principles of Imam Khomeini'.[1] Iran saw the closure of many reformist newspapers, and the assassination of some of the reformists, to spread terror among their ranks. However, these practices were halted after the head of the Revolutionary Guards voiced his allegiance to Khatami. After this precedent, Imam Khamina'i himself condemned the reign of terror and assassinations that targeted the reformists.

One of the main fiascos of the reformists was their failed attempt to strip the *wali al-faqih* of some of his prerogatives and transfer these to the institution of the presidency. The reformists wanted to empower the institution of the presidency at the expense of *wali al-faqih*. But Khatami realised after the end of his first tenure that his objective would not be achieved. So, he changed course and supported the centrality of the stature of the *wali al-faqih* in the system and the constitution. This deference was reciprocated by the *rahbar*, Khamina'i, who voiced his support for reforms from within the Islamic system, especially after the bloody confrontations in Tehran University and its vicinity.

That is why the reformist trend led by President Khatami in his second tenure tried to adjust to the leadership of the *rahbar*, avoiding a direct confrontation. Khatami reverted to his call for freedom, respect of the law and to 'Islamic Civil Society'. Khatami's groundbreaking speech on the twenty-second anniversary of the victory of the Islamic Revolution on 10 February 2001 attacked fanatics on both sides. He called for moderation and stressed the continuation of his reformist project, in both the domestic and foreign spheres, without directly confronting the *rahbar* or his prerogatives – even though many reformists wished that he did so.

Khatami's concessions led a number of reform-minded Iranians, particularly the youth, to become disillusioned with his leadership. When the students in Tehran University took to the streets a second time at the end of June 2003, in an unprecedented move, they did not attack the conservatives, except for the ritual of bashing the *rahbar*; rather they called for Khatami's resignation.[2] Khatami stressed the right of the students to voice their opinion as a democratic feature; however, he condemned the degeneration into chaos and breaking the law.

These confrontations led to an expansion of the circle of criticism of the leaders of the system, increasing the social economic and cultural problems that the youth were suffering from, and the flocking of the student movement around Iranian

---

1   'Atrisi, *Al-Jumhuriyya*, pp. 197–8.
2   *Reuters*, 16 June 2003.

intellectuals who constructively criticised the system of the Islamic Republic, such as Abdolkarim Soroush, Agha Jari and Muhsin Kadivar. This movement had previously found in Khatami a personification of its desires for change and reforming the system. That is why millions had lent their support to Khatami when he employed the slogans of civil society and political development. However, after Khatami's limited successes in both the political and economic sphere, the student movement reduced its support for Khatami during his second term and even called for his resignation, because he had 'failed' to deliver the promises that he made to the students and the populace. They were especially angry that he had not confronted the clerical establishment that controls the most powerful state institutions, which could be regarded as a measure of an 'open' public sphere in an 'open society'.

However, since street politics led to mayhem and the destruction of private and public property, Khatami backed off from resorting to this technique, even though he was severely criticised by some of the reformist cadres for failing to manipulate such a movement to the end of ousting, or at least reducing, the prerogatives of the dominant state institutions. After Khatami finished his first term in office, the reformist movement resorted to another strategy. Instead of employing street politics, they directed their pressure towards the institutions of the state *per se*. In this regard, reformist MPs in the Majlis al-Shura or parliament attempted to amend laws, most notably the law of the press, the delineation of the prerogatives of the Expediency Council, and the Council of Guardians. They pressed for a constitutional mechanism that clearly stated why the Council of Guardians prohibited some candidates from candidacy to the Shura Council or the presidency, rather than keeping the mechanism of choice discrete. By these measures, the reformists endeavoured to reduce the prerogatives of these councils. At the same time the reformists favoured increasing the prerogatives of the president who, as Khatami contended, 'does not have prerogatives more than any citizen in Iran'.

However, the reformists failed to achieve the required legal amendment regarding reform of the Council of Guardians, nor could they pass a new press law. Due to these fiascos, the student movement started to move its support even further away from President Khatami after his second term was about to end, and after he had failed to deliver his promises. As such, the wedge between Khatami and the reformist trend increased. The more than 20 million people who voted for Khatami in the second round were still hopeful that the system would be amenable to reform through their efforts and those of their leaders. However, the obstruction of prominent state institutions to the reformist aspirations on the ground led Iranian citizens to regret offering their votes to Khatami; 85 percent of the Iranian voters opted not to vote in the municipal elections.[1]

Khatami realised that he was losing grip and came to the conclusion that there

---

1   'Atrisi, *Al-Jumhuriyya*, p. 212.

was a gap between himself and his reformist allies. He defended himself against accusations that he had deviated from the principles of reform, accusing the reformists of doing so. Meanwhile he was still adamant in defending the freedom and independence of the Islamic Republic, while taking into consideration the most salient prescription of keeping the system intact, come what may.

Khatami propagated what came to be termed as the phenomenon of 'rising expectations'[1] where a space is opened and promises and pledges are made without real capability to deliver, which would eventually lead to popular discontent. In the case of Khatami, he whetted the people's appetite when he opened the political space and could not open up more, and as people were pressing for more rapid changes he could not deliver, thus leading them into disappointment.

IS DEMOCRATISATION TAKING PLACE IN IRAN?

One could pose the legitimate question of what the reformists accomplished in Iran after Khatami's two terms for eight years and after four years of broad popular trust and support, delegated authority (*tafwid*) from the people in the Parliament and municipalities. What would the future hold for the reformists after their support dwindled among the youth and the students who even went as far as asking Khatami to step down because he did not deliver his promises? What would the reformists do after they lost in the 2004 parliamentary elections where the conservatives gained control? How did the reformists explain the abstinence of the biggest student union (*Maktab Ta'ziz al-Wihda*) from participating in the presidential election of 2005 and parliamentary polls in 2004, in spite of the presence of reformist candidates such as presidential contender Dr Mostapha Moeen?

What would be the implications of the failure of the reformists to succeed Khatami and retain the presidency, which was lost to Mahmud Ahmadinejad in 2005? Why had more than one reformist[2] contested the 2005 presidential election, thus not only limiting their chances of success but also failing to secure the required number of votes for the second round, after Hashemi Rafsanjani, the head of the Expediency Council, and Ahmadinejad, the mayor of Tehran, made it to the second round? Would reform remain part of the Iranian political, social and cultural scene? Or would the reformists' influence dwindle after Khatami ended his second tenure?

These and similar issues call into question the degree of democratisation in the Islamic Republic, especially after the tug of war between the reformists and the conservatives resulted in tilting the balance toward the latter, who continue

---

1   See Samuel Huntington, *Political Order of Changing Societies*.
2   Mostapha Moeen and Mahdi Karrubi, the reformist ex-Speaker.

to wield considerable power in most of the institutions of the Islamic Republic, including the presidency.

After their defeats in 2005 and 2007, the reformists tried to evaluate what had happened, and they gave various explanations. At the time, Khatami considered the achievements that the reformists had made as an important step in the right direction on the long road towards changing the system. He contended that one of the main successes was the crystallisation of the basic foundations of Iranian civil society: many political groups received official recognition, more than 400 non-governmental organisations came to the fore, and hundreds of independent publications emerged, which reached a peak of 700 in major cities and thousands of publications in the provinces. Khatami added that the reformists had become an effective lobbying force for the promotion of human rights.[1]

In turn, Sayid Muhamad Ali Abtahi, President Khatami's Chief of Staff, noted other important tangible accomplishments, such as controlling the intelligence by purging it from the inside in order to stop any possible political assassinations. Abtahi also noted that intelligence was curbed from their prior strong influence over the revolutionary system of courts, and in fact the entire judiciary system. He stressed that the price of change was the arrest of hundreds of reformists, the closures of tens of newspapers and other repressive measures. But Abtahi credited the reformist movement with putting Iran on the modernity track.[2]

Members of the reformist movement stressed the cultural aspects that the reformists had successfully achieved, in both quality and quantity in the domains of theatre, literature, movies and industry, amongst other spheres. They credited their movement with changing the political milieu in the Iranian public sphere, whereby the conservatives ended up using the same concepts that the reformists were advocating for, such as championing the sovereignty of the law, pluralism and respect for human rights.

However, Said Hajjarian, a prominent Iranian reformist, conceded that there were still many accomplishments that had yet to be achieved. One was the founding of a unified leadership of the reformist movement, one with a common strategy and means to affect change in the balance of power and to tilt the status quo towards the reformists. He conceded that the precept of practice suggested that revolutionary accomplishments could be revoked through popular pressure.[3]

As such, Hajjarian contended that the reformists' bitter defeat in the legislative elections in 2004 and their loss of the presidency in 2005 led to the 'death of reform'. Especially dispiriting was the absence of a viable political programme that addressed people's needs and at the same time ensured the continuation of

---

1   'Atrisi, *Al-Jumhuriyya*, p. 210.

2   Ibid., pp. 210–211.

3   'Iran, Bilan presidential', *Le Monde Diplomatique*, June 2001.

the pace of reforms.[1] However, most reformists did not agree with Hajjarians's analysis, since some were still promoting the strategy of going back to the people, the main wielders of legitimacy. They argued that this could be done through the activation of three priorities: restructuralisation, reinforcing ties with civil society and NGOs, and the formation of a new reformist coalition. There was also a trend among some reformists to solicit foreign intervention in order to achieve their aims, though this would later prove to be a detrimental decision.[2]

Another reason that was often cited for the failures of the reform movement was the increasing external pressure that was placed on the Iranian regime. Shirin Ebadi, for example, pointed out that as a rule of thumb, governments tend to exploit national security in order to compromise people's freedom.[3] That is why she and other Iranian women activists believe that bombing Iran would derail the reforms in the Islamic Republic, thus providing a pretext for the government to choke public liberties. According to Ebadi, this would lead to an opposite consequence to what the government ought to perform, namely to respect people's rights and foster democracy in Iran.[4]

This line of argument perhaps explains why the Iraq-Iran war was viewed as a Western-Arab onslaught against Iran's nascent Islamic Republic, and one that gave the upper hand to conservatives to clamp down on social liberties and political freedom. The perception of a threat led to a certain kind of hyper-vigilance on the part of the system. And socially the system had become more hardline, with a 'decontamination' drive due to fears of cultural infiltration.

Sanei'i, whose progressive fatwas championed the rights of women, argued that regardless of any external pressure or internal crisis in Iran, the Islamic Republic would eventually become more democratic. He contended that the prerogatives of the *wali al-faqih* was constrained by the elected institutions, which in turn highlighted the importance of flexibility in interpreting the constitution.[5]

In spite of all the ups and downs witnessed during the Khatami era (1997–2005) and afterward, Iran in the first decade of this century undeniably experienced a cultural-intellectual awakening, in which new and multiple discourses emerged to the fore. Many of these new discourses denoted 'a departure ... from an Islamist ideological package which is characterised by universalism, monopoly of religious truths, exclusivism, and obligation, in principles and practice.'[6]

---

1 Ibid.
2 'Atrisi, *Al-Jumhuriyya*, pp. 211–213.
3 This is the case even in the United States, where many have criticised the USA Patriot Act as having restricted civil liberties and freedoms.
4 *Al-Sharq Al-Awsat* 29, 10342, 17 March 2007, p. 6.
5 *Al-Sharq Al-Awsat* 29, 10336, March 2007, p. 6.
6 Asef Bayat, *Islamism and Democracy: What is the Real Question?*, Amsterdam: Amsterdam University Press, 2007, p. 20.

The 2009 Election and its Aftermath

The reformists approached the 12 June 2009 presidential election as an opportunity to apply the lessons that they had learned in the bitter aftermath of Khatami's presidency. Unlike previous election campaigns in 2005 and 2007 in which reformists divided into a variety of competing camps, reformist leaders were for the most part allied with one another during the 2009 election campaign.

The run-up to the hotly contested election saw the birth of *mowj-e-sabz*, or the 'green wave,' a campaign to support the presidential bid of Mir Hossein Mousavi, who was the strongest of three contenders trying to unseat the incumbent Mahmoud Ahmadinejad. Importantly, his campaign gained the backing of Khatami, who had earlier announced his intention to run in the election, but who withdrew his candidacy after Mousavi said that he would stand as a candidate. The only other reformist candidate in the polls was Mehdi Karrubi,[1] who opinion polls suggested was trailing far behind Mousavi before the election. It was thought that the entrance of a fourth candidate, Mohsen Rezaie, a man with firm conservative credentials, might lose the incumbent Ahmadinejad some support from his base. And this in turn, suggested analysts, would offset any electoral losses to the reformist camp created by Karrubi's candidacy.

Despite this effort to consolidate reformist support, and despite massive participation in the polls, Ahmadinejad was declared the official winner. Many observers have raised doubts about whether the election was fair, or whether some form of fraud was committed during the polls, though even highly credible Western research has supported the assertion that Ahmadinejad was the

---

1 A lawyer by training, former parliamentary chairman and former member of the Expediency Council, since 2005 he has headed of the Etemad-e-Melli, or National Trust party.

legitimate winner.[1] The task of proving or disproving these allegations is beyond the scope of this research, but it is important to note, however, that this issue became a matter of open debate in Iran in the immediate aftermath of the polls and remains a point of contention within the public discourse.[2]

After Mousavi was deemed to have been defeated in the election, the *mowj-e-sabz* campaign was transformed into a massive social movement that began demonstrating against the official results of the election and openly pressing for greater civil liberties. The Western media tended to portray this movement as a budding counter-revolution, or an anti-regime effort that could eventually result in the toppling of the Islamic Republic. Not only is this assessment inaccurate, its widespread and repeated mention in the Western media has arguably damaged the reformists' credibility and thereby undermined their cause.

IRAN'S GREEN WAVE: REFORMISTS OR COUNTER-REVOLUTIONARIES?

In the Western narrative, a false dichotomy has been used to describe the post-election period, which has been broadly depicted as a struggle between two subsets of Iranians: the regime and counter-regime forces. Opposition leaders such as Mousavi and Karrubi have been portrayed as anti-regime elements whose apparent goal is to topple the Islamic Republic and create a Western-style democracy. Nothing could be further from the truth and perhaps nothing has been more damaging to the reformists' credentials in the internal Iranian political sphere. A more accurate description is to see the situation as one in which a variety of different actors are engaged in a contest for control of the existing regime, as well as its future direction.

Mousavi himself is an unlikely counter-revolutionary. A participant of the 1978–9 Islamic Revolution, Mousavi played an active role in the toppling of the shah's regime and was even briefly detained for his role in organising street

---

1   For example, an analysis of multiple public opinion polls conducted by the Program on International Policy Attitudes at the University of Maryland concluded that Ahmadinejad was likely the legitimate winner. Analysing polls taken a week before and a week after the election, the study noted that all polls showed that a majority said they planned to vote for Ahmadinejad, with numbers ranging from 52 to 57 percent immediately before the election and 55 to 66 percent after the election. The analysis is available online at http://www.worldpublicopinion.org.

2   In the immediate aftermath of the election, all three losing candidates alleged fraud. But by the time of this publication, Rezaie's position had changed, and he had embraced the view that there were only a limited number of anomalies witnessed during the polls, and that these did not affect the official outcome. Karrubi was initially outspoken on the matter of alleged fraud, but he abandoned these allegations after Khamina'i officially endorsed the election results. Mousavi still publicly alleges that fraud took place, and cites the need to reform certain measures that are in place for contesting official election results.

protests against Reza Pahlavi. Along with Mohammad Beheshti, he founded the Islamic Republic Party, which pressed for overthrow of the Iranian monarchy and the establishment of an Islamic Republic in Iran. And as the revolution gained momentum, Mousavi was appointed by Khomeini to the Iranian Council of Islamic Revolution.

His loyalty to the revolution and to Khomeini was rewarded after the creation of the Islamic Republic. He served for eight years as prime minister while Khamina'i was president and was widely praised for his handling of the economy during the height of the Iran-Iraq war. During his premiership, he was a key figure in secretly negotiating the Iran-Contra affair, helping the United States free American hostages in Lebanon in exchange for US weapons and spare parts needed in the Iran-Iraq war.

Indeed, Mousavi's revolutionary credentials were regarded as his strongest asset during the campaign, and perhaps contributed to Khatami's decision to withdraw from the race. In campaign messages and advertisements, Mousavi's supporters frequently highlighted the former prime minister's close relations with the late Ayatollah Khomeini, as well as his service to the country during the time of the Iran-Iraq war.

During the campaign, Mousavi was keen on perpetuating his reputation as a moderate architect of the revolution and distanced himself from other politicians who were calling for radical change. For example, he publicly disavowed calls for an 'Iranian,' rather than an Islamic, republic.

Even in the immediate aftermath of the vote, Mousavi maintained his pro-regime rhetoric and sought to dispel any notion that he was seeking to disrupt the existing power structure. He repeatedly emphasised the need to act within the confines of the Islamic Republic in order to effect change. On 22 July 2009, for example, he emphasised in a message to his supporters posted on his website the need to act within the law: 'If we move out of the constitution's framework then we would face uncontrollable anarchy.'[1]

What was perhaps most interesting about this post-election period is that it saw various players engaged in a contest to lay claim to an Islamic moral high ground. The tenets of Islam were cited by all and sundry to support their own arguments during much of the debate in this phase. Both Ahmadinejad's camp and Mousavi's supporters sought to portray themselves as the more devout adherents of Islam and used Islamic references to support their arguments. In this regard, the vote touched off a public discussion about what constitutes an Islamic polity.

For example, a heated debate emerged after the election about the alleged mistreatment of prisoners in detention centres. Reformists did not resort to Western human rights rhetoric to support their arguments, but rather denounced these

---

1   Mousavi's website, http://www.mir-hosseinmousavi.com/

misdeeds as contradictory to Islam. In response to the allegations of torture, Mousavi Karrubi and Khatami wrote a joint open letter on 25 July 2009 to the country's *marja' al-taqlid* in Qom urging them to speak out against the crackdown on postelection protests and describing the treatment of prisoners as contradictory to Islam. They wrote: 'What can justify repeated torture of those who live under the flag of Islam? How can one claim the system to be forgiving and follow Muhammad's religion when there is silence in the face of all this violence and savagery?'[1]

The three also compared the post-election crackdown to the repression of the shah and warned against the dangers of allowing the Islamic Republic to engage in acts of tyranny: 'We call on you, the *marja' taqlid* ... to remind the relevant authorities of the damaging consequences of employing unlawful methods and warn them about the spread of tyranny in the Islamic republic system,' said the letter.[2] It added that government officials 'have resorted to illegal, immoral and un-Islamic methods to obtain confessions'. Furthermore it asked: 'What legal, Islamic or human rights code can justify the repeated torture of those who live under the banner of Islam?'[3]

More importantly, Iranian reformists were during this period keen on emphasising that they were not seeking to overthrow the regime. As Karrubi wrote in his party's newspaper, *Etemad-e Melli*, on 24 June 2009: 'Most of those who have objected to the trend of the presidential election in the country and its result are those who fought for the establishment of the Islamic system in Iran.'

But as Hooman Majd, a scholar on Iran, now based in New York, has argued, the *mowj-e-sabz* movement has been widely misunderstood by the Western media as an effort to overthrow the regime. The movement, he wrote, should be seen 'not as a revolution but as a civil rights movement – as the leaders of the movement do see themselves'.[4] Majd noted that the reality of Iran's *mowj-e-sabz* movement might 'disappoint both extremes of the American and Iranian political spectrum ... especially US neoconservatives hoping for regime change,' because the 'movement's aim is not for a sudden and complete overthrow of Iran's political system.'[5]

---

1   The original Farsi letter was posted on Mousavi's Ghalamnews website, as well as the website of Karrubi's political party, Etemad e-Melli. For a partial English translation, see 'Iran's clerics urged to help 'stop oppression', Agence France Presse, 25 July 2009.

2   For an English translation of parts of the letter, see Ali Akbar Dareini, 'Iranian opposition appeals to clerics', Associated Press, 25 July 2009; and 'Iran clerics urged to halt spread of oppression', Agence France Presse, 25 July 2009.

3   Ibid.

4   Hooman Majd, 'Think Again: Iran's Green Movement', *Foreign Policy*, 6 January 2010.

5   Ibid.

THE SUBVERSION OF THE *MOWJ-E-SABZ* MOVEMENT

The fact that the Western media has sought to portray the *mowj-e-sabz* movement as a counter-revolution has allowed Ahmadinejad and his supporters to levy the damaging accusation that the movement was purely a foreign plot to trigger a 'colour' revolution similar to the Orange Revolution, Rose Revolution or other movements that overthrew existing regimes. From the onset of the post-election unrest, opponents of the pro-reform camp sought to undermine the reformist leadership by pointing to their alleged contacts with Western leaders or intelligence apparatuses.

On 4 July 2009, for example, Hossein Shariatmadari, the editor in chief of the conservative *Kayhan* daily, wrote a commentary that denounced reformist leaders, accused them of acting on the orders of the United States and called for their prosecution in a court of law. 'An open court, in front of the people's eyes, must deal with all the terrible crimes and clear betrayal committed by the main elements behind the recent unrest, including Mousavi and Khatami,' he wrote, adding: 'All they did and said was in line with the instructions announced by American officials in the past.'[1]

The reformists' quandary in dealing with these accusations was exacerbated by the fact that terrorist elements saw the post-election unrest as an opportunity to engage in violent acts against the state. Each of the early demonstrations in the aftermath of the vote saw the destruction of public and private property, including banks, street signs, cash machines, vehicles, and Basiji[2] offices, acts that provoked confrontations with security forces. It is important to note that these activities were carried out by a small group of demonstrators. Footage broadcast on YouTube and opposition websites showed several incidents in which larger groups of peaceful demonstrators intervened to prevent these more radicalised minority elements from beating or otherwise attacking security forces. However, acts of vandalism and other violations of the law served to portray the *mowj-e-sabz* demonstrations in a negative light in larger parts of the Iranian public.

Perhaps most damaging of all in terms of the Green Movement's public relations with the Iranian citizenry were the acts of vandalism and profanity that occurred during the Ashura commemoration on 27 December 2009. Like previous demonstrations, the Ashura protests saw multiple acts of violence such as the destruction of property, arson, burning of tires and torching of motorcycles.

---

1   For English excerpts of the article, see Fredrik Dahl and Hossein Jaseb, 'Hardline Editor calls for Mousavi to face trial', Reuters, 4 July 2009.
2   Literally meaning 'mobilisation', the Basiji were formed in November 1979 on Imam Khomeini's orders as a paramilitary volunteer militia. They have grown considerably since then, and besides providing social services they also help enforce internal security, and are known to aggressively police morals and suppress dissidents. With offices in virtually every city in Iran, they are said to be particularly loyal to Ayatollah Khamina'i.

But what was different about these Ashura rallies is that many of the acts of violence and vandalism were widely seen as crossing a red line because they targeted Imam Hossein and the Ashura commemoration itself. Many of the motorcycles that were burned, for example, belonged to ordinary citizens who were coming to attend the annual mourning ceremony.[1] Moreover, groups of protesters burned *katibeh*, or mourning banners that commemorate the martyrdom of Imam Husayn, and *ta'zieh*, or the stages upon which theatrical commemorations of Imam Husayn's martyrdom are staged. YouTube and mobile phone videos that were circulated among Iranians via the internet and bluetooth showed demonstrators shouting profane slogans against Imam Husayn.[2]

The Iranian media reported an incident in central Tehran at Jumhuri Square in which HojetolIslam Salihan, an Ashura prayer leader, was wounded and bloodied when he and other worshippers were pelted with stones by green-clad protesters, who also burned the garbage dumpsters around the square.[3]

In another incident in North Tehran, at Tajrish Square, pro-Mousavi demonstrators were seen clapping and whistling, while burning *katibeh,* or banners commemorating Zahra, Husayn and Abbas, as others shouted obscenities.[4]

In Wali Asr Square, *katibeh* were shredded by angry demonstrators, who were also said to be wearing green.[5] The state-owned news agency IRNA drew a comparison between these demonstrators and the supporters of Husayn's killer, Yazid,[6] by reporting, 'we see history is being repeated' and warning that Mousavi, Karrubi and Khatami were responsible for the incident and calling them 'partners in these crimes'.[7]

This profanity, desecration of religious imagery and disrespect for religious symbols was deeply offensive to the general public's sensibilities. Many Iranians were also upset by the celebratory atmosphere of the *mowj-e-sabz* protests, in which green-clad demonstrators were seen applauding, whistling and engaging in other cheerful displays during the normally sombre Ashura.

These incidents of disorder provoked unanimous condemnation from the

---

1 Borna News Agency, 28 December 2009.

2 Similar footage was broadcast on Simaya Azadi, Mojahid-e Khalq's satellite television station. Interview with Iranian journalist and researcher Reza Golpour, conducted in Beirut, 6 January 2010.

3 This particular incident held added significance because the square is very near to Khamina'i's home. The news agencies Fars, Tabnak and Gorna, 29 December 2009.

4 Ibid.

5 IRNA, 28 December 2009.

6 Yazid ibn Mu'awiya, second Caliph of the Ummayad Caliphate, who lived between 645 and 683 CE, and ruled from 680 until his death. Yazid's reign is notorious amongst Shi'is, and even amongst many Sunnis, for its waste, misjudgements and brutality, not least the massacre at what became the holy Shi'i city of Karbala. In Shi'i terminology, 'Yazid' is a byword for evil and dictatorial tendencies

7 IRNA, Ibid.

country's *marja' al-taqlid,* including many who had hitherto lent their support, whether quietly or overtly, to Mousavi and Karrubi, including Makaram Shirazi, Javadi Amoli and Mousavi Ardebili.[1] This represented a dramatic shift in the stances of those *marja' al-taqlid,* who had not previously shown a proclivity to favour one camp over another and had tended to remain above the post-election fray. In the immediate aftermath of the vote, for example, only one of nine *marja' al-taqlid* congratulated Ahmadinejad as the winner of the election, as had previously been a routinely observed custom, and three others spoke out against the crackdown on opposition protesters, namely Sanei', Montazeri and Ardebili.[2] However, after the events around Ashura, lower-ranking clerics also joined the condemnation of the demonstrations, including all members of the Jam'ieh Robaniyat, or the Clerics Societies of Qom, Mashhad, Isfahan and Tehran.[3] All of the *hawziyeh,* or centres of Islamic learning in Qom, closed in protest.[4]

A wide array of civil society groups also expressed outrage at the incidents, including the society of Iranian doctors, university student groups, the Iranian Parliament, Oil Industry Workers, the Iranian Women's Culture and Education Society, the Society of Iranian Teachers, the Iranian Professors Society, provincial governors, municipalities and bazaars, all of which were closed after the Ashura demonstrations.[5] The organisation Veterans of the War with Iraq, key leaders of which had been important supporters of Mousavi during the election and its immediate aftermath, also voiced their condemnation.[6]

Many of these groups publicly called for the prosecution of opposition leaders.[7] A number of Iranian media outlets compared the Ashura protesters to the supporters of Imam Husayn's murderers Yazid and Shamer, who according to Shi'i Hadiths had also clapped and whistled during the original days of Ashura.[8]

These incidents provoked outrage among Iranian citizens, many of whom participated massively in a pro-government rally on 30 December that was seen as a resounding rejection of the Ashura violence. Hundreds of thousands of people took part in the demonstrations, chanting slogans against opposition leaders Mousavi and Karrubi, and calling for harsh punishment in response to the violence.[9] Widespread public outrage over the behaviour of demonstrators on

---

1 The *marja' al-taqlid* included: Ayatollah Makaram Shirazi, Ayatollah Nouri Hamadani, Ayatollah Subhani, Javadi Amoli, Ayatollah Mozaheri, Ayatollah Wa'iz Tabasi, Alavi Gorgani and Hosseini Zanjani, among others. Fars News Agency and Tabnak News Agency, 29 December.
2 Ali Akbar Dareini 'Iranian opposition appeals to clerics', , in Associated Press, 25 July 2009.
3 Fars News Agency, 29 December 2009.
4 Fars News Agency and Tabnak News Agency, 29 December.
5 Ibid.
6 Ibid.
7 Ibid.
8 Raja News, 29 December 2009.
9 Parisa Hafezi 'Hundreds of thousands at pro-government rallies in Iran', Reuters, 30 December 2009.

Ashura had increased the pressure on Khamina'i and other leaders to deal more firmly with the *mowj-e-sabz* movement as a whole.

Abdolkarim Soroush, a founder of the reform movement, acknowledged that the rally had altered perceptions of the post-2009 election reform movement: 'After [the protests on] Ashura on 27 December, we came to realise that it was a real turning point. It was at that time that the regime decided to crack down on the Green Movement.'[1]

Evidence suggests that the most egregious acts were committed by only a handful of minority elements. Kazem Jalali, the spokesman of the Parliament's National Security Commission, said that Mojahid-e Khalq and pro-monarchist groups were to blame; likewise, the Iranian intelligence service said that those arrested in the Ashura unrest had direct ties to Mojahid-e Khalq, an outlawed terrorist group that has killed scores of Iranian civilians in its repeated attacks.[2] But in the eyes of the public, a link had been drawn between such terrorist groups and the *mowj-e-sabz* demonstrators.

In the weeks after Ashura, Mousavi and other opposition leaders sought to distance themselves from Iranian terrorist groups, as well as foreign elements who were being blamed for the Ashura unrest. On 8 February 2010, for example, Mousavi said during a speech to a group of Iranian scholars: 'They [our political opponents] are saying we have relations with countries outside Iran. And with this talking they want to turn the *marja' al-taqlid* against us. But clearly, this movement and myself have no connections outside Iran ... We only want to return to the principles of the Islamic Revolution, and one of those is independence, so we never want foreigners to use us as their agents. All of these assertions [about our foreign connections] are unfounded accusations.'[3]

In an open letter to British Prime Minister Gordon Brown, Massoud Khodabandeh, of the Middle East Strategy Consultants in Leeds, urged the British government to stop incitement to violence being broadcast by Mojahedin-e Khalq in London. Khodabandeh warned in his letter that the 'Iranian people's courageous, peaceful demonstrations to achieve their natural freedoms and rights' were 'being fatally undermined from within the UK' as a result of the terrorist group's activities.[4]

Khodabandeh was referring to Sima-ye Azadi, a satellite channel owned by Mojahedin-e Khalq that was using its broadcasts from London to urge Iranians to take to the streets in order to overthrow the Iranian regime, as well as repeatedly airing offensive footage from the Ashura demonstrations. In his open letter,

---

1   Abdolkarim Soroush, 'The Goals of Iran's Green Movement,' Global Viewpoint Network/ Tribune Media Services, in *Christian Science Monitor*, 6 January 2010.

2   Fars News Agency and IRNA, 4 January 2010.

3   The speech was posted on Mousavi's *Kalemesabz* website, as well as his Facebook site.

4   'Open Letter to Prime Minister Gordon Brown,' PR Newswire/ US Newswire, 4 January 2010.

Khodabandeh urged the British prime minister to 'remove from the Iranian hardliners their main excuse for crushing the people's legitimate protests to bring about change in their own country.'

THE FUTURE OF REFORM

There is no question that the Ashura rallies marked a turning point and perhaps even the demise of the *mowj-e-sabz* movement, as reformist leaders were put on the defensive in the aftermath. What would be the implication of this setback on the future of the reform movement?

The period after Ashura has seen reform leaders evaluating the situation and trying to outline a set of specific objectives for the future. Several prominent reformists in exile issued a manifesto on 3 January 2010 which outlined a series of specific reforms that the movement as a whole should strive to achieve. The signatories include the reformist cleric, Muhsin Kadivar; former parliamentarian and Islamic Guidance Minister Ataollah Mohajerani; investigative journalist Akbar Ganji; Abdolali Bazargan, an Islamic thinker and son of a former prime minister; and the reform movement founder and scholar Abdolkarim Soroush. The document calls, among other things, for the resignation of Ahmadinejad, the release of political prisoners, an investigation into allegations of torture at Iranian detention centres, the recognition of law-abiding political and non-governmental organisations, labour unions, greater freedom of press and independence of the judiciary by electing, rather than appointing, its head.

Their demands were as follows:

(1) Resignation of Mr Mahmoud Ahmadinejad [as the president] and holding a new presidential election under the supervision of neutral organs; abolish the vetting process of candidates [by the Guardian Council] and formation of an independent election commission that includes the representatives of the opposition and protestors, in order to draft the rules and regulations for holding free and fair elections.

(2) Releasing all the political prisoners, and investigating the torture and murder of the protestors over the past several months in open courts in the presence of a jury and the attorneys of their [the victims'] own choice, and compensating those who have been hurt and their families.

(3) Free means of mass communication, including the press, the internet, voice [radio] and visage [television]; abolishing censorship and allowing banned publications [such as dailies] to resume; expanding non-governmental TV and satellite channels; ending the filtering of the internet and making

it easily accessible to the public; and purging liars and provocateurs from [national] radio and television.

(4) Recognising the rights of all the lawful political groups, university student and women movements, the NGOs and civil organisations, and labour unions for lawful activities and the right to peaceful protest according to Article 27 of the Constitution.

(5) Independence of the universities [from political meddling and intervention]; running the universities democratically by the academics themselves; evacuating the military and quasi-military forces from the universities; and abolishing the illegal Supreme Council for Cultural Revolution [that interferes in the affairs of the universities].

(6) Putting on trial all those that have tortured and murdered, and those who ordered the past crimes, particularly those over the past several months.

(7) Independence of the judiciary by electing [rather than appointing] its head; abolishing illegal and special courts [such as the Special Court for the Clergy]; purging the judiciary of unfair judges, and banning judiciary officials from giving political speeches and carrying out orders of higher officials [the president and the Supreme Leader], instead of implementing the laws fairly and neutrally.

(8) Banning the military, police, and security forces from intervening in politics, the economy, and culture, and ordering them to act professionally.

(9) Economic and political independence of the seminaries, and preventing politicising the clerics to support the government, and banning the use of Friday prayers sermons for issuing [by the clerics] illegal and anti-religious orders.

(10) Electing all the officials who must become responsive to criticisms, and limiting the number of terms that they can be elected.

Not meeting these [legitimate] demands of the Green Movement and increasing the [violent] crackdown and oppression will not only not help us to pass the [present] crisis, but will also deepen the crisis with painful consequences, for which only the supreme leader will be responsible.[1]

Although the demands are many, reform leaders privately acknowledge that even limited progress on any of the issues identified would mark an improvement from the status quo. Commenting on the document during an interview with Global Viewpoint, a syndicated commentary and interview service, Soroush asserted

---

1   The manifesto was published in Farsi on 3 January, 2010, on the pro-reform Jaras website. For an English translation , see 'Abdolkarim Soroush: The Goals of Iran's Green Movement,' *Christian Science Monitor*, 6 January, 2010.

that 'if even one of these demands is fulfilled – such as freedom of press – that will be enough to change drastically the political scene and atmosphere of the country. If they accept one of these ten demands – and not the rest – it will revolutionise the whole country.'[1]

Another major demand that remains a key priority for reformists is for the powers that be to scale back the role of the Council of Guardians in vetting candidates for parliamentary and presidential elections. Karrubi, for example, has called for a referendum on whether the council should have the right to ban candidates, asking, 'What kind of parliament is it that … operates under the fear of the Council of Guardians?'[2]

Many aspects of the public debate still taking place in the aftermath of the 2009 vote serve to illustrate that the contentious question persists, of whether *wilayat al-faqih* should be seen as being based on popular or Islamic legitimacy. The argument over the exact role of the *wali al-faqih*, and whether, as theology professor Dr. Habib Fayyad explained, he should be seen as being chosen through a process of revelation (*kashif*) or appointment (*nasib*), continue to this day. In his last days before his death, Montazeri warned that the Islamic Republic's legitimacy would be undermined if the people's demands were ignored, insisting that 'resisting people's demands is religiously prohibited.'[3] Likewise, Grand Ayatollah Yousuf Saanei' has continued to weigh in on this ongoing debate: 'I remind you that no instruction or command can be a permission or excuse to violate people's rights and this could be a great sin,' he said on 4 July 2009.[4]

In the West, the struggle between the reformist movement and the current leadership has been portrayed as a dichotomy in which there must eventually be clearly demarcated camps of winners and losers. But the reality of Iranian society is not a dichotomy; rather it is an arena that has seen interplay among various elements that are engaged in contributing to the Iranian public discourse. Even though the reformists are currently not in power, this interplay has succeeded in shifting and expanding the discourse on a number of important issues.

For example, although reformists failed to regain the presidency in the 2009 election, one of the principles that they had long championed, the idea that women ought to be allowed to play a role in governance, has gradually gained broader public acceptance, though it remains a matter of heated debate in some quarters.

This shift in discourse is evidenced, for example, by the fact that upon his re-election, Ahmadinejad selected three women to serve in his cabinet – the first time in the country's history that women had ever been nominated as ministers.

---

1 Soroush, 'Goals', ibid.
2 Karrubi's appeal was published on the pro-reform Saham News website. For an English translation, see Associated Press report of 22 February 2010.
3 Reuters, 21 June 2009.
4 Fredrik Dahl and Hossein Jaseb, Reuters, 4 July 2009.

One of them, Marzieh Vahid Dastjerdi, gained parliamentary approval to head the country's health ministry, and has now become Iran's first-ever woman minister.[1] This illustrates that the call to give women a greater role in governance, previously a taboo in Iranian society, has gained acceptance in Iranian politics, even among conservatives.

Likewise with regards to the authority of the *rahbar*, some would argue that Ahmadinejad has himself tested and attempted to expand the limits of the powers of the presidency vis-à-vis the office of Khamina'i. For example, upon his re-election in 2009, Ahmadinejad appointed Esfandiar Rahim Mashaei, a controversial figure in Iranian politics whose daughter is married to Ahmadinejad's son, to the office of first vice president, a decision that Khamina'i opposed in a letter to the president that ordered Mashaei's resignation. Ahmadinejad initially defended his decision, saying it 'would not be revisited', in what some say was an act of defiance and an assertion of the perogatives of the president. It was not until the letter was read aloud on state television days later that Ahmadinejad partially complied: but rather than dismissing Mashaei entirely, he instead appointed him as his chief of staff.[2] A similar contest of authority ensued when in 2010 Ahmadinejad appointed Mashaei and three other allies to newly created offices of special envoys for foreign affairs in what was widely regarded as an attempt to create a parallel diplomatic apparatus to the Foreign Ministry, which falls under the authority of the *rahbar*.[3] Ahmadinejad only partially reversed the decision under heavy pressure from conservatives, demoting his special envoys to advisors. Thus the question of the extent of the powers of the *wali al-faqih* remains contested, even under the administration of Ahmadinejad.

Therefore the broadening of the boundaries of acceptable discourse continues to enable a vibrant civil society to apply the tools of grassroots pressure to promote democratic reforms. In short, Iranians are leading an organic process that could be labelled as democratisation. This process has been far from linear and has met with successes and failures. It has proceeded in jumps and starts, and at times has gone into reverse. But even when the reform movement has suffered defeats, there is no doubt that internal social forces have continued to play a prominent role in the promotion of democratic reforms and democratisation in the Islamic Republic.

---

1   Although her political positions could be labelled conservative, Dastjerdi has strongly advocated the role of women in governance, and has insited that 'women must have a greater role in the country's affairs.' For an English-language interview with Dastjerdi, see Simon Tisdall, 'Iran appoints first female cabinet minister for 30 years', the *Guardian*, 3 September 2009.

2   'Islamic leader's letter regarding Mashaei has been sent to the president', ParlemanNews.com 21 July 2009.

3   'Ahmadinejad changes special envoys to advisors', *Tehran Times* 16 September 2010.

Acknowledgements

This book is based on my dissertation defended at Birmingham University, UK, under the supervision of Professor Jorgen Nielsen. This product would not have come into completion without the much appreciated financial support from Al-Tajir Trust Foundation for which I am very grateful.

Throughout the course of compiling this book, I benefited from the insights of Professor Scott Lucas of Birmingham and Professor L'Arbi Siddikki of Exeter. I would like to extend my gratitude to Dr Hiba Rauuf and Dr Yaser Elwi for their insights that served as a source of intellectual inspiration. I owe journalist Kristin Dailey, who, much appreciatedly, spent long hours in reading the document and coming up with practical suggestions.

I would like to wholeheartedly thank the anonymous reviewers of Saqi Books for their kind suggestions and sharp insights.

While this book is far from being perfect, I take the blame for any shortcomings.

Finally, I would like to thank all those who gave me moral support, especially my family.

Bibliography

Abrahamian, Ervard, *Khomeinism: Essays on the Islamic Republic,* London: I.B. Tauris and Co. Ltd, 1993.

Abu Zahra, Sheikh Muhammad, *The History of Islamic Mazaheb* (Religious Trends), vol. 1, Beirut: Dar Al-Fikr Al-Arabi, 1985.

Ajami, Fouad, *The Vanished Imam: Musa al-Sadr and the Shi'i of Lebanon,* London: I.B. Tauris and Co., 1986.

Akhavi, Shahrough, 'The Ideology and Praxis of Shi'ism in the Iranian Revolution,' *Comparative Studies in Society and History* 25, 2 (April 1983): 203.

Al-Allamah, Al-Na'ini, 'Tanbih Al-Ummah Wa Tanzih Al-Mullah' in *Al-Ghadir Journal* 12 and 13 (1991).

Al-Ansari, Muhammad Hussein, *Al-Imama Wal-Hokomua fi Al-Islam* (Imamate and Governance in Islam), Tehran: Matbouat Maktabat Annajah, 1998.

Al-Ansari, Abdul Hamid Ismail, *Shura and its Impact in Democrcay.* Third Edition. Beirut: Al-Maktaba Al-Asriyyah.

Al-Ansari, Al-Sheikh Murtada, *Faraid al-Usul, Muassasat Al-Nashr Al-Islami Al-Tabi'a Li Jama'at Al-Mudarressin,* Qom, Iran: 1405AH, Volume 2, 275ff, section on *ijma'.*

Al-Asadi, Mukhtar, *Al-Thawra fi Fikr Al-Imam Al-Khomeini* (Revolution in Imam Khomeini's Thought), third edn, Tehran: Muassasat Tandhim wa Nashr Turath Al-Imam Al-Khomeini, 2003.

Ali, A.Yusuf, *The Holy Qur'an: Translation and Commentary,* Lahore: Islamic Propagation Centre International, 1993.

'Amid Zinjani, Sheikh 'Abbas 'Ali, *Al- Idara Al-Siyasiyyah wa-Al-Dusturiyya fi Al-Jumhuriyya Al-Islamiyya* (Political and Constitutiuonal Administration in The Islamic Republic), in Nizam Al-Idara, *Al-Hukumiyyah fi Al-Islam* (The Administrative System of Islamic Government)

— 'Majalis Al-Shura Al-'Amud Al-Fiqari Li Al-Nizam Al-Siyasi Al-Islami (Shura councils: The Backbone for the Islamic Political System)', Proceedings of the Fourth Convention on Islamic Thought, (place, date?)

Amili, Sheikh Abdullah Jawadi, 'Wilayat al-Faqih and Republicanism' in *Silsilat Al-Wilaya Al-Thaqafiyya*, 35 (1998).

Amuli, Ayatollah Javadi, *Wilayat al-Faqih: Wilayat al-Faqaha wa Al-'Adala* (The Governance of the Jurisprudent: Mandate and Justice), Beirut: Dar Al-Rasul Al-Akram, 2002.

Arjomand, Sai'd Amir, 'The Constitution of the Islamic Republic', in *Encyclopedia Iranica*, vol. 6, 1993.

Asadullahi, Mas'ud, *Wilayat Al-Faqih wa Al-Dimuqratiyya: Darasa Muqaran* (Wilayat Al-Faqih and Democracy: A Comparative Approach), Beirut: Dar Al-Mahajja Al-Bayda', 2007.

Al-Sayyid, Radwan, *Masalat Al-Shura bein Al-Nas wa Al-Tajrobah Al-Tarekhiyyah Li Al-Ummah* (The issue of Shura: Between the Religious and Historical Practice of The Ummah), first edn, Beirut: Dar Al-Kitab Al-'Arabi, 1997.

— *Siyasat Al-Islam Al-Mouaser: Morajaat wa Moutabaat* (Politics of Contemporary Islam: Reviews and Follow-ups), Beirut: Dar Al-Kitab Al-'Arabi, 1997.

'Atrisi, Talal, *Al-Jumhuriyya Al-Sa'ba: Iran fi Tahawulatiha Al-Dakhiliyya wa Siyasatiha Al-Iqlimiyya* (The Difficult Republic: Iran in its Domestic Changes and Regional Politics), Beirut: Dar Al-Saqi, 2006.

'Awdeh, Abdul Qadir, *Al-Islam wa Awda'una al-Siyasiya* (Islam and Our Political Situation), Beirut: Mu'assasat Al-Risalah, 2008.

Ayubi, Nazih, *Political Islam: Religion and Politics in the Arab World*, London: Routledge, 1991.

— 'State Islam and Communal Plurality', in *Annals of the American Academy of Political and Social Science* 524 (November 1992).

Al-Bahadli, Ali Ahmad, *Al-Hawza Al-'Ilmiyya fi Al-Najaf: Ma'alimaha wa Harakataha Al-Islahiyya (1920-1980)* (The Religious Seminary in Najaf: Features and Reformist Trends), Beirut: Dar Al-Zahra', 1993.

Bahkshi, Ali Agha, *The Dictionary of Political Science*, Tehran: Centre for Iran's Scientific Information and Documentation, 1995.

Barakishian, Mahmud, 'Republicanism from Imam Khomeini's Perspective', in *Sunlight Monthly* 19 (October 2002).

Bashiriyyeh, Husayn, *A Contribution in Iranian Political Sociology: The Stage of the Islamic Republic*, Tehran: Contemporary Outlook Publication, 2002.

Bayat, Asef, 'The Coming of a Post-Islamist Society', in *Critique: Critical Middle East Studies*, Minnesota: University of Hamline, No. 9, Fall 1996.

— *Islamism and Democracy: What is the Real Question?*, Amsterdam: Amsterdam University Press, 2007.

Bosworth, C.E., van Donzel, E., Lewis, B., and Pellat, C.H., eds, *The Encyclopedia of Islam*, new edn, vol. 1, Leiden: E.J. Brill, 1991.

Calder, Norman, 'Accommodation and Revolution in Imami Shiʻi Jurisprudence: Khomeini and the Classical Tradition', in *Middle East Studies* 18 (1982).

Cole, Juan R.I. and Keddie, Nikki R., eds., *Introduction to Shiʻism and Social Protest*, New Haven and London: Yale University Press, 1986.

Dairat Al-Marif Al-Shiʻiyyah Al-Islamiyyah (The Encyclopedia of Shiʻi Islam), vol. 1, on the Third Hadith, 1997.

Fadlullah, H., 'Islamic Leadership inside the State' in *Al-Thaqafa Al-Islamiyyah* 37 (May-June 1991).

— Vice President of the Consultative Centre of Studies and Documentation, Hizbullah's think tank, interviewed by author, Beirut, 2 March 2006.

Fayyad, Professor of Theology at Tehran University, interviewed by author, Tehran, 23 May 2006.

Al-Ghanushi, Rashed, 'Political Jurisprudence' in *Al-Muntalaq* 110 (1995).

Al-Hai'iri, Kadhem, *Asas Al-Houkomah Al-Islamiyah, Dirasah Istidlaliya Mokaranah bein al-Dimokratiyyah wa al-Wilayat fi Al-Islam*, fifth edn, Beirut: Islamiyah Publishing House, 1979.

Hajarian, Saʻid, 'Republicanism as a Framework for Freedom', in *Sunlight Monthly* 13 (March 2002).

Al-Hakeem, Mohammad Baqir, *Al-Alaqa bein Al-Shoura Wa Al-Eilayah Fi Al-Islam* (The relation between the Shura and the Wilaya in Islam), Beirut: Al-Aaraf Publishing House, 1993.

Al-Hakim, Al-Sayyid Muhammad Taqi, *Al-Usul al-ʻAmah li-l-Fiqh al-Muqaran*, second edn, Beirut: Muʼassasat al-Bayt li-l-Tibaʻah wa al-Nashr, 1979.

Haroun, Abdulsalam, *Tahzeeb Sirat Ibn Hisham,* tenth edn, Beirut: Mouassasat Al-Risalah, 1984.

Al-Hashemmi, Mahmoud, *Masdr Al-Tashree Wa Nizam Al-Hokm* (The Source of Legislation and Governance System).

Hashimi, Sayyid Muhammad, *The Constitutional Law for The Islamic Republic of Iran: General Principles and the Pillar of The System*, vol 1, 1. Tehran: Shahid Beheshti University, 1995.

— *The Constitutional Law of the Islamic Republic of Iran: Sovereignty and Political Institutions*, vol. 2, Tehran: The Higher Educational College in Qom, 1996.

Haydar, Mahmud, Lebanese intellectual and opinion leader, journalist and editor-in-chief of *Madarat,* interviewed by author, Beirut, 5 May 2007.

Al-Husseini, Muhammad, 'The Different Lutherism and the Alleged Secularism Project' in *Al-Hadaf,* 22 November 1992: 41.

Ibrahim, Fuaʼd, *Al-Faqih wa Al-Dawla: Al-Fikar Al-Siyasi Al-Shiʻi (The Jurisprudent and the State: Shiʻi Political Thought)*, Beirut: Dar Al-Kunuz Al-Adabiyya, 1998.

Ibrahim, Fuaʼd, Saudi intellectual Shiʻi dissident, interviewed by author, 28 January 2007.

Iran, 'Bilan presidential', *Le Monde Diplomatique* (June 2001).

Iranian Arab Affairs Quarterly 10 and 11 (Fall 2004 and Winter 2005).

Jaber, Hasan, Professor of History at the Lebanese University, interviewed by author, Beirut, 7 January, 2007.

Al-Jaberi, Muhammad Abed, *Democracy and Human Rights,* first edn, Beirut: Markaz Derast Al-Wehda Al-Arabiyya, 1994.

Jradi, Sheikh Shafic, Director of M'arif Hikamiya College, interviewed by author, Tehran, 6 June 2006.

Al-Kawtharani, Ali Khalifa, et al, *Al-Istibdad fi Nuzum Al-Hukm Al-Arabiyya Al-Muasira* (Tyranny in Contemporary Arab Political Systems), Beirut: Markaz Dirasat Al-Wihda Al-Arabiyya, 2005.

Khomeini, Imam Ruhollah, *Al-Hokouma Al-Islamiyyah* (Islamic Government), second edn, Beirut: Markaz Baqiyyat Allah Al-A'zam, 1999.

— *Al-Kawther: A Collection of Imam Khomeini's Speeches,* vol. 3, Tehran: Mu'assasat Tanzeem Wa Nashr Athar al-Imam Khomeini, 1996.

— *Majmu'at Al-Nur,* vol. 2, 3, Tehran: Centre for Cultural Documents of the Islamic Republic, 1995.

— *Sahifat Al-Nur* (Messages of Light), a collection of Khomeini's speeches, messages and writings, Tehran, vol 3, 2006.

Kadivar, Khaykh Muhsin, *Nazariyyat Al-Dawla fi Al-Fiqh Al-Shi'i: Buhuth fi Wilayat Al-Faqih* (The Theory of the State in the Shi'i Jurisprudence: Research in the Rule of the Religious Jurisprudent), Beirut: Dar al-Jadid, 2000.

— *Nazariyyat al-Dawla fi al-Tashri' al-Shi' i* (Theories of State in the Shi'i Legislation), Tehran: Nay Publications, 1997.

— *The Government of Wilayat Al-Faqih,* Tehran: Nay Publications, 1998.

Katuzian, Nasir, *The Principles of Public Law.* Tehran: Gostar Publishing House, 1998.

Kelidar, 'Abbas, 'The Shi'i Imami Community and Politics in the Arab East', in *Middle East Studies* 19, 1983.

Khishtainy, Khalid, 'Shi'ism and the Islamic Revolution', in *Contemporary Review* 247, 1985.

Kohlberg, Etan, *Belief and Law in Imami Shi'ism,* Hampshire, Great Britain: Variorum, 1991.

Kristol, William and Kagan, Robert, *Present Dangers: Crisis and Opportunity in American and Defense Policy,* San Francisco: Encounter, 2000.

— 'Toward a Neo-Reaganite Foreign Policy', in *Foreign Affairs* 75, 4, 1996.

Lapidus, Ira M., *A History of Islamic Societies,* Cambridge: Cambridge University Press, 2005.

Maghniyye, Sheikh Mohammad Jawad, *'Ilm Usul Al-Fiqh fi Thawbihi Al-Jadid,* (Science of Usul Al-Fiqh in its New Dress) second edn, Beirut: Dar Al-'Ilm Li Al-Malayeen, 1980.

— *Al-Shia wa al-Hakimoun,* (The Shi'i and the Rulers), Beirut: Dar Al-Hilal, 1966.

Mahallati, Muhammad Surush, 'Nasihat A'immat Al-Muslim', (Advice for Islamic Leaders) in *Qadaya Islamiyya Muassira* (The Giving Council to the Muslim Clergy), 1996.

Mallat, Chibli, *The Renewal of Islamic Law: Muhammad Baqer as-Sadr, Najaf and the Shi'i International,* Cambridge: Cambridge University Press, 1993.

Al-Mawdudi, Abu Alaala. *Nazariyat Al-Islam Wa Hadyehi fi Al-Siyasah Wa Al-Qanoun Wa Al-Doustour* (Islamic Theory: Guidance in Politics, the Law and the Constitution), Beirut: Mouassasat Al-Risalah, 1980.

McLane, Ian, ed., *Oxford Political Dictionary,* Oxford: Oxford University Press, 1996.

Momen, Moojan, *An Introduction to Shi'i Islam: The History and Doctrines of Twelver Shi'ism,* New Haven: Yale University Press, 1985.

Moussalli, Ahmad, *Al-Usuliyya Al-Islamiyya: Al-Khitab Al-'Aydiyuluji 'ind Sayyid Qutb* (Islamic Fundamentalism: The Ideological Discourse of Sayyid Qutb), Beirut: American University of Beirut, 1992.

Al-Mumin, 'Ali, *Qadaya Islamiyyah Mu'asira* (Contemporary Islamic Issues), Beirut: Dar Al-Hadi, 2004.

Montazari, Husayn, *Dirasat fi Wilayat al-Faqih wa Fiqh Al-Dawlah Al-Islamiyyah (Studies in Wilayat al-Faqih and The Jurisprudence of The Islamic State),* vol. 4, second edn, Beirut: Al-Dar Al-Islamiyyah, 1998.

Musa, Farah, *Shamseddine Bein Wahj Al-Islam Wa Jaleed Al-Madheb* (Shamseddine between the Glare of Islam and the Freeze of the [Islamic] Schools of Law), Beirut: Dar Al-Hadi, 1993.

— *The Necessities of the Regimes and the Choices of the Ummah according to Sheikh Shamseddine,* first edn, Beirut: Dar Al-Hadi, 1995.

Al-Musawi, Muhsin Baqir, *Al-Shura wa Al-Dimuqratiyya,* Beirut: Dar Al-Hadi, 2003.

Al-Najafi, Al-Sheikh Muhammad Hasan, *Jawahir Al-Kalam* (The Jewels of Discourse), 22 Beirut: Dar Ihya Al-Turath Al-Arabi.

Al-Naraqi, Ahmad, *Wilayat Al-Faqih,* with introduction and commentary by Yassine Musawi, Beirut: Dar Al-Taaruf Li Al-Matbouat, 1990.

Norton, Augustus Richard, ed., *Civil Society in the Middle East,* vols. 1 and 2, Leiden: E.J. Brill, 1995, 1996.

Pur Azeghdi, Rahim, Iranian intellectual, interviewed by author, Iran, 6 May 2006.

Rahhal, Husayn, *Ishkaliyyat al-Tajdid: Dirasah fi Daw 'ilm ijtim'a alma'rifah* (The Dialectic of Modernity: A Study in the Domain of the Sociology of Knowledge), Beirut: Dar al-Hadi, 2004.

Rahimi, Mustapha, *The Principles of Republican Government,* Tehran: Amir Kabir Publishing House, 1979.

Rajaee, Farhang, 'A Thermidor of "Islamic Yuppies"? Conflict and Compromise in Iran's Politics.' *Middle East Journal* 53, 2 (Spring 1999): 217-231.

Rapoport, David, 'Messianic Sanctions for Terror', in *Comparative Politics* 20, (January 1988).

Reuters, 16 June 2003.

Rishahri, Muhammad, *Al-'Aql wa al-Jahil fi al-Kitab wa al-Sunna* (Reasoning and Ignorance in the Qur'an and the Sunna), Beirut: Dar Al-Hadith, 2000.

Rose, Gregory, 'Velayet-e-Faqih and the Recovery of Islamic Identity in the Thought of Ayatollah Khomeini', in Nikki Keddie, ed., *Religion and Politics in Iran*, New Haven and London: Yale University Press, 1983.

Roy, Olivier, 'The Crisis of Religious Legitimacy in Iran', in *Middle East Journal*, Vol 53. No. 2 (Spring 1999), pp. 201-216.

Al-Ourabi, Hasan Abdullah. *Nazarat Fi Al-fiqh Al-Siyasi* (Glimpses of Political Jurisprudence). Kharhtum: Al-Sharikah Al-Alamiyyah li Khadamat Al-Iilam, 1998.

Al-Tabataba'i, Muhamad Hussein, *Nazariyat Alhokm wa Siyasah fi al-Islam*, third version, translated and introduced by Assefi Mohammad Mahdi, Tehran: Publications of the Grand Islamic Library and the Foreign Information on Islam, the Theory of Power and Politics section of the Baatha Institution 1402H (1981).

Sachedina, Abdulaziz, 'Activist Shi'ism in Iran, Iraq and Lebanon', in *Fundamentalism Observed*, Martin E. Marty and R. Scott Appleby, eds., The Fundamentalist Project, vol. 1, Chicago and London: The University of Chicago Press, 1991.

Al-Sadr, Muhammad Baqir, *Lamha Tamhidiyyah an Mashrou Dostour Al-Jamhouriyyah Al-Islamiyyah: Al-Islam Yakud Al-Hayat (A Preliminary Insight on the Project of Islamic Republic Constitution; Islam Guides Life)*, second edn, Beirut: Dar Al-Taaruf Li Al-Matbouat, 1979.

— *Sura 'an Iqtisad Al-Mojtamaa Al-Islami, sulsulat Al-Islam Yaqud Al-Hayat (An Image about the Economy of the Islamic Society: Series of Islam Guiding Life)* Beirut: Dar Al-Taaruf Li Al-Matbouat, 1979.

—*Thaqafat Al-Dawaa Al-Islamiyya, Hizb Al-Dawaa Al-Islamiyyah, Al-Qism Al-Siayasi* (The culture of the Islamic call, Al-Dawaa Islamic Party, the Political Wing), vols. 1 and 2, Iran, 1984.

— *Manabi Al-Kodra fi Al-Dawla Al-Islamiyyah* (The Sources of Power in the Islamic State), Beirut: Dar Al-Taaruf Li Al-Matbouat, Beirut, 1979.

— 'Usul Al-Dostur Al-Islami', (Origin of the Islamic Constitution) in Chibli Mallat, edited volume, *Muhammad Baqir Al-Sadr between Najaf and the Shiites of the World,* first edn, Beirut: Dar Al-Nahar, 1979.

— *Bahth hawl Al-Wilayah, (Research on the Wilaya)*, Dar Al-Taaruf Li Al-Matbouat, Beirut, 1990.

Al-Sayf, Tawfik, *Did al-Istibdad* (Against Tyranny), Beirut: al-Markaz al-Thaqafi al-Arabi.

Al-Sayyid, Radwan, 'Shura between Nass and Experience', *Al-Muntalaq* 98 (1993)

Sa'i, Habib, 'Islamic Republic?', in *Iranian Echo Monthly* Vol. 3, Issue 10 (July-August 2002).

Schulze, Reinhard, 'The Ethnization of Islamic Cultures in the Late 20th Century or from Political Islam to Post-Islamism', in George Stauth, ed., *Islam: Motor or Challenge of Modernity*, Yearbook of the Sociology of Islam, Hamburg, Vol. 1, 1998.

Shamseddine, Sheikh Muhammad Mahdi, *Al-Ummah Wa Al-Dawlah Wa Al-Harakah Al-Islamiyyah*, first edn, Alghadeer book series, Alghadeer Magazine publisher, The Higher Shiite Islamic Council, Lebanon, 1994.

— *Nizam Al-Hukum wa Al-Idara fi Al-Islam* (The Order of Governance and Adminstration in Islam), seventh edn, Beirut: Al-Muassasa Al-Dawliyya Li Al-Dirasat wa Al-Nashr, 2000.

— *The Book on Secularism*, Beirut: Dar Majd, 1983.

— *Al-Ijtihad wa Al-Taqlid: Bahith Fuqhi Istidlali Muqaran* (Ijtihad and Emulation: A Comparative Fuqhi Istidlali Research), Beirut: Al-Dawliyya Al-Mu'assat, 1998.

Al-Sharq Al-Awsat, 29, 10336, 10342 (17, 20, 21 March 2007): 1, 6.

Shqayr, Sheikh Muhammad, interviewed by author, Beirut, 15 January 2007.

Soroush, Mohammad, 'Republicanism? Islamism?' in *Iranian Echo Monthly* Vol. 3. Issue 9 (April/May 2002).

Spuler, Bertold, *The Age of The Caliphs: A History of the Muslim World*. Princeton: Markus Wiener Publishers, 1999.

Tabataba'i, Sayyed Mohammad Hussein, *Nazariyyat Assiyasah Wal Hokm fi Islam* (The Theory of Politics and Power in Islam), Beirut: Al-Dar Al-Islamiyyah, 1982.

Yassine, Abdulsalam, *Hiwar ma Al-Fudalaa Al-Demikratiyyeen* (A Dialogue with the Deocratic Notables), Casablanca: Al-Mouallef, 1994.

Zubaida, Sami, *Islam: The People and the State*, London and New York: I.B. Tauris and Co. ltd., 1993.

Index